STUDIES IN AMERICAN LITERATURE

Volume IX

REALITY AND IDEA
IN THE
EARLY AMERICAN
NOVEL

by

DAVID H. HIRSCH

1971
MOUTON
THE HAGUE · PARIS

LIBRARY OF CONGRESS CATALOG CARD NUMBER: 76-166976

Printed in The Netherlands by Mouton & Co., Printers, The Hague

TO MY FATHER AND MOTHER

PREFACE

The serious American writers who composed novels during the post-Revolutionary and pre-Civil War periods were deeply concerned with the relation of the human form to ideas of revolution and order, republicanism and monarchy, and their interest in these ideas inevitably found its way into their fiction. I have attempted to locate some of these ideas in specific novels and to trace the ability of individual writers to convert them into fiction without violating the formal demands of art.

Before settling down to my discussions of separate novels, however, I have found it necessary to come to grips with a number of problems that have been raised by literary theorists and critics who have been preoccupied with the form of the novel. My first chapter, therefore, is an attempt to test the thesis that the novel is a direct outgrowth of the stable world-view of the British empirical philosophers. The second chapter calls into question the notion that the novel, which is presumably a faithful representation of "reality", belongs to England, while the exclusive domain of American writers has been, and is, romance, essentially a flight from "reality".

Beyond this, I am primarily interested in the novels themselves and not in any thesis that may be squeezed out of them or imposed upon them. I shall not pretend to be able to find disease in the collective American psyche, nor yet to declare its good health. Similarly, I am not especially concerned with the good or ill health of the individual authors I deal with but with what they have created.

I am indebted to the Summer Stipend Committee of Brown

University for several grants which have enabled me to use my summers to good advantage, and to Mark Spilka, who helped me to procure an award from the Faculty Research Fund of Brown University to pay for the typing of the final manuscript.

In the course of completing this book I have run up many personal debts. When I started this work as a doctoral dissertation, the late William Charvat was my adviser. Julian Markels gave me encouragement when it was greatly needed. The soul searching of John Gabel and Milton Kessler deepened my spiritual development at a crucial period of my life. In recent years I have learned much from George Monteiro. His influence on my critical practices and attitudes has been incalculable. Hyatt Waggoner was kind enough to read and comment on portions of the text. Harold Fisch and Eli Pfefferkorn of Bar-Ilan University have made perceptive suggestions on the Yojo section of my Melville chapter. Ely Stock and Jane Donahue have read the final version in its entirety and have helped me with their valuable comments. A word of thanks to Jacqueline Taylor, whose expertise in the preparation of manuscripts helped to make my life a little easier.

A final debt of very long standing I owe to the late Sidney Berenzweig. His manly intelligence and courage were an inspiration to all who knew him.

Parts of this book have appeared in somewhat different form in *Texas Studies in Language and Literature, The Sewanee Review, Books at Brown,* and *The Critical Quarterly.*

TABLE OF CONTENTS

I

THE EMPIRICAL ORIGINS OF THE ENGLISH NOVEL

1

When Lionel Stevenson writes that "the essential quality for an acceptable novel is the illusion of reality",[1] he is expressing a view to which few students, or even casual readers, of the novel would take exception. But he also raises questions that have been the despair of theoreticians of fiction: What do we mean by reality? What do we mean by the "illusion of reality"? And how is it possible that the single most important criterion for the excellence of a work of imagination should be not its imaginativeness but its "realism"? No one has addressed himself to these questions with greater aplomb than Ian Watt, who writes that ". . . the correspondence between the literary work and the reality it imitates is an issue which the novel raises more sharply than any other literary form . . ."[2] Watt's purpose in his authoritative study, *The Rise of the Novel*, is to establish a firm and viable connection between the rise of the middle class and the development of empirical philosophy on the one hand and the process of imitation embodied in the novel as a genre on the other. His method, basically, is to describe the social and intellectual milieu and then to fit the emergence of the novel into that milieu. In presenting his picture of eighteenth-century thought, Watt stresses three major developments: a newly emerging concept of "personal identity"; the introduction of a consciousness of "Time process" (p. 22); and the tendency to define ". . . the individual particular case . . . by reference to two coordinates, space and time" (p. 26).

---

[1] *The English Novel: A Panorama* (Cambridge, Mass., 1960), p. 7.
[2] *The Rise of the Novel* (Berkeley and Los Angeles, 1964), p. 11. Hereafter page numbers are given in text.

Watt's summary of the empirical philosophy expounded by John Locke is impressive in its clarity and lucidity. Yet, it is exactly this clarity and lucidity that must be called into question. Locke's philosophy was not as clear and distinct as Watt would have it. As a matter of fact, Locke, as David Hume, among others, recognized, was a most problematic philosopher. Though he believed himself to be clarifying many of the obscurities of Scholastic philosophizing, it became apparent to later thinkers that what he had done was to shift the obscurities into a new framework. Instead of solving the problem of what we can know, he raised, implicitly, the question of whether we can know anything at all.

Watt's discussion of "personal identity" may provide a good example of the way in which he tends to smooth out problems inherent in the early eighteenth-century world-view. "Locke", he writes, "had defined personal identity as an identity of consciousness through duration in time; the individual was in touch with his own continuing identity through memory of his past thoughts and actions. The location of the source of personal identity in the repertoire of its memories was continued by Hume: 'Had we no memory, we never should have any notion of causation, nor consequently of that chain of causes and effects, which constitute our self or person.' Such a point of view is characteristic of the novel ..." (p. 21).

As Watt has presented the matter, then, the concept of personal identity was not a problem for Locke, and it was also a concept on which Locke and Hume were in agreement, Hume simply having "continued" in Locke's footsteps. To consider Locke's own words, however, is immediately to see how vexed and vexatious a problem personal identity is. In the paragraph that Watt cites in his footnote (*An Essay Concerning Human Understanding*, Bk. II, ch. 27, sects. ix, x.), Locke had actually written

For it being the same consciousness that makes a man be himself to himself, personal identity depends on that only, whether it be annexed only to one individual substance, or can be continued in a succession of several substances. For as far as any intelligent being can repeat the idea of any past action with the same consciousness it had at first, and with the same consciousness it has of any present action; so far it is the same personal self. For it is by the consciousness it has of its present thoughts and actions that it is *self* to *itself* now, and so will be the same self, as far as the same consciousness can extend to actions past or to come; and would be by distance of time, or change of substance no more two persons, than a man be two men by wearing other clothes to-day than he did yesterday, with a long or short sleep between: the same consciousness uniting those distant actions into the same person, whatever substances contributed to their production.

It is true that Locke implies that identity can be conceived in terms of a continuity of consciousness and that that in turn implies that personal identity is dependent on the "repertoire of its memories". But the passage also introduces a myriad of vexing problems. For one thing, Locke seems to be saying that personal identity is not only the memory of past thoughts and actions but the individual's ability to feel with equal intensity a simultaneous consciousness of both his present existence and his past experience. But if it is possible to do this, if it is possible for an "intelligent being" to "repeat the idea of any past action with the same consciousness it had of it at first, and with the same consciousness it has of any present action", then there would seem to be no way of separating what is being remembered from what is being directly perceived, and as a consequence there would seem to be no way of distinguishing immediate experience from remembered experience, or reality from illusion. Hume tried to cope with this problem when he distinguished between "impressions" and "ideas", the latter being only "faint images" of the former, while the impressions themselves are "those perceptions, which enter [the mind] with most force and violence".[3] Other problems arise out of Locke's attempt to settle the problem of metempsychosis by comparing a consciousness in two bodies with a man in two suits of clothes, which suggests that the consciousness can exist apart from the body that experiences sensations. Furthermore, Locke assumes what he is trying to prove when he says the "same consciousness" exists now, in the past, and in the future, for it is questionable whether consciousness is static, that

[3] *A Treatise of Human Nature*, Bk. I, pt. 1, sect. i.

is, always the same, and is not crucially affected and changed by the experiences through which it passes.

R. I. Aaron affirms that "we find here no adequate analysis of the concept of identity. Locke merely shows that the term is vague and carries with it more than one meaning . . . . If it be said that a person merely *is* the consciousness of present and past experiences this is an interesting theory, but I do not think that it is Locke's either in this chapter or elsewhere. It is not possible to say what Locke thinks a person to be".[4]

In addition to the problems of consciousness and identity inherent in the cited passage there is also the problem of memory. It is no secret that the task of defining memory was in itself one that gave Locke a good deal of difficulty. In the first edition of the *Essay*, Locke had defined memory as ". . . the power to revive again in our minds those ideas which, after imprinting, have disappeared, or have been as it were laid aside out of sight . . . . *Memory* is, as it were, the storehouse of our ideas. For the narrow mind of man not being capable of having many ideas under view and consideration at once, it was necessary to have a repository to lay up those ideas, which at another time it might have use of".[5] But when it was pointed out that Locke's position here was inconsistent with his earlier attack on innate ideas, he added the following "elucidatory" passage to the second edition:

But our ideas being nothing but actual perceptions in the mind, which cease to be anything when there is no perception of them, this laying up of our ideas in the repository of the memory, signifies no more but this, that the mind has a power, in many cases, to revive perceptions which it has once had, with this additional perception annexed to them, – that it has had them before. And in this sense it is that our ideas are said to be in our memories, when indeed they are actually nowhere, but only there is an ability in the mind, when it will, to revive them again, and as it were, paint them anew on itself, though some with more, some with less difficulty; some more lively, and others more obscurely.[6]

---

[4]   *John Locke* (Oxford, 1965), p. 152.
[5]   Bk. II, ch. 10, sect. ii.
[6]   *Ibid.*

The contortions that Locke has to go through to clarify his position are revealing. He cannot decide whether to locate remembered ideas in the mind or outside of it. Either way he is in trouble, because if the ideas are in the mind without our being conscious of them, then the mind, as one of Locke's contemporaries observed, contains ideas which are not actual perceptions, that is to say the mind then contains innate ideas. But Locke's attempt to eliminate this difficulty presents new difficulties that are no less stubborn. For if the ideas that "are said to be in our memories . . . are actually nowhere . . .", then the implication is that it is possible for ideas to exist, not only outside of a mind, but outside of anything conceivable (i.e., "nowhere"). And if the ideas can exist outside of an individual mind there would then seem to be no necessary connection between the ideas and any individual identity. The argument here is analogous to Locke's attempt to explain secondary qualities, such as color, by asserting that they are ". . . in truth nothing in the objects themselves, but powers to produce various sensations in us . . .".[7]

Locke's concern with personal identity, it should be added, was more legalistic than metaphysical. "Throughout the discussion", James Gibson notes, "he has in mind its practical application to the question of moral responsibility, and the justification of a system of rewards and punishments. Human justice, he recognizes, cannot rely without reserve upon the principle that responsibility only extends as far as the consciousness of an identical self, because of its liability to be deceived in any attempt to apply this purely inward principle".[8] But if Watt were right in saying that Locke had unequivocally defined personal identity as the individual's "continuing identity through memory of his past thoughts and actions", there would still remain the problem of whether an individual in a dreamless sleep or suffering from amnesia retains his own personal identity.

It was difficulties of this nature that Hume engaged in *A Treatise of Human Nature*. Far from continuing the "location of

[7] Bk. II, ch. 8, sect. x.
[8] *Locke's Theory of Knowledge and Its Historical Relations* (Cambridge, Eng., 1931), p. 117.

the source of personal identity in the repertoire of its memories", Hume strenuously denies the possibility of defining personal identity only in terms of memory. The context of the sentence quoted by Watt above makes this clear:

Had we no memory, we never shou'd have any notion of causation, nor consequently of that chain of causes and effects, which constitute our self or person. But having once acquir'd this notion of causation from the memory, we can extend the same chain of causes, and consequently the identity of our persons beyond our memory, and can comprehend times, and circumstances, and actions, which we have entirely forgot, but suppose in general to have existed. For how few of our past actions are there, of which we have any memory?[9]

Hume writes, further, that "the identity, which we ascribe to the mind of man, is only a fictitious one . . .", and ". . . identity is nothing really belonging to these different perceptions, and uniting them together; but is merely a quality, which we attribute to them, because of the union of their ideas in the imagination, when we reflect upon them".[10]

T. H. Green concludes that for Hume, ". . . the identity of a mind, which has been already defined as a succession of perceptions, is a contradiction in terms".[11] Whatever conclusion philosophers may ultimately come to with regard to Hume's views on personal identity, what is evident is that the problem itself was by no means as clear and simple for the eighteenth-century thinkers as Watt indicates. Personal identity was a matter that the philosophers found extremely elusive. That is not to say, however, that characterization in the novel does not owe a great debt to the empirical philosophers but that the debt is not accurately described by Watt. No doubt the novel rose out of its intellectual milieu, but that milieu is more complex than Watt indicates, and insofar as the novel may be said to have risen from this milieu, we should not expect to find it portraying character as a clear, coherent, unified structure, but rather as something highly prob-

---

[9] Bk. I, pt. iv, sect. 6.
[10] *Ibid.*
[11] "General Introduction to Hume's Treatise", T. H. Green, T. H. Grose, eds. (London, New York, Bombay and Calcutta, 1909), I, 295.

generally accepted that our temporal consciousness is essentially dependent upon the apprehension of movement in space, and is directly determined by its objective occurrence. Motion, he insists, can only give rise to an idea of duration if, and in so far as, it occasions a constant succession of ideas; and such a succession may be experienced without the apprehension of movement".[13] R. I. Aaron comes to a similar conclusion. Locke, he asserts, finds that "it is a mistake . . . either to identify time with motion or to suppose that time is simply the measure of motion".[14]

Watt, in speaking of time, goes on to contrast the ancient and modern views on the subject as follows:

Both the philosophy and the literature of Greece and Rome were deeply influenced by Plato's view that the Forms or Ideas were the ultimate realities behind the concrete objects of the temporal world. These forms were conceived as timeless and unchanging, and thus reflected the basic premise of their civilisation in general that nothing happened or could happen whose fundamental meaning was not independent of the flux of time. This premise is diametrically opposed to the outlook which has established itself since the Renaissance, and which views time, not only as a crucial dimension of the physical world, but as the shaping force of man's individual and collective history. (pp. 21-22)

Whatever may be the outlook that has established itself since the Renaissance, it seems fairly accurate to say that Locke did not view time as a "crucial dimension of the physical world". It may even be no exaggeration to say that the principal weakness in his attempts to account for matter is his inability to account for its temporal dimension. Simple ideas, for instance, once they enter the mind, seem never to change. They are stored away, and when the individual exercises his power to revive them, they are revived, apparently as they were originally. Similarly, consciousness, though it may go through the most portentous experiences, remains always identical, until it ceases to be conscious any longer. In this respect, Locke remains Platonic. For him, as much as for Plato, ideas are unchanging, though they are not necessarily "ultimate

---

[13]   *Locke's Theory*, p. 80.
[14]   *John Locke*, p. 163.

lematic, and we should expect personal identity to emerge
the novel (as indeed it does from *Tristram Shandy*) not
simple reservoir of memories but as something essentially
terious and indefinable.

As vexing to the empirical philosophers as the proble
personal identity was the problem of time. Here again, hov
Watt tends to be reductive. He asserts that

time is an essential category in another related but more extern
proach to the problem of defining the individuality of any objec
'principle of individuation' accepted by Locke was that of existe
a particular locus in space and time: since, as he wrote, 'ideas b
general by separating from them the circumstances of time and
so they become particular only when both these circumstanc
specified. (p. 21)

It need not be pointed out that the converse of a positive
ment is not always true. If "ideas become general by sepa
from them the circumstances of time and place", it doe
necessarily follow that ideas can "become particular only
both these circumstances are specified". Can we, for exa
make the idea of truth particular by saying that it was c
northeast corner of 42nd Street and Fifth Avenue at 3 P.
January 23, 1968? Nor is it clear anywhere in Locke th
would subscribe to this reversal, for it would imply that part
ideas could be deduced from general ideas instead of bei
ceived directly from the sensations, a notion that would be
thetical to Locke's entire epistemology. It is doubtful, fu
whether Locke's epistemology allows for a "locus in spac
time", since in Locke's thinking the two seem to exist on dif
planes.

For Locke, as one writer puts it, "space becomes the f
work of body, and duration or time the structure of mind,
inner sense".[12] This matter of Locke's conceiving time as a
"inner sense" is one on which students of Locke agree. G
writes, "In maintaining the subjective origin of our ideas of
tion and succession, Locke directly controverts the view

[12] James Gordon Clapp, "John Locke", *The Encyclopedia of Philo
Paul Edwards, ed. (New York, 1967), IV, 494.

realities", and though they can be directly located in the mind and not in a special world of forms.

There is, moreover, nothing in Locke's epistemology to suggest that he conceived time as a force in human affairs, as Watt maintains. There would seem to be nothing more alien to Locke's thought, or to empirical thought in general, than the notion that time is a "shaping force of man's individual and collective history". What we know is duration, or the succession of ideas flowing through the mind, which can best be measured by "the diurnal and annual revolutions of the sun", and "this consideration of duration, as set out by certain periods, and marked by certain measures or epochs, is that, I think, which most properly we call time".[15] Insofar as time may be said to be external, then, Locke conceives it as an indeterminate quantity which can be divided into measurable parts but which has no substantiality in itself and therefore can exert no influence in human affairs. But whether it is internal or external, nowhere does Locke conceive time as a "force" of any kind.

Locke's recalcitrance on this point is crucial because it is on its ability to convey a sense of temporal development that Watt rests his definition of the novel as a distinctly modern form different from all else that had gone before. "We have", he writes,

already considered one aspect of the importance which the novel allots the time dimension: its break with the earlier literary tradition of using timeless stories to mirror the unchanging moral verities. The novel's plot is also distinguished from most previous fiction by its use of past experience as the cause of present action ... Even more important, perhaps, is the effect upon characterisation of the novel's insistence on the time process .... The novel in general has interested itself much more than any other literary form in the development of its characters in the course of time ...

Shakespeare's sense of the historical past ... is very different from the modern one. Troy and Rome, the Plantagenets and the Tudors, none of them are far enough back to be very different from the present or from each other. In this Shakespeare reflects the view of his age ... (pp. 22, 23)

[15]   Bk. II, ch. 14, sects. xvii, xix.

But if the novel is, as Watt finds it, a direct embodiment of the eighteenth-century world-view, a world-view most fully expressed in the writings of Locke, how are we to reconcile the centrality of the consciousness of time in the novel with Locke's rather cavalier treatment of, and apparent scant interest in, the problem of time? And how are we to account for the astonishing suggestion that the characters of Defoe and Richardson show a greater development than the characters of Shakespeare because the eighteenth-century writers had a more profound understanding of the importance of the historical past?

2.

The existence of these questions points to a glaring weakness in Watt's book, his inability to bring about a coalescence between the philosophical outline and actual literary works. Having established a philosophical base on which modern definitions of the real and realism may be grounded, Watt, in his discussions of individual novels, cannot avail himself fully of the definitions that grow out of the empirical philosophy. The philosophical definitions of the real that he establishes in his opening chapter do not finally help Watt to establish what is real or even realistic in a literary text. He writes, for example, that "Pamela's residences in Lincolnshire and Bedfordshire are real enough prisons ..." (p. 26).

It is not unfair, I think, to ask what it means to say that Pamela's "residences . . . are real enough prisons", and how this use of the word "real" is related to the new realism of the empiricist philosophers. Is it that the prisons are "real" because they have "existence at a particular locus in space and time"? Surely not, for these prisons do not have any existence in such a locus, nor does the sophisticated reader believe that they do. Are the residences "real enough prisons", then, because they resemble prisons that do exist in time and space and that have been previously experienced by the reader? Perhaps, but this would presuppose that all readers will have had an experience of residences in Bedfordshire and Lincolnshire that have been turned into prisons. The fact is that these prisons exist in time and place only insofar as the imagination may be said to exist in time and place (or perhaps insofar as time and place exist in the imagination), and there is no stronger evidence to demonstrate the reality of the prisons than Watt's assertion that they are "real enough".

Similar problems arise when Watt maintains about Defoe's fictional world that "its pains, like its pleasures are as solid as those of the real world" (p. 95). Immediately apparent is a shift from a reality that is ostensibly objective (the "real enough prisons" that presumably exist in a locus of place and time outside the mind of Richardson, Pamela, and the reader) to a reality that is wholly subjective. But what, we are led to ask, does it mean to speak of "solid" pains and pleasures? Are the pains and pleasures of the "real world" solid or are they intangible, the one inescapable nightmares, the other fleeting fantasies? Or, to put the question differently, are the pains and pleasures of Defoe's fictional world "solid" in the same way that the prisons in *Pamela* are "real enough"? Or, can we distinguish between them in the same way that we would distinguish between a headache and a house in the phenomenal world?

The same kind of confusion is also evident in Watt's contention that "the main reason why Richardson's erotic scenes are so much more suggestive than Boccaccio's is merely that the feelings of the actors are so much more real" (p. 204). First, we must resist easy acceptance of the claim that Richardson's erotic scenes are more suggestive than Boccaccio's, unless suggestive is being used in a limited sense. That is, one can say, perhaps, that Richardson sublimates and conceals the sexual appetites of his female characters, whereas Boccaccio, in the tradition of true bawdy, portrays such appetites openly. It then follows that Richardson's erotic scenes are suggestive because he is not explicit. But this would have nothing to do with the reality of the feelings of the actors. It would mean only that different sets of feelings are being described, one no more real than the other.

Sometimes, to add to the confusion, the term reality refers to neither the objective nor the subjective. For example, in *Moll*

Flanders, "Defoe does not so much portray his heroine's character as assume its reality in every action, and carry his reader with him . . ." (p. 108), and those who think *Moll Flanders* a great novel ". . . discern behind it a firm grasp on the realities of human behaviour" (p. 118). Here, the reality of the fictional character and the feelings of the fictional character are part of a mysterious or even mystical trans-linguistic, trans-representational communication between author and reader. The empirical criterion of a locus in time and space is quite beside the point. Reality is arrived at by means of an intuitive leap on the part of both reader and author. It is also clear that in none of these instances is time a factor at all, neither as measured duration nor as a "shaping force".

I should like to demonstrate this disparity between the reality established philosophically and the reality of fiction by citing a passage in some detail. What follows is a quote from *Moll Flanders*, along with Watt's commentary on the passage.

The next thing of moment was an attempt at a gentlewoman's gold watch. It happened in a crowd, at a meeting house, where I was in very great danger of being taken. I had full hold of her watch, but giving a great jostle as if somebody had thrust me against her, and in the juncture giving the watch a fair pull, I found it would not come, so I let it go that moment, and cried as if I had been killed, that somebody had trod upon my foot, and that there was certainly pickpockets there, for somebody or other had given a pull at my watch; for you are to observe that on these adventures we always went very well dressed, and I had very good clothes on, and a gold watch by my side, as like a lady as other folks.

.   .   .   .

It is very convincing. The gold watch is a real object, and it won't come, even with 'a fair pull.' The crowd is composed of solid bodies, pushing forwards and backwards, and lynching another pickpocket in the street outside. All this happens in a real, particular place. It is true that, as is his custom, Defoe makes no attempt to describe it in detail, but the little glimpses that emerge win us over completely to its reality. A dissenting meeting-house is a piquant choice for these activities, to be sure, but Defoe does not arouse suspicion that he is a literary man by drawing attention to its ironic inappropriateness. (pp. 96-97)

Watt's commentary raises a myriad of questions. What does it mean to say that a description (rather than an argument or a legal brief) is convincing? Who is convinced? Is it only Watt or a hypothetical reader, as well? What is it that Watt or a hypothetical reader is convinced of? And what is it that is convincing? Is it the truth of the description that is convincing? Is it the accuracy? Is it its beauty that convinces? Perhaps it will appear that I am quibbling, and it may be that I am. Nevertheless, it seems ludicrous for Watt to have gone to such lengths to establish a philosophical definition of "reality" if in the end he cannot demonstrate that something is real in terms of his own definition but is forced to fall back on unreasoned authoritative assertion. In effect, Watt establishes a philosophical meaning for the word "real", and proceeds to free it of meaning when he applies it to literature.

"The gold watch", we are told, "is a real object". In what way is it "a real object"? Surely we cannot touch it or tell time by it. Neither is it particularized. More to the point, perhaps, why is it important that the watch be a "real object"? Does it make *Moll Flanders* a "better" work of art, or a more beautiful work, or a more perfect work, or a truer work, if everyone agrees that the watch is indeed "real"? Oddly enough, Watt does not stop to entertain this question. He seems to assume that if he says something fictional is real, and no one is present to question his assertion, then he has established a value. That is, we are apparently to infer that *Moll Flanders* is a better, truer, more beautiful, and more perfect work for having a real watch in it, which is stolen in "a real, particular place". Or if the "real watch" does not do all these things for the novel, then why bother to mention it? And yet, why we should accept "real things" as value indicators, this Watt never bothers to tell us. Nor does he stop to ask himself whether such a measure of values is worthwhile. All we need to know is not that beauty is truth, truth beauty, but that "reality" is a supreme value. This we must never question.

And yet, Watt cannot demonstrate what is "real" in a work of fiction. Of what relevance is the detail, to which Watt seems to attribute so much importance, that the watch will not come loose, even with "a fair pull"? Is it this detail that finally makes the watch a "real object"? Would the gold watch have been less "real" if the description had continued, "it came off easily"?

Watt goes on to say that "the crowd is composed of solid bodies". But this is to beg the important question, which is, what makes these "solid bodies"? Certainly there is nothing in the description itself to establish their solidity. "All this", Watt feels, "happens in a real, particular place", even though "Defoe makes no attempt to describe it in detail". But if particularity depends on detail, how are these two assertions to be reconciled? Moreover, the "real, particular place" appears to be more a function of Watt's imagination than Defoe's creation. Where is this "particular place"? At a meeting house. But where is the meeting house? Someplace in London. But where in London? Well, no place in particular. Moll is at the meeting house. But where is she? Is she in the front or in the back? Is she in the middle of the meeting house or along the sides? Is she close to a door (an important detail for a pickpocket)? Given all this vagueness, how are we won "over completely to [the] reality" of this place?

Finally, how is it possible to say that Defoe "does not arouse suspicion that he is a literary man by drawing attention to [the] ironic inappropriateness" of having the thievery go on in a meeting house? Is not Watt's own comment testimony to the fact that suspicion has been aroused? And does not Defoe draw our attention to the irony precisely by telling us that it is a meeting house that Moll chooses for her activities? Is it not also possible that Defoe may have omitted other details because he was more intent on stressing this irony than on presenting a "full and authentic report"?

Later, Watt adds that "Defoe gets into the middle of the action", with "I had full hold of her watch . . ." (p. 97). But is it Defoe or Moll who gets into the middle of the action? If we can be so absolutely confident that it is Defoe rather than Moll, must we not then conclude that the "realism" has failed, and that Defoe has not successfully created a fictional character? Elsewhere, Watt holds that Defoe was not able to moralize directly in the novel because "such editorial intrusion . . . would have interfered with Defoe's primary purpose, that of giving the impression that

Moll Flanders is a literal and authentic autobiography, and the method was therefore unacceptable" (pp. 116-117). But if Defoe's mask is so transparent that we can say with assurance that he is narrating the events and that he gets himself into the middle of the action, then it is clear that we do not have "the impression that *Moll Flanders* is a literal and authentic autobiography". If we can dispense with Moll as a narrating persona it indicates that we do not believe in her authenticity, and therefore we cannot be said to believe in the authenticity of the report.

Finally, it is interesting that Watt can describe Defoe's realism without mentioning the temporal dimension. Indeed, he cannot mention the temporal dimension because Defoe's realism does not employ it. The scene takes place late in Moll's career, but we do not know exactly how late. We do not know what year it is or how old Moll is. We are not told whether the adventure takes place morning or evening, winter or summer. Neither are we given any sense of "internal" time. We know that many years have passed since Moll first yielded her virginity, but her reactions and emotions have not changed at all. Indeed, Moll, it might well be said, is ageless. Time does not make any inroads on her. Time and all Moll's many adventures do not leave any mark on her inner person.

Watt's difficulties in bridging the gap between the philosophical definitions of reality and personal identity on the one hand and the literary representation of reality and personal identity on the other do not disappear when he turns his attention to Richardson, the writer who, in his opinion, brought the methods of literary realism in the novel to perfection. In trying to defend Richardson against Fielding's criticism of the moral implications of *Pamela*, Watt writes,

There is at least no doubt that Mr. B. finds Pamela's virtuous resistance infinitely more provocative than any compliance could have been, and thus provides an involuntary tribute to the efficacy of the new feminine role in encompassing its ultimate aim.

That, however, does not justify us in assuming, as the Fielding interpretation suggests, that Pamela is only modest because she wants to entrap Mr. B. It is surely better to regard her as a real person whose actions are the result of the complexities of her situation and of the effects, both conscious and unconscious, of the feminine code. Steele pointed out that prude and coquette are alike in that they have 'the distinction of sex in all their thoughts, words and actions': the code that commanded the allegiance of Pamela and her author is itself open to either interpretation. Similarly, although Pamela's acceptance of Mr. B. as a husband suggests that she regards his early advances as less heinous than she could publicly admit at the time, the inconsistency can be fully explained as the result of the falsity of the public code, rather than of her own character. Certainly, if we condemn Pamela for such departures from absolute openness and sincerity in courtship, we must not forget how widely the charge could be brought against others in similar circumstances, both in her age and in ours. (pp. 169-170)

This mixture of the fictional and historical worlds is reminiscent of the utmost perplexities of quixotism. Is there assuredly "no doubt that Pamela's resistance is more provocative than any compliance could have been?" How do we arrive at such certainty? We know that Mr. B. finds Pamela provocative, but how can we know how he would have reacted if Pamela had behaved differently? Can we infer an answer from a general fund of human experience? Experience, it is true, reveals the urgency of unsatisfied desires. But it is also true that human appetites have a way of renewing themselves and of growing by what they feed on. How does the action of the book "provide an involuntary tribute to the efficacy of the new feminine role in encompassing its own aim"? Surely, we are not to believe that it is only since the appearance of such a code in the eighteenth century that men have been "trapped" by their own lust and woman's guile.

We may also ask why we are to "regard [Pamela] as a real person". Is it because she has the same kind of reality as Defoe's gold watch or is Watt's fiat sufficient in itself? What is the implication of saying that the same code commanded the allegiance of both Pamela and Richardson? Does that put them on the same level of existence? Is there any indication that Richardson would have expected this new code to be an ameliorating force in the novel, which would exonerate Pamela?

Watt's indiscriminate mixing of history, sociology, and fiction puts him on very shaky ground. He has projected the ethic of nineteenth- and twentieth-century liberalism back onto an eighteenth-century conservative Protestant writer. Richardson himself would doubtless have been appalled by Watt's justification of Pamela's behavior. Clearly, Richardson intended to show that Pamela is, as a moral agent must be, free to choose either the way of virtue or the way of degradation and sin. She chooses virtue and in her choice, as far as Richardson is concerned, she is wholly admirable and in no way duplicitous. Watt's defense, however, is that Pamela's behavior may indeed be duplicitous, as Fielding and others rightly saw, but Watt goes on to argue that her duplicity is not reprehensible because it is common practice in eighteenth- as well as twentieth-century society, and therefore can be taken as the outcome of irresistible predetermining social forces. But it is unthinkable that Richardson would have accepted the contention that the operation of such forces relieves the individual of moral responsibility. Watt, twentieth-century man that he is, sees morality as relative, and virtue as a quality defined by society, whereas for Richardson just the opposite is true. Morality is absolute, and virtue is good for its own sake, the reward (in Pamela's case, blissful marriage above her station) being incidental.

What Fielding saw so clearly and ridiculed so effectively was the limitation implicit in Richardson's vision and in his moral position, a limitation that became glaringly manifest in the disparity between conscious intention and artistic result. Fielding perceived, as one must assume Richardson did not, that an absolute morality that deals in ephemeral rewards (even incidental ones) is inherently absurd. Watt seeks to obfuscate this disparity between intention and achievement by taking as a "real person" the character Richardson created, and judging her by the moral values of nineteenth-century liberalism. But Richardson was not an enlightened liberal, and he thought of his fictional character not as a "real person" but as an exemplar of bourgeois virtue. In a letter to Johannes Stinstra, Richardson candidly declared that his purpose was to "instruct handsome girls, who were obliged to go out to Service . . . how to avoid the Snares that might be laid against their Virtue . . .".[16] At any rate, whatever Richardson intended, it is clear that Watt cannot tell us what it means to say that Pamela is a real person or why we should regard her as one. Certainly, the locus of time and place and the reservoir of memories have nothing to do with the matter.

There is one other means of establishing reality or unreality that Watt calls on that should be mentioned, which is the appeal to "probability". In attempting to affirm the "reality" of the action in *Pamela*, Watt cites some statistics. "The outlook for servant girls was particularly bad", he writes.

> There were, it is true, some glorious catches, although none of them provide an exact parallel to the supreme one made by Pamela. But the normal fate of domestic servants was much less happy: they were usually bound to stay with their employers either until they were twenty-one or until they married; many employers forbade their servants to marry under any circumstances; and in fact the number of unmarried servants in London was said to be 10,000 out of a total of 25,000 in 1760. Pamela's only chance of escaping servitude until her majority might well therefore have been the marriage to her employer which she actually made . . . (pp. 143-144).

Here is the empirical method with a vengeance. Numbers will make us believe in the probability of fictional events that at first glance seem improbable. But what do these numbers mean? First, it must be pointed out that Watt has presented the figures incorrectly. The source from which the numbers come, a biography of Jonas Hanway, states that 10,000 of 25,000 *pairs* of servants were unmarried. The point that the author of the biography is making is, that because servants were not encouraged to marry but were, at the same time, expected to hire out in pairs, Hanway thought the system "conducive to immorality and instability among menials".[17]

Watt's use of sociological and statistical evidence, then, is misleading. The major "improbability" in Richardson's novel is not whether a squire would marry a servant but whether it is likely

---

[16]   Quoted in A. D. McKillop, *Samuel Richardson* (Chapel Hill, 1936), p. 16.

[17]   John H. Hutchins, *Jonas Hanway* (London, 1940), p. 150.

that a Pamela could have been found among the servant class. Moreover, had there been an eighteenth-century servant girl as beautiful and intelligent and charming and articulate and chaste as the servant girl Richardson created, and that girl was also determined to see herself married, then it would seem that she would not have encountered excessive difficulties in joining the happy sixty percent. But Richardson did not intend to portray an average "lifelike" servant girl. He was out to create an exemplary case that would stand as a universal paradigm of virtuous feminine behavior. His purpose as he stated it was to instruct as well as amuse. To achieve this goal he showed life not as it is but as it should be. If he imitated, he imitated the ideal, so that he might edify his readers. That he would have tried to achieve any kind of fidelity to statistical truth seems highly unlikely.

One other instance of Watt's attempts to cope with the problem of probability is revealing. According to Watt, probability is something that eludes Fielding:

Fielding's most obvious imitation of the epic model in the action of his novels – the mock-heroic battles – is also somewhat at variance both with the dictates of formal realism and with the life of his time. Either because the events themselves are inherently improbable – as is the case, for instance, with the fight between Joseph Andrews and the pack of hounds that is pursuing Parson Adams – or because they are narrated in such a way as to deflect our attention from the events themselves to the way that Fielding is handling them and to epic parallels involved. (p. 253)

Unfortunately, Watt does not specify just how the mock-heroic battles in Fielding are "at variance . . . with the life of [Fielding's] time". Granting the triumph of the middle class and the eclipse of the heroic in eighteenth-century life, one would think the mock-heroism, by Watt's own standards, to be very much coincident with the times. Instead of a superhuman Beowulf or St. George battling a supernatural dragon we have a hero who is considerably less than superhuman battling dogs who have nothing of the supernatural about them. Far from being at variance with the life of his time, Fielding's account seems to be very much in accord with the world of Lockean sensationalism and the bourgeois descent from the heroic ages, and it is through the mock-heroic that this descent from supernaturalism and heroism is recorded. Moreover, Watt does not tell what it is in the events themselves that is "inherently improbable". How one establishes the probability or improbability of a clergyman's being set upon by the dogs of a sadistic master is not mentioned. Apparently, there are no statistics against which to measure the events. But if our standards of probability are to be applied, then knowledge of eighteenth-century character (the apparent joy taken in such sports as cock-fighting, bear-baiting, bull-baiting, and prize-fighting women), derived from nonfictional documents, suggests that such sadism in a squire would be more easily found than the sentimentality of a Mr. B.

3.

The consequence of Watt's method, of first providing a definition of reality rooted in empirical philosophy and then showing that the representation of reality in the novel is an outgrowth of the philosophical definition, is that he is forced into the position of having to make a leap from "reality" as he thinks it is defined by the empirical philosophers to the "reality" of fiction. And this leap, no matter how hard he tries, Watt simply cannot make successfully. Like Dr. Johnson, he can only kick rocks and tell us that he knows from the pain in his toe that the rocks are real. But since he is dealing with fictions and not rocks, his assertions are not particularly impressive. Presumably, we will all feel pain in our toes if we kick rocks, but we do not necessarily all feel the things that Watt says we are supposed to feel when we read the fictions he discusses. It is one thing to say that matter is "real" because it occupies a locus in time and place and resists any intrusion of other matter; it is another to say that a fictional watch is "real" because it is a "real watch", or that a fictional character is "real" because that character's "actions are the result of the complexities of her situation and of the feminine code". If the watch in *Moll Flanders* never had material existence, then how can it be empirically "real", or if the complexities of Pamela's situation are themselves fictions, how can they make Pamela real?

Watt has not answered these questions, nor can he. Although he attempts to demonstrate that reality can be sufficiently defined as particulars situated in a locus of time and place, and though he asserts that realism in the novel descended from the legacy of the empirical philosophers who ostensibly defined reality as particulars located in time and place, yet when Watt comes to speak about realism in the novel he can speak of it only as a feeling or a belief or an intuition. That is to say that Watt, who represents himself as a wholly objective critic, is in truth a most subjective critic. This subjectivity is concealed beneath such stylistic subterfuges as authoritative expletives and declarations of reality, and by appeal to a supposedly universal emotional and intellectual response by a mysterious "we". But who has given Watt the authority to declare reality? And who is this "we" that always feels and believes and intuits and responds in the same way as Watt? Suppose that one reader, if even for the sake of perversity, refuses to join this company of perceptive men, and says, "I am not convinced, I refuse to believe, I do not feel this or that". What happens then to Watt's elaborately presented "reality"? Does it not disappear? And may not this disappearance suggest that fictional reality must always be conceived, in the words of Wallace Stevens, as "an activity of the most august imagination"?

II

EMPIRICISM AND THE AMERICAN NOVEL

1

The English novel, as literary historians generally agree, is the direct ancestor of the American novel, though where the one ends and the other begins remains a vexing question. Although many attempts have been made to discover the essential characteristic that differentiates the American novel from its parent, the theory that has been most influential has its seed in Lionel Trilling's essay, "Manners, Morals, and the Novel". Like Watt, Trilling subscribes to the view that the novel is (or should be) a faithful record of a world whose reality resides in the empirical world-view, what Trilling calls the "social field". He finds, therefore, that "the novel in America diverges from its classic intention, which . . . is the investigation of the problem of reality beginning in the social field."[1] Like Watt, Trilling takes too narrow a view of "the problem of reality".

"All literature", he advises, "tends to be concerned with the question of reality – I mean quite simply the old opposition between what really is and what merely seems" (p. 202). The statement is very clear. There is "reality" and there is "appearance", "what is", and "what seems", and the two are always opposed. But if this were the case there would be no problem, for all we would have to do would be to accept everything as the opposite of what it seems, an obvious absurdity. The confusion, of course, stems initially from the tautological statement that reality "really is". This leads Trilling to limit "reality" by positing a "what" that "really is". The difficulty in making such a sup-

[1] *The Liberal Imagination* (Garden City, New York, 1957), p. 206. Hereafter, page numbers are given in text.

position is beautifully expressed by G. E. Moore, who defines reality as "Determined being, and not being determined as 'what'. For to determine being as 'what' is to circumscribe and relate it in a universe of existence which denies its universality".[2] Trilling, by denying the possibility that appearance and reality *may* coincide, seems to be depriving appearance of *any* claim to existence. Even so adamant an idealist as Francis H. Bradley must concede that "reality, set on one side and apart from all appearance, would assuredly be nothing".[3]

A close examination of Trilling's concrete illustrations reveals the way in which he actually avoids the "problem of reality":

'Don't you *see?*' is the question we want to shout at Oedipus as he stands before us and before fate in the pride of his rationalism. And at the end of *Oedipus Rex* he demonstrates in a particularly direct way that he now sees what he did not see before. 'Don't you see?' we want to shout again at Lear and Gloucester, the two deceived, self-deceiving fathers: blindness again, resistance to the clear claims of reality, the seduction by mere appearance. The same with Othello – reality is right under your stupid nose, how *dare* you be such a gull? So with Moliere's Orgon – my good man, my honest citizen, merely *look* at Tartuffe and you will know what's what. So with Milton's Eve – 'Woman, watch out! Don't you see – any one can see – that's a snake!' (pp. 201-202).

All of this, however, is an excellent example of what does *not* constitute exploring the question of reality in literature. Not that Shakespeare, Sophocles, Molière, et al. ignore the problem, but their concern with it is more than Trilling suggests it is. Trilling maintains that in the instances he cites the problem is one of *seeing*. But seeing is only part of the problem. It is not only sight that is defective in Gloucester, Othello, Lear, Orgon, Oedipus, and Eve; it is judgment. Moreover, the recognition that reality is not being explored is implicit in Trilling's construction of the matter, for he assumes that the auditor or reader, and, by implication, the author, know at all times precisely what is "real" and what is "apparent". If this is so, if "reality" is always palpably

---

[2] James Mark Baldwin, ed., *Dictionary of Philosophy and Psychology* (New York, 1940), II, 240.
[3] *Appearance and Reality* (New York, 1908), p. 114.

"there", open to the view of all who can penetrate sham and pretense, then the question that Trilling raises in all these works is not one of "reality", but of human hypocrisy and the fallibility of human judgment. The essential flaw in Trilling's argument is that he cannot make up his mind whether to locate "reality" in the subject or in the object. He states, for example, that

there are two movements of thought in *Don Quixote*, two different and opposed notions of reality. One is the movement which leads toward saying that the world of ordinary practicality *is* reality in its fullness. It is the reality of the present moment in all its powerful immediacy of hunger, cold, and pain, making the past and the future, and all ideas of no account. When the conceptual, the ideal, and the fanciful come into conflict with this, bringing their notions of the past and future, then disaster results . . . .

Thus one movement of the novel. But Cervantes changed horses in midstream and found that he was riding Rosinante . . . . Cervantes begins to show that the world of tangible reality is not the real reality after all. The real reality is rather the wildly conceiving, the madly fantasying mind of the Don: people change, practical reality changes, when they come into its presence.[4] (p. 202)

We have seen that on the one hand (Othello, Lear, Orgon, etc.) Trilling posits reality as "what is" rather than "what merely seems", that is, as the phenomenon opposed to the idea, the object opposed to the subject. But now he goes on to say that the two "opposed" realities of *Don Quixote* are: the "powerful immediacy of hunger, cold, and pain" and "the wildly conceiving, the madly fantasying mind of the Don". Neither of these "realities" is identical with the "reality" Trilling mentions in the previous citation, but both are identical with each other. Both are *subjective*. Pain, especially, but hunger and cold as well, may be

---

[4]   As regards the alternate movements, Leo Spitzer, in his brilliant analysis of Cervantes' novel, writes, "Thus the interpolations of these episodic short stories, whose reality is at least as fantastic as the most daring dreams of the mad knight, offer another revelation of the perspectivism of Cervantes; we have to do not only with the opposition between prosaic reality and fantastic dreams: reality itself can be both prosaic and fantastic". "Perspectivism in 'Don Quijote' ", *Linguistics and Literary History* (New York, 1962), p. 62.

delusions, may be present in the mind only, and therefore no more "real" than any of the Don's "fantasies". What Trilling conceives as "opposed notions of reality" are not opposed at all. The opposition is between Trilling's first tautological definition of reality as "what really is" and his later implication that all reality is in the mind.

From his oscillating assumptions about reality Trilling infers that "the novel . . . has never really established itself in America. . . . The fact is that American writers of genius have not turned their minds to society. Poe and Melville were quite apart from it; the reality they sought was only tangential to society. Hawthorne was acute when he insisted that he did not write novels but romances – he thus expressed his awareness of the lack of social texture in his work" (p. 206). In the light of the fact that it was Trilling who first scored Vernon Parrington for playing fast and loose with the term "reality" in *Main Currents in American Thought*, this is a remarkable statement for him to make. In his article, "Reality in America", Trilling had demonstrated most incisively that Parrington's "errors are the errors of understanding which arise from his assumptions about the nature of reality". He went on to attack Parrington for having believed reality to be "one and immutable, . . . wholly external, . . . [and] irreducible". For Parrington, Trilling had maintained, "Men's minds may waver, but reality is always reliable, always the same, always easily to be known. And the artist's relation to reality he conceives as a simple one. . . . Sometimes the artist spoils this ideal relation by 'turning away from' reality. This results in certain fantastic works, unreal and ultimately useless" (pp. 2-3).

One would expect that, having seen so acutely and condemned so unreservedly the gravity of Parrington's sins, Trilling himself would avoid them. He does not. He winds up making the same assumptions about "reality" that Parrington makes, but Trilling makes them not as Parrington did, out of a commitment to populist ideology, but out of a commitment to the virtues of rigid class stratification. In the early essay Trilling had attacked Parrington for his inability to see that Hawthorne did *not* ignore reality: "The fact is that Hawthorne was dealing beautifully with realities, with substantial things. The man who could raise those brilliant and serious doubts about the nature and possibility of moral perfection, the man who could keep himself aloof from the 'Yankee reality' and who could dissent from the orthodoxies of dissent and tell us so much about the nature of moral zeal, is of course dealing exactly with reality" (p. 7). In the later essay, however, Trilling himself, almost echoing Parrington, accuses Hawthorne of "turning away from reality", – not from the reality of contemporary social ills, but from the reality that begins "in the social field", the reality of "cultivated" society.

Trilling's belief in "manners" as the only reality capable of reflecting and embodying the most exhilarating heights of Western intellect and culture induces him to denigrate the artistic legitimacy of any other kind of representation of reality. He seems to feel, moreover, that the novel, as the chronicle of manners, must accept the stability of the social order it records, and that it cannot, indeed, exist without a relatively static hierarchy of "social facts" *to* record. Pushed to a not wholly illogical extreme, Trilling's position culminates in the belief that the essence of the tradition of American fiction is a total disregard not only of the social but of the physical world as well, and an uncurbed flight into a world of fancy totally unrelated to the ordinary facts of human existence.

2.

Just such an assumption is made by Richard Chase, who develops at length the thesis that the tradition of American fiction is, in a peculiar way, the romance rather than the novel. Speaking about American fiction in such phrases as "radical forms of alienation, contradiction, and disorder", "contradictions among extreme ranges of experience", "acceptance . . . of radical disunities", and "profound poetry of disorder", Chase uses the term "romance" to indicate a pathological condition in the American psyche or in the American social order.[5] Following Trilling, he

[5]   The symptoms were first described and the disease diagnosed by D. H. Lawrence in *Studies in Classic American Literature* (1923).

seeks the roots of this diseased condition (the supposed tendency of American literature to "pursue the possibility" of discovering "a putative unity *in* disunity or to rest at last among irreconcilables") in the barrenness of the American milieu and in "the Manichaean quality of New England Puritanism". Stuck in the wilderness, with no society and no manners to portray, the American novelist turns to the one subject available to him, and available only to him in its purest state: the "Puritan version" of the abstract struggle between good and evil, light and darkness, spirit and flesh.

Chase's principal contribution, however, is his attempt to establish the distinction between novel and romance by defining the terms. "The main difference between the novel and romance", he writes, "is in the way in which they view reality. The novel renders reality closely and in comprehensive detail . . . . By contrast the romance, following the distantly medieval example, feels free to render reality in less volume and detail".[6]

The distinction seems clear, but the clarity is largely illusory. Chase states that the novel and romance are distinguished by the fact that each has a different view of reality; he goes on to say, however, that the distinction lies not in the way in which the two forms *view* reality, but in the way they *render* it. And then it turns out that the distinction is not actually in the way they render reality, but in the volume of reality they render. The potential confusion inherent in Chase's definitions can be seen by applying to *Clarissa* and *Moby-Dick* his dictum that "the novel renders reality closely and in comprehensive detail [while] the romance . . . feels free to render reality in less volume and detail". Since the latter is crammed, to the point of tedium for some readers, with "real", verifiable cetological details, it must, by Chase's criteria, be classified a novel. The former, however, which contains very few, if any, "verifiable" details, must be classified a romance.

A similar weakness inheres in Chase's account of the way in which the two forms handle character. In the novel, according to

---

[6]   *The American Novel and Its Tradition* (Garden City, New York, 1957), p. 12.

Chase, "we come to see these people in their real complexity of temperament and motive. They are in explicable relation to nature, to each other, to their social class, to their own past". In the romance, on the other hand, "The characters, probably rather two-dimensional types, will not be complexly related to each other or to society or to the past".[7] What Chase apparently has in mind is something like E. M. Forster's distinction, in *Aspects of the Novel*, between flat and round characters. But he has added some twists of his own that upset the delicate equilibrium established by Forster, who is quite careful to limit the terms flat and round so that both apply only to the fictional structure itself. Flat characters, Forster writes, "in their purest form, ... are constructed round a single idea or quality: when there is more than one factor in them, we get the beginning of the curve towards the round".[8] To speak in this way of relative complexity in fictional characters is one thing, to say that "we come to *see*" characters "in their *real* complexity ..." is another. What Chase does is to dichotomize not between two different genres or two different ways of writing fiction but between literature and life, and in such a way as to confuse one with the other. Fictional characters may be complex, and their complexity may persuade the reader into believing that the characters bear a close resemblance to "real people", but the complexity itself – like the characters – is "fictional", the mutual creation of the writer's imagination and the reader's response. The unwillingness to distinguish between life and art is apparent in Chase's belief that fictional characters should be "in explicable relation" to both "nature" and "their own past", as though "nature" (*not* the novelist's representation of nature) and the past of a fictional character (not *the* past) were equivalent.

The same kind of juggling occurs when Chase asserts that the characters in the romance "will not be complexly related ... to society or the past", for now the terminology has shifted to "society" rather than "their social class" and "*the* past" rather than "their own past". In the first instance, "their social class" and

7   Pages 12-13.
8   New York, 1954, p. 67.

"their own past" seem to relate to qualities within the work of fiction that adhere to and help to define characters (as, presumably, Squire Western is defined by his being a country gentleman, though, interestingly enough, the foundling Tom Jones is defined by neither his mysterious past nor his non-existent class). But in the case of the romance, "the past" and "society", as Chase uses the terms, seem to be phenomena outside the sphere of the fiction to which the fictional work bears no clear relation. As with Trilling, so now with Chase, manners and a rigid and well defined class structure have become the only legitimate agents which can be used to communicate reality, and insofar as a work of fiction cannot be directly related to or superimposed upon an empirically verifiable, highly stratified social structure, to that extent it has veered away from "reality" and toward "romance". The necessary inference is that the writer unfortunate enough to live in a classless, mannerless society can never cope with reality. "Reality", then, turns out to be a function of the writer's social milieu, never of style or imagination.

What is true of "reality" is also true of "complexity". Just as American writers have been unable to convey "reality" so they have also been unable to achieve "complexity". Chase feels that "the complexity of the American novel has been much exaggerated. With the exception of one or two of James's novels no American fiction has anything like the complexity of character and event of *Our Mutual Friend* ...".[9] In the absence of any elucidative commentary, one must assume that Chase is equating complexity with quantity of detail. Presumably, what makes *Our Mutual Friend* more complex in "character and event" than *Moby-Dick* or *The Scarlet Letter* is the fact that there is so much of both in Dicken's novel – so many characters and so many things happening. But quantity and complexity may not always be synonymous.[10] In the course of his brilliant analysis of the

[9] Page 5.
[10] This, of course, is not to deny that characters and events are complex in *Our Mutual Friend*. But Chase does not specify what the complexity of the novel consists in, nor why *Our Mutual Friend* provides a better example of complexity than, let us say, *Bleak House* or *Great Expectations*, or *Dombey & Son*, or any other Dickens novel.

sparsely detailed Biblical text which sets forth the "testing" of Abraham, Erich Auerbach discusses Abraham's complexity:

Human beings in the Biblical stories have greater depths of time, fate, and consciousness than do the human beings in Homer; although they are nearly always caught up in an event engaging all their faculties, they are not so entirely immersed in its present, that they do not remain continually conscious of what has happened to them earlier and elsewhere; their thoughts and feelings have more layers, are more entangled. Abraham's actions are explained not only by his character (as Achilles's actions by his courage and his pride, and Odysseus' by his versatility and foresightedness), but by his previous history; he remembers, he is constantly conscious of, what God has promised him and what God has already accomplished for him – his soul is torn between desperate rebellion and hopeful expectation; his silence is multilayered, has background.[11]

The narrative that Auerbach deals with is deceptively simple. Details of place and time, from an empirical point of view, remain always vague and undefined, especially when set against the closely textured, luminous details of the Homeric epic. Abraham, like the characters in what Chase calls "romance", is not in "explicable relation" to nature or a social class or even, in a superficial way, his own past (of his boyhood and youth we know relatively little). Neither is he surrounded by a host of characters drawn from all walks of life. As he appears to us in Genesis 22 he is in relation to two things only – God, with Whom he has already made a covenant, and Isaac, his son, his only son, whom he loves. But far from making him a "two dimensional character", this sparsity of material detail is precisely what gives him "background" and renders him more complex than Odysseus. As Auerbach points out, the narrator's extreme restraint in the presentation of detail, and the way in which certain details are underscored, make each detail presented vibrate with ethical significance. Abraham's complexity (as Biblical commentators through the centuries, and Kierkegaard most strikingly in the nineteenth century, have made clear) lies in his behavior as an ethical being.

[11] *Mimesis: The Representation of Reality in Western Literature*, trans. Willard Trask (Garden City, New York, 1954), p. 9.

The same may be said of Ahab, though his behavior is more ambiguous than Abraham's. Milton O. Percival, in his study, *A Reading of Moby-Dick*,[12] has set forth the ideological relationship between Melville's Ahab and Kierkegaard's Abraham as the knight of faith. Equally intriguing, however, are some of the aesthetic resemblances between the Biblical Abraham and Melville's Ahab as representations. Ahab's actions on that momentous whaling voyage described by Ishmael cannot be fully explained by the happenings of the present moment nor by recourse to his character, for like Abraham he is impregnated by certain events of his past and by his intense consciousness of those few events. While his past never explains Ahab, it is, nevertheless, a constant incitement to him. His initial fateful encounter with the White Whale is outside the range of Ishmael's actual observations, and yet that encounter, like the Whale himself, is always a palpable factor in the events being described. What the reader must not forget and what Ahab cannot forget is that God has made a kind of covenant in reverse with Ahab. The one fact of his existence that conditions his entire being in Ishmael's narrative is his mutilation, possibly a parodic parallel to Abraham's circumcision. Ahab, like Abraham, exists, so to speak, ethically. He is defined always in relation to the White Whale on the one hand and to the members of the crew on the other.

Of Ahab's childhood we are told only that his naming was "a foolish ignorant whim of his crazy widowed mother, who died when he was only a twelvemonth old". In *Moby-Dick* as in the Biblical narrative all other details are subordinated to those with "ethical" significance. In his name Ahab goes back to one of the historical kings of Israel; in his very existence he is associated with a king who is a paradigm of ethical misconduct. "*He's Ahab*, boy; and Ahab of old, thou knowest, was a crowned king!" Peleg tells Ishmael. "And a very vile one", Ishmael rejoins. "When that wicked king was slain, the dogs, did they not lick his blood?" The effect of Melville's method of naming and of underlining the ethical considerations implicit in names is to give Ahab (like Ishmael) a deeper past, to mingle the historical and the legendary

[12] Chicago, 1950. Reprinted, New York, 1967.

with the purely fictional, and to set in brilliant relief individual men acting out in merciless complexity and desperate urgency the most tantalizing and most deeply ensconced human dilemmas.

It may be that Ahab is "simple" to the extent that he is mad. But madness, even Ahab's monomania, does not necessarily exclude the possibility of complexity. Ahab, after all, is mad in a special way. He is mad in the same way that Don Quixote is mad, and Hamlet, and Raskolnikov, and in the same way that Abraham, perhaps, would be thought mad had he lived in the modern era. A standard modern commentary on Abraham's attempted sacrifice of Isaac states that any modern man who even thought of doing what Abraham did, ". . . if his thoughts were detected, would be put in a mental hospital. Any man who actually carried it out would be convicted of murder and executed".[13] Kierkegaard had said as much in the nineteenth century in *Fear and Trembling*, and also that Abraham himself ". . . was greater than all, great by reason of his power whose strength is impotence, great by reason of his wisdom whose secret is foolishness, great by reason of his hope whose form is madness, great by reason of the love which is hatred of oneself".[14] The form of Abraham's hope is madness, and so is the form of Ahab's despair. Furthermore, Ahab's hope is *in* his despair. The paradoxes that constitute Ahab cannot be explained any more than those that constitute Abraham.

All of which is not to say that Ahab is Abraham, nor only that the complexity of Ahab – an ethical complexity rooted in the deepest recesses of his being – is of the same nature as the complexity of the Biblical Abraham, but that Ahab's complexity and "reality" both owe something to Melville's direct response to Biblical literature, to the "reality" of Abraham as a representation – historical or legendary. Speaking of the English Puritans of the seventeenth century, Harold Fisch says that ". . . for Tyndale, the Scottish covenanters, for Milton and Herbert, the reading of Scripture was . . . a matter of being exposed to a direct, even blinding spiritual illumination . . . . The tremendous effect which the Bible had upon men, the awe, the terror, and

---

[13]   *The Interpreter's Bible* (New York, 1952), I, 642.
[14]   Garden City, New York, 1954, trans. Walter Lowrie, p. 31.

ecstasy which it undoubtedly inspired, should be sufficient to convince the sceptic that the men of the Reformation were concerned
with real and mighty facts of experience. The Bible ... was an
experiential factor no less than the new empirical sciences and the
new humanism of the Renaissance".[15]

F. O. Matthiessen has demonstrated the indebtedness of American writers of the mid-nineteenth century to the seventeenth-
century British writers – to Milton as well as Thomas Browne
and the Platonists.[16] For the writers of the American Renaissance,
as for the English writers of the seventeenth century, the Bible
was not merely a literary source, or the "unfortunate" inspiration
for an anachronistic and misguided Manichaeism; it was, rather,
a real and mighty fact of experience, no less awesome and immediate than other experiential factors.

But by the middle of the nineteenth century the skepticism of
the scientific method, abetted by the empirical epistemology of
Locke, had become critical in the extreme. The analytic criticism
of the Biblical text was already well under way, and in order to
cope with the dual impact of secular humanism and religious
humanism, Melville (following Hawthorne's lead) turned, not
away from reality and the novel to romance, but rather to the
novel in its "classical" form as the most radically skeptical and
self-ironizing of literary genres. As Bruce W. Wardropper puts
it in a perceptive and happily worded essay on the first great
modern novel:

Don Quixote does not disentangle the story from the history, but
points its telescope at the ill-defined frontier itself. It presents the
evidence for the uncertainty of truth and says to the reader: 'You be
the judge.' 'Tu lector, pues eres prudente, juzga lo que te preciere,'
says Cide Hamete Benengeli in a marginal note, after casting doubt
on the authenticity of the Cave of Montesinos episode (II, xxxiv).
This awareness of the ill-defined frontier between history and story,
between truth and lie, between reality and fiction is what constitutes
Cervantes' *Don Quixote*, is what constitutes the novel as distinct from
the romance. The novel is the most self-conscious, the most introverted
of literary genres. Unlike the Alexandrian romance, it is sensitive to

---

[15]   *Jerusalem and Albion* (London, 1964), pp. 3-4.
[16]   *American Renaissance* (New York, 1941).

its origins in historiography and aware of the need to handle its claim to historical accuracy with massive doses of irony.[17]

In this sense, the fiction writers of the American Renaissance did write "novelistically". Sometimes they succeeded in producing great works of art, though very often they failed to hit the mark they were aiming at. But their failures were not the consequence of a turn away from reality. On the contrary, what they did was to attack "reality" at its most vital center and in a most meaningful way. Even their adoption and transformation of Walpole's Gothic machinery was a way of attacking the problem of reality. Responding to the real and mighty fact of experience that was the Bible, and returning also to the formal examples of Cervantes, Laurence Sterne, and the Gothic novelists, they attempted to obliterate ". . . the dividing-line between the actual and the potential, the real and the imaginary, the historical and the fictional, the true and the false", and to eliminate "the critical scrutiny of evidence".[18] That is to say, in their concept of what the novel should do, writers like Hawthorne and Melville were much closer to Cervantes than to the promulgations of Watt, Trilling, and Chase. They sought to encompass reality, but not the reality of Locke. In fact, they were often consciously rejecting and attacking the world that Locke built; though they may not have accepted the world as Locke presented it, they were very much aware of what he had created.

Hawthorne, of course, called his longer works of fiction romances, but one need not assume that he intended this as an advertisement of his "turning away from reality", or as an inability to face Locke's world. Since it was common practice in both England and America at the time to use such subtitles as "A Tale Founded on Fact", "A Tale of Truth", "A Historical Narrative", or simply "A Romance", it would perhaps be unwise to lay too much stress on Hawthorne's subtitles. Moreover, in "The Custom-House", usually taken, along with the Preface to *The House of the Seven Gables*, as the classic statement of his

---

[17] *"Don Quixote*: Story or History?", *Modern Philology*, LXIII (August, 1965), 5.
[18] *Ibid.*, p. 6.

method as a "romancer", Hawthorne establishes not a turning away from reality but the novelist's tendency to obliterate "the dividing-line between the actual and the potential, the real and the imaginary, the historical and the fictional . . .". One of Hawthorne's reasons for prefacing the narrative of adultery with the Custom-House essay was, as Austin Warren observes, to employ "A traditional device of novelists . . . to offer a fiction as a true story, a document".[19] And what Hawthorne does in the essay is to mingle the contemporary actual (Brook Farm, Channing, Emerson, Thoreau), the remotely historical (Surveyor Pue), the quasi-historical (Hawthorne's disapproving Puritan ancestors), and the purely fictional (the discovery of the capital A, "each limb" of which "proved to be precisely three inches and a quarter in length" and of the "several foolscap sheets, containing many particulars respecting the life and conversation of one Hester Prynne . . .").[20]

Hawthorne makes this mingling explicit when he writes that ". . . the floor of our familiar room has become a neutral territory, somewhere between the real world and fairy-land, where the Actual and the Imaginary may meet, and each imbue itself with the nature of the other".[21] The room with which the author started, "the chamber which I most absurdly termed my study", has itself become something else. The room that Hawthorne describes seems to be an imitation of the room in which he composed, and yet it is clearly something more than that. It is not only what Hawthorne explicitly calls it, "a neutral territory . . . where the Actual and the Imaginary may meet", but a dramatized living example of the way in which the novelist may intertwine the one with the other. The "actual" room has been transformed into an imaginary room and the narrator has, without ostentation, changed his identity from the Custom Surveyor satirizing actual people and manners to a purely creative imagination, a process reminiscent of the preface to "Kubla Khan", in which the author describes the metamorphosis in the opposite direction, as a trans-

---

[19]   Introduction, Rinehart ed., *The Scarlet Letter*, p. vi.
[20]   Bobbs-Merrill (Ohio State University text), pp. 32-33.
[21]   *Ibid.*, p. 36.

formation from a purely creative imagination (the opium dreamer) to a bumbling worldling who permits himself to be "detained . . . by a person from Porlock" until the world of imagination has been effectually overshadowed by the material world. In Hawthorne's account, the ordinary details of quotidian existence have been impregnated until they yield up their "reality" in an additional dimension.

Hawthorne, then, did not ignore reality. And the reality he sought can be considered "tangential to society" only if it is assumed that problems of society, like Nature and knowledge in general, "can be explained in terms of their own conditions".[22] But Hawthorne, like Melville (and the seventeenth-century Puritans) found both society and reality "fraught with background", to use Auerbach's phrase. The Puritan acceptance of the Hebraic Covenant-idea in which ". . . man is miraculously elected to be the partner of Deity in an historical enterprise" added, for the Puritan, another dimension to both reality and society. The spirit of the Covenant, as Fisch writes, "leads us back to a dramatic encounter, a confrontation of our own individuality with a transcendent otherness – an I/Thou confrontation". It is through the binding together of "Revelation, Salvation, and Creation" in the Covenant, he adds, that "the three orders of reality – Man, God, and Nature" become meaningful.[23]

Hawthorne and Melville, however, are no longer Puritans. They are as much the heirs of eighteenth-century rationalism as of Puritan dogma. And it is the intermixture of the two streams that issues in the kinetic reality of their novels. For Horace Walpole, a public figure writing in England in the eighteenth century, *The Castle of Otranto* could come into being as an unrestrained

[22] A similar point is made by D. E. S. Maxwell, who writes that Hawthorne's ". . . territory was the human soul, not in isolation or in its transcendent relations only, but in the bearings of social life." *American Fiction: The Intellectual Background* (London, 1963), p. 188.
[23] Chapter 7 of Fisch's book provides a most penetrating account of the spirit and implications of the Covenant-idea. Quotations from pp. 107, 108, 111-112. The definitive discussion of Covenantal theology in New England is Perry Miller's *The New England Mind: The Seventeenth Century* (Boston, 1961), Book VI.

eruption of subconscious irrational forces, a kind of automatic writing in which imagination uninhibited burst the bonds of reason. But his novel of the supernatural remained for Walpole essentially a safety valve, a temporary escape from the immediate pressures of politics. The picture he presented was as distant as he could make it from the frustrations of "real life", and no one, apparently, was more surprised than Walpole himself by the warmth and enthusiasm with which the novel was received by a "rational" public.

The American writers who borrowed from Walpole and his imitators were much more calculating and deliberate in their use of the tools he bequeathed them, more aware, it would seem, of the wider implications of Gothic devices, and more sensitive to the way in which Gothic machinery could be combined with other literary traditions to present a "perspectivistic"[24] picture of reality. "Reality" comes to encompass both the unknown and the intangible, the world of ideas and dreams as well as the material world. Taking their cue from Emerson, Hawthorne and Melville become less interested in man the thinker than in "Man Thinking".

In three early novelists, none of whom succeeded in writing a great novel, there is a pronounced groping toward the "novel of ideas". Hugh Henry Brackenridge, Charles Brockden Brown, and James Fenimore Cooper were all, oddly enough, more interested in conveying ideas than in telling a story. Their struggles to use the novel as a platform for their own "philosophies" without destroying the form are readily apparent. All, to a greater or lesser extent, heirs of the Enlightenment, they clearly try to please and instruct at the same time. Hawthorne and Melville discovered

[24]   In his analysis of *Don Quixote*, Leo Spitzer says of Cervantes that he ". . . must see that the world, as it is offered to man, is susceptible of many etymologies; individuals may be deluded by the perspectives according to which they see the world as well as by the etymological connections which they establish. Consequently, we may assume that the linguistic perspectivism of Cervantes is reflected in his invention of plot and characters . . . . In [the] lexicological variants Cervantes must have seen not a striving toward the approximation of an ideal, but only the variegated phantasmagoria of human approaches to reality: each variant has its own justification, but all of them alike reflect no more than human 'dreams' " (pp. 50, 56).

that it was possible to introduce ideas into the novel without making them discursive. In *Moby-Dick* the method of generating thought through allusion, metaphor and symbol reaches a level of intensity unmatched in the novel in English until the second decade of the twentieth century.

III

BRACKENRIDGE: IDEAS AND THE MAN OF REASON

The last decade of the eighteenth century marked the acceptance, if not the triumph, of the novel, or, more specifically, of the sentimental romance, in America. In spite of the fact that novels received little or no critical notice until the second decade of the nineteenth century,[1] the audience continued to grow for those writers, mostly women, who insisted that they were social historians, purveyors of truth, whose purpose was the edification of the young females who were their principal readers. Writing for a literate but unlearned audience, the authors themselves made no pretence to learning or to any interest in ideas. The most popular of them, Susanna Rowson, candidly asked, in the preface to *Mentoria; or the Young Lady's Friend* (1794), "Alas! What may not be my fate? whose education, as a female, was necessarily circumscribed, whose little knowledge has been simply gleaned from pure nature, and who, on a subject of such importance, write as I feel, with enthusiasm".

Mrs. Rowson, like the majority of her colleagues, felt called upon to fulfill the needs not of the cold intellect but of the tender heart. In this there was little departure from the contemporary novel in England, as is evident from a brief comparison of titles. Some English titles were *Felicia to Charlotte: being Letters from a Young Lady in the Country to her Friend in Town* (1744);[2]

---

[1] See William Charvat, *The Origins of American Critical Thought: 1810-1835* (Philadelphia, 1936), p. 136. See also Terence Martin, *The Instructed Vision; Scottish Common Sense Philosophy and The Origins of American Fiction* (Bloomington, 1961). Lillie D. Loshe, *The Early American Novel, 1789-1830* (New York, 1958).

[2] Other editions in 1755 and 1788.

Ela: or the Delusions of the Heart. A tale founded on Facts (1780); and *The Friend, a Sentimental History: describing love as a Virtue, as well as a Passion* (1754). They had as their American counterparts *Trials of the Human Heart* (1795), *The Power of Sympathy* (1789), *Amelia; or the Faithless Briton* (1798), and so on. As a matter of fact, the aforementioned Mrs. Rowson was born in England and there published her most popular and enduring novel (28 editions in 35 years),[3] *Charlotte Temple.* Much of the action of the novel, however, took place in America, as did, also, most of the sales.

The picture at this point seems fairly clear. Available to the novelists of the late eighteenth century were the works of such great predecessors as Fielding, Smollett, Sterne, and Richardson. The productions of the last two, however, provided the ladies with models to work from. Sterne supplied a pure ore of sentimentality and feeling, while Richardson provided plot (about-to-be-seduced virgin, villainous would-be seducer, and all the embellishments derivable from a social system in which inter-class marriage was frowned upon), form (epistolary), and vision (the beauty, goodness, and truth of bourgeois morality). The history of how the sentimental novelists altered what they borrowed is recorded in H. R. Browne's *The Sentimental Novel in America.* For our purposes it is enough to know that while the men were busy trying to build a new nation, the indefatigable women were becoming the custodians of the novel.

Among the builders, though by no means as prominently as he would have liked, was Hugh Henry Brackenridge. Unlike Mrs. Rowson, Brackenridge could not complain of a sketchy education. Born in Scotland in 1748, of poor parents, he showed an early disposition to learning, becoming sufficiently proficient in the

---

[3] Susanna Rowson, *Charlotte Temple, A Tale of Truth*, ed. Francis W. Halsey (New York, 1905), pp. xcvii-c. The years referred to are 1790 (the first English edition) to 1825. In all, Mr. Halsey found 104 editions up to 1905. Also, R. W. G. Vail, "Susanna Haswell Rowson, The Author of *Charlotte Temple*: A Bibliographical Study", *Proceedings of the American Antiquarian Society*, n.s. XLII, pt. 1 (Mass., 1933), pp. 62-68 and 91-130. Mr. Vail estimates over 200 editions, of which 160 are described. Of 161 known editions, only nine are not American.

classics at the age of fourteen to gain admittance to Princeton University. There he was a classmate of Philip Freneau and James Madison. After graduation in 1771, he tried his hand at pedagogy, theology, and letters, before finally settling on the law. But in all his groping after a profession he never lost his interest in ideas and literature.

Neither by education nor temperament was Brackenridge suited to the novel of sentimentality. His early love of the classics suffered no diminution in later life, and he confessed, in *Modern Chivalry*, that "I have forgot almost all the reading of my middle age; and recollect chiefly my academic studies. Hence it is that the classics are more in my head, than Shakespeare; or Milton".[4] But even when the classics were not in his head, it was certainly not *Pamela* which replaced them. "In the English language", he wrote, "that of Hume, Swift, and Fielding, is the only stile that I have coveted to possess". And in the matter of fiction, he maintained that "Except memoirs of person's own times, biographical sketches by contemporary writers: Voyages, and Travels, that have geographical exactness, there is little of the historical kind, in point of truth, before *Roderick Random*; or *Gil Blas*" (p. 406). But the book to which he was primarily indebted for his most significant literary work was *Don Quixote*.

No amount of critical legerdemain can make *Modern Chivalry* (1792-1815) out a great novel, for its flaws are too serious. For one thing, Brackenridge constantly intrudes to speak in his own person in such a way as to cause an unintended confusion between himself and the fictional character, Captain John Farrago. Albert Van Nostrand, in *The Denatured Novel*, comments on James Fenimore Cooper's practice of separating entertainment and instruction by writing "a chapter for the reader, then a chapter for Cooper. The violent action would move the characters around for awhile, then they would all sit down and have a serious thought".[5] Brackenridge indulges in a similar practice, except that he writes a chapter for the reader, then two for himself. The

---

[4] Hugh Henry Brackenridge, *Modern Chivalry*, ed. Claude M. Newlin (New York, 1937), p. 464. Citations in my text are from this edition.
[5] (Indianapolis, Indiana, 1960), p. 30.

result is that the balance of the novel breaks down. Brackenridge originally seems to have conceived Farrago as a Quixote-like character – a man steeped in book learning who is ridiculously ignorant of the world around him, but certainly not "mad". Brackenridge's opening description shows him as

a man of about fifty-three years of age, of good natural sense, and considerable reading; but in some things whimsical, owing perhaps to his greater knowledge of books than of the world; but, in some degree, also, to his having never married, being what they call an old bachelor, a characteristic of which is, usually, singularity and whim. He had the advantage of having had in early life, an academic education; but having never applied himself to any of the learned professions, he had lived the greater part of his life on a small farm, which he cultivated with servants or hired hands, as he could conveniently supply himself with either. (p. 6)

A little later, Brackenridge confirms that "Captain Farrago was a good man, but unacquainted with the world. His ideas were drawn chiefly from what may be called the old school; the Greek and Roman notions of things" (p. 53).

What Brackenridge apparently had in mind was to create a series of absurd juxtapositions between a pedant and the ignorant masses. Both of these constituted a threat to a democratic system of government, the former because of an inability to cope with the practical problems of life, and the latter because of an inability to understand the history and tradition of a democratic society. But if Farrago is impractical and pedantic, his mind is not, like Quixote's, deranged by his reading. It may be interesting to note, also, that the reading which "afflicts" him is not, as with Quixote, chivalric romances but the classics.

At any rate, the Quixote concept is sustained only briefly.

A strange idea came into the head of Captain Farrago about this time. . . . The idea had come into his head, to saddle an old horse that he had, and ride about the world a little, with his man Teague at his heels, to see how things were going on here and there, and to observe human nature. For it is a mistake to suppose, that a man cannot learn man by reading him in a corner, as well as on the widest space of transaction. At any rate, it may yield amusement. (p. 6)

(I take it, at this point, that the "cannot" is a textual or printing error. The statement makes more sense if it reads "It is a mistake to suppose that a man *can* learn man by reading him in a corner . . .".) Farrago, then, like Quixote, decides to enter the world, taking a Sancho Panza with him. But the nature of his character seems to become blurred in his first encounter, which is with some jockeys about to bet on a horse race. They mistake Farrago's nag for a thoroughbred, and no amount of argument on his part can convince them of their error. The trouble with the scene is that for an impractical pedant Farrago is all too practical. It is he who recognizes what is actually the case, that his horse "is but a common palfrey, and by no means remarkable for speed or bottom; . . . a common plough horse which I have used on my farm for several years, and can scarce go beyond a trot" (p. 6). When the jockeys refuse to accept the empirical evidence, insisting that the nag must have been sired by a blooded steed, "the Captain . . . could not avoid answering".

Gentlemen, said he, it is a strange thing that you should suppose that it is of any consequence what may be the pedigree of a horse. For even in men it is of no avail. Do we not find that sages have had blockheads for their sons; and that blockheads have had sages? It is remarkable, that as estates have seldom lasted three generations, so understanding and ability have seldom been transmitted to the second. There never was a greater man, take him as an orator and philosopher, than Cicero: and never was there a person who had greater opportunities than his son Marcus; and yet he proved of no account or reputation. This is an old instance, but there are a thousand others. . . . I will venture to say, that when the present John Adamses, and Lees, and Jeffersons, and Jays, and Henrys, and other great men, who figure upon the stage at this time, have gone to sleep with their fathers, it is an hundred to one if there is any of their descendants who can fill their places. Was I to lay a bet for a great man, I would sooner pick up the brat of a tinker, than go into the great houses to chuse a piece of stuff for a man of genius. (pp. 7-8)

At the conclusion of the speech, the jockeys merely think him a fool, "and gave themselves no more trouble about him" (p. 8). Farrago's problem is that for all the good sense of his speech he does not realize that there is no point in casting pearls before swine. Nothing in the speech is actually "foolish". He does not, as does Don Quixote on occasion, mistakenly think he is addressing royalty or another knight. Nevertheless, it is unrealistic to exhibit such erudition before ignorant men.

The Captain's speech is revealing in other ways too. First, it affirms his faith, a faith similar to Jefferson's, in nature's ability to produce her own aristocrats. Secondly, his admiration for Cicero both as an orator and philosopher indicates an admiration, as well, for the self-made Ciceronian gentleman. Finally, the speech shows the Captain himself to be a man of classical learning, albeit, at this point, one who does not quite know how to carry that learning before ignorant men.

Brackenridge expatiates on this flaw of Farrago's in a chapter of commentary which immediately follows. "The first reflection that arises, is, the good sense of the Captain; who was unwilling to impose his horse for a racer; not being qualified for the course. . . . The second reflection that arises, is, the simplicity of the Captain; who was so unacquainted with the world, as to imagine that jockeys and men of the turf could be composed by reason and good sense . . ." (p. 11).

This strange combination of ingredients in Farrago,[6] naiveté mingled with learning and common sense, becomes a serious drawback. Brackenridge seems unable to decide whether to ridicule Farrago, or society through him, and the result is that the Captain never quite comes through as a character. He remains an odd mixture of literary conventions: Quixote, Uncle Toby, Parson Adams. But eventually, Brackenridge himself becomes the most important character in the novel. For before long, the fictional disguise becomes too burdensome to maintain, whereupon the author simply takes to expressing his ideas directly. The ideas, perhaps, press too hard. Brackenridge himself affirms, "I have taken courage to write on, and thought that if it did give offense, I might as well be hanged for an old sheep as a lamb. The truth is, I had not written myself out; but, many more ideas springing up in my brain, and crouding together in a narrow compass, wanted egress, and demanded to see the light" (p. 576).

[6] Brackenridge must have been aware of this, as the name, Farrago, indicates.

As Brackenridge's alter ego, Farrago becomes above all an eighteenth-century man of reason. "Force", he insists at one point, "proves nothing but the quantum of force. Reason is the only argument that belongs to man" (p. 88). His belief in reason, as one might expect, is most salient in Farrago's attitude toward religion. "His ideas on the subject of religious toleration were correct; and though he disapproved of founding religion in passion, it being a thing of reason, judgment, and habit, yet he had seen that by directly opposing this error of the understanding, the pride of the multitude is enlisted in its service" (p. 609).

Farrago conceives reason, moreover, as an instrument of moderation. This is directly reflected in a belief in the values of compromise and in a distaste for extremes.

In a bedroom scene reminiscent of Restoration farce, Teague O'Regan, Farrago's servant, tries to rape a chambermaid in her quarters. Her screams bring several other lodgers including an innocent clergyman. O'Regan quick-wittedly manages to cast suspicion on the clergyman, whose mortification and temporary muteness convince the others, among them Farrago, of his guilt. The Captain's first instinct is to relieve the clergyman's embarrassment by taking the whole affair lightly.

> The Captain, interrupting him, and wishing to save his feelings, began by excusing or extenuating the offence. It is no great affair, said he, after all that is said or done. The love of women is a natural sin, and the holiest men in all ages have been propense to this indulgence. There was Abraham that got to bed to his maid Hagar, and had a bastard by her, whom he named Ishmael. Joshua, who took Jericho by the sound of ram's horns, saved a likely slut of the name of Rahab, under a pretence that she had been civil to the spies he had sent out, but in reality because he himself took a fancy for her. I need say nothing about David, who wrote the Psalms, and set them to music; and yet in his old days had a girl to sleep with him. Human nature is human nature still; and it is not all the preaching and praying on earth can extinguish it. (p. 31)

Farrago takes the stance of a man of the world who can tolerate "minor" vices so long as they do not disrupt the order of the universe. But when the clergyman informs Farrago that the affair may wreck his clerical career, the Captain, because of "a real love of humanity and justice", proceeds to force O'Regan to assume the guilt.

Teague, said he, from what I know of your disposition, I have no more doubt than I have of my existence, that it was yourself who made that uproar with the girl at the tavern where we lodged; though I could not but give you credit for your presence of mind in throwing it upon the clergyman. But whether the matter lies with you or him is of no consequence. You can take it upon you, and lay up treasure in heaven. . . . It will be no harm to you, for your character in this respect is as bad as it can well be.

Teague said he did not care much; but thought the priest ought to pay a little smart money; for it was a thankless matter to do these things for nothing. Said the Captain, these people are not the most plenty of money; but I will advance half a crown towards the accommodation. Teague was satisfied, and ready to acknowledge whatever was demanded of him. (pp. 33-34)

The arguments and actions of the Captain here are interesting. Certainly, he does not display any passion for absolute justice, nor does he seem to be interested in righteousness for its own sake. These matters are not his business. He is concerned, rather, to see the world operate as smoothly and conveniently as possible. He cannot be positively, though he may be reasonably, certain of Teague's guilt. But it does not matter to the Captain even if he is wrong. Since Teague has nothing to lose by confessing the crime, and the clergyman a great deal to gain, encouraging Teague to assume the guilt is obviously the most sensible course of action for the Captain to arrange. And when Teague holds out for his pound of flesh, the Captain does not rise in moral indignation to crush the monster, but instead, again takes the smoothest path. He cheerfully pays a nominal extortion fee in order to expedite a satisfactory conclusion of the episode.

Absent from the Captain's makeup is messianic zeal. Eminently a man of reason, he does not, like the French revolutionaries, make a goddess of it. Logic for him is not, as it is for the romantic intellectuals, a cup of gall to be drained to the last painful and bitter drop. It is a lubricant for the machinery of life. And the Captain, as a consequence, approaches most situations pragmatically. On one occasion, for example, two men appeared, the one of a grave aspect, with a black coat; the other without the same clerical colour of garb; but with papers in his pocket which announced his authority to preach, and officiate as a clergyman. The man with the black coat, averred, that coming over together, in a vessel from Ireland, they had been messmates; and while he was asleep one night, being drowsy after prayers, the other had stolen his credentials from his pocket. The man in possession of the papers, averred they were his own, and that the other had taken his coat, and by advantage of the cloth, thought to pass for what he was not. (p. 99)

The Captain proposes to solve the problem by having both men preach a sermon. When the populace's preference is divided equally between the fraud and the genuine clergyman, the Captain, who had recognized the imposter immediately, speaks out:

Gentlemen, said he, the men seem both to have considerable gifts, and I see no harm in letting them both preach. There is work enough for them in this new country; the first [who is the genuine] appears to me, to be more qualified for the city, as a very methodical preacher; but the last is most practical; and each may answer a valuable purpose in their proper place. (p. 104)

As in the abortive rape scene, principle is a minor consideration. The Captain seeks not an absolute answer to the problem but a functional solution. He is not hell-bent on purging the imposter and punishing him for his imposition. Instead, he is satisfied to settle the issue to everyone's satisfaction, if that is possible.

When, on another occasion, a mob tries to tear down a church because the preacher "is not an American republican, but quotes the English commentators in his sermons . . ." (p. 369), the Captain replies:

Religion . . . is of no government. Wines are the better for being brought over seas, and our best brandies are from monarchies. Where was the cloth of that coat made? Will you reject a good piece of stuff because it came through the hands of an aristocratic weaver? These are false ideas of what is right, and useful to mankind. The common law is not the worse for having been the common law of England, and our property and birth right which our ancestors brought with them; nor is our Bible the worse for having been translated under James the first of England, which translation we still use, and from

which we repeat all sentences of scripture. Nor are systems of theology, or harmonies of the evangelists the worse for having been written
in another country. Why do we use the English language? Is it not
because we cannot easily substitute another; or have no better to substitute. (p. 370)

If we accept as the pragmatist position that "that is true which
is best for us to believe", then Farrago clearly anticipates it. In
theory, the product of evil is evil. We should not, if we are to
remain pure, make bargains with the devil. But Farrago is not
concerned with theory; only with product. If, as we can see by
our reason and experience, the common law works, if it insures
the maintenance of order and rational freedom, then by all means
we must not reject it, no matter what its source. This anticipation
of the pragmatic frame of mind is even more startling when
Brackenridge drops Farrago. At one point, speaking in one of
his own little private essays, he says, "Even supposing the representations of our theologists to be an illusion, why dissipate the
vision? Does it not constitute a great portion of our happiness?
Are those men supposed to have done nothing for the world who
have raised fabricks of this kind to the imagination *even upon
false grounds?* Has it not contributed at least to amuse in this
life? It is an opiate under pain, *and eases the mind without affecting the nerves*" (p. 573).

Diametrically opposed to this position is the denunciatory
comment attributed to Karl Marx, religion is the opiate of the
masses. For all its triteness now, the remark is none the less
revealing. In its very fury, in its passion to see "truth" clearly,
and establish it in all its purity on earth, the comment is characteristic of the revolutionary and romantic intellectual throughout the nineteenth century. It is also, one must add, what marks
the intellectual in European fiction. Be he liberal or conservative,
he is obsessed by an irresistible drive to convert intellectual ideals
into physical realities, and there seems, as a consequence, no end
to his capacity for or delight in picking intellectual scabs. This
mental scab-picking is characteristic of one of the most power-
fully portrayed intellectuals in all fiction, Raskolnikov. It is not
enough for him to perceive intellectually that all great men are

ruthless; he must experience the intellectual perception in action. And once the action has been performed it is not enough to let it go at that. He must torment himself in his little verbal game with the inspector, shamelessly regurgitating the foulest contents of the depths of his mind.

Such passion does not afflict Farrago. Though he is highly interested in matters of government and political power, he is as reasonable in them as in questions of religion. The right of revolution the Captain is quick to recognize. But he recognizes it only as an extreme measure to be undertaken as a last resort.

... Is it [revolution] conducive to an amelioration of the state of life, [he asks,] and likely to produce a greater sum of happiness, to innovate upon established forms, or to let them remain? It is true, indeed, that when we consider the throes and convulsions with which a change in government is usually attended, it ought not to be lightly attempted; and nothing but an extreme necessity for a reform can justify it. It is almost as impossible comparing a physical with a moral difficulty, to change a government from despotism to liberty, without violence, as to dislodge a promontory from its base, by any other means, than mining and gunpowder. (p. 315)

Farrago's concept of revolution, then, is essentially conservative and utilitarian. In itself revolution is far from desirable, and is justifiable only insofar as it contributes to the greater happiness of the people. Therefore, though the Captain approves revolution when it is absolutely necessary, he does not revel in it for its own sake. He perceives and deplores the extremes to which it can be carried. Describing the stay of his "bog-trotter" in revolutionary France, he states:

He has seen the folly of the people of France ... in reducing all things to the first elements instead of accommodating to existing establishments; of deracinating from the foundation church and state, and bandying the term liberty until ignorance and usurpation, terminated in despotism. For though at the commencement of a revolution, active and uninformed spirits, are useful, or perhaps absolutely necessary, like the subterranean fire throwing up continents; yet as in this case, the fostering dews, and the breath of the atmosphere, are necessary to give soil and impregnate with vegetation; so after the stirrings of men's minds, with a political convulsion, deliberate reason, and prudent temperament are necessary, to preserve what is gained, and turn it to advantage. (p. 348)

In this belief in controlled revolution, Farrago is certainly a man of his time. All men are created equal, but the masses are not to be trusted too much, for their tendency is to overthrow, rather than build on, the foundations of society. The people *en masse* are too susceptible to overflow of emotion, and it is this kind of extremism, passion unwatered by reason and prudence, that leads from tyranny right back into despotism. This is the lesson the Captain learns from the French Revolution: "Whence sprung the emperor that now *affects the French*? From the *mountain* of the national assembly. It is the madness of the people that makes emperors. They are not always aware when they are planting *serpents teeth*" (p. 449).

It is one of the functions of the learned gentlemen in a democracy to be aware, to be alert to the dangers that beset a liberal form of government when a tendency arises to resolve the liberal tension into one of the extremes (right or left) of despotism. "Reflecting men", the Captain says, "saw the emperor, in the insurrections of Paris: in the revolutionary tribunals; in the dominancy of the clubs; in the deportations to Cayenne. Whether it springs from the seed, or grows from the plant, . . . *despotism is not of a day*; it is of gradual increase. Will not the people give him credit that can point out to men, *where a germ of it exists*" (p. 449).

The answer to this question is a resounding No! The people like to be courted by the demagogue, not chastised by the sage. They want to have their passions enflamed to further extravagance rather than cooled to rational compromise. In a tavern conversation overheard by Farrago, one of the speakers points out that "It is natural to distrust him who proposes to stop short of what seems a complete reform. The sovereign people is as liable to the impulse of passion, and as open to the insinuations of flatterers as the individual tyrant. The courtier devoid of principle, in the democratic hall, gets the ear of the populace, as he would that of a Prince, and abuses it" (p. 382). It is significant that though the speaker does not romanticize "the people" neither does he apotheosize the Prince. Both are corruptible, but it is the corruptibility of the former that is the special headache of a democracy.

The Captain himself, in one of his meditations, wonders,

How do you distinguish the demagogue from the patriot? The demagogue flatters the clown, and finds fault with the sage. The patriot, and the sage, unless you mean the vain philosopher, [sic] mean the same thing. The Jewish prophets were all of them sages. They were seers, or *men that saw far into things*. You will find they were no slouches at blaming the people. 'My people Israel, is destroyed for lack of knowledge.' *I am wounded* in the house of my friends.' *This may be said of liberty, when republicans give it a stab*. The lamentations of Jeremiah are but the weepings of a patriot over the errors of the people. Yet the people are always right, say the demagogues. I doubt that. *Tom fool*, may laugh at the expression, 'save the people from themselves.' Never the less, there is something in it. It is a Scripture phrase, 'go not with a multitude to do evil'; which would seem to imply that the multitude will sometimes do wrong. (p. 415)

The question raised in this meditation is crucial to democracy. How is it possible to find the equilibrium point between oppression of the people and false glorification of them for selfish ends. The great danger is that the demagogues who flatter the clown and berate the sage are many, while men with vision and the courage to denounce the people to themselves are few. And yet, there is as little merit in encouraging the people in their wrong as in encouraging princes in theirs. But what is most surprising in the meditation is Farrago's choice of sage. It is difficult to imagine any single group more different in spirit from the eighteenth-century man of reason than the Hebrew prophets. In their total commitment, their fiery denunciations of the evils of this world, even in their concept of knowledge ("lest they see with their eyes, hear with their ears, and understand with their hearts . . ." Isaiah 6:10), they are far removed from the rationalism and classical restraint that are such admirable qualities in Farrago's eyes. But Cicero will not do as model here, for his denunciations are pretty much limited to the ruling class. The full force of the paradox implicit in Farrago's admiration for the nay-saying religious zeal of the prophets can be felt when it is set alongside his distrust of the passion and fervor of revolutionary zealots:

A journal was published in France, [Farrago recalls,] by Marat, under the direction, or, with the assistance of Robespierre, entitled '*L'ami du peuple*.' There could not be a more seducing title; and yet this very journal was the *foe of the people*; I have no doubt, but that Marat meant well to the people; but he had not an understanding above the public, and judgment to correct the errors of occasional opinion. He was of the multitude himself, and did not overtop them *by having higher ground from whence to observe. He had not been a sage before he became a journalist.* Hence he denounced the Girondists, the philosophers of the republic; Condorcet, and others who had laid the foundation of the revolution. He denounced them because they suggested a confederate republic, such as Montesquieu projected, and America has realized. Marat took up with the simple, *the one and indivisible*; the populace understood this, but not the complication, and it prevailed; but the republic went down. (pp. 423-24)

An even more perplexing problem, then, than distinguishing between demagogues and patriots is distinguishing true prophets from false. The difference is that the former are sages (though whether their sagacity is that of the Hebrew prophet or the eighteenth-century rationalist is not quite clear). The trouble with Marat, according to Farrago, was not his lack of sincerity but his lack of judgment. And this zealous sincerity when it is attended by a lack of judgment can be disastrous. Brackenridge takes the problem up in more detail when he considers Robespierre and the Reign of Terror.

I never had a doubt with the Captain, but that the bulk of the jacobins in France meant well; even Marat and Robespierre considered themselves as denouncing, and trucidating only the enemies of the republic ... Doubtless ... both [Robespierre and his brother Peregrine] were innocent ... of meaning ill. 'The time shall come, when they that kill you, shall think they are doing God service.' ...

Marat the journalist and Robespierre were pushed gradually to blood; by the principle, which governed them, of taking it for granted that all who thought differently upon a subject were traitors .... It is a truth in nature, and a maxim in philosophy 'that from whence our greatest good springs, our greatest evils arise.' ... That activity which was useful in the first effort, is unwilling to be checked in further employment; and under the idea of a *progressing reform*, turns upon the establishment which it has produced, and intending good, does harm. . . . Fresh hands especially, are apt to over-do the matter. . . . Prudent people do not like rash hands. States have been best built up, *by the wise as well as the honest.* (pp. 425-26)

Farrago and Brackenridge are quite incisive at this point. They do not, as less reasonable observers might, question the good intentions of the revolutionary zealots. But it is the very sincerity of these intentions that is the source of danger. The process that Brackenridge describes subsequently bears a remarkable resemblance to the process that Michael Polanyi has called "moral inversion": a growing willingness, and finally a conviction that it is absolutely necessary, to shed rivers of blood indiscriminately for the sake of achieving absolute right. In this process, violence as a method of moral persuasion inevitably descends from a means to an end in itself. Furthermore, the passion for absolute right tends to culminate in the final conviction that only one man knows the right, and that therefore the revolution must be resolved into a totalitarian unit rather than into a republican pluralism which allows a margin of error.

This process of "moral inversion" is typical of the romantic intellectual who shifts eventually from the eighteenth-century belief in Reason to a belief in total Ego. In politics and religion as well as aesthetics, the lamp replaces the mirror, and the concept of the law-giver as the greatest of men becomes an obsession in the nineteenth-century mind. The movement is from God and Tradition to Reason to "I".[7] Individual conscience becomes the final measure of human action, and by a final ironic twist, the man with the most sublime conscience becomes the "law-giver" who must impose his own will over every other man's. The image of the "law-giver" becomes a fixture in the European romantic consciousness.

In his funeral oration on Benjamin Franklin, Abbé Fauchet soared to the heights of eulogy in declaring that Franklin was the

---

[7]   For a discussion of the transition from Tradition (Divine Law) to Reason (Natural Law) to Conscience (Ego), see Ernst Cassirer, *The Philosophy of the Enlightenment* (Boston, 1955), pp. 234-74.

". . . foremost lawgiver of the world".[8] It is difficult to believe that Franklin himself would have welcomed the apotheosis which took place in France after his death. Nor is it conceivable that he would have taken the title of "foremost lawgiver" as his due. But the words Fauchet chooses to indicate the highest praise are revealing. Almost fifteen years later, Napoleon was to take them for himself, first issuing the Napoleonic Code and then crowning himself emperor. This image of the law-maker, now embodied in Napoleon, persisted in the European imagination. Julien Sorel, Stendhal's hero in *The Red and the Black*, is haunted by it. So is Raskolnikov. And Nietzsche has Zarathustra speak: "Behold the good and just. Whom do they hate most? Him who breaketh up their table of values, the breaker, the law-breaker: – he, however, is the creator . . . . Companions, the creator seeketh, not corpses – and not herds of believers either. Fellow-creators the creator seeketh – those who grave new values on new tables".[9]

But the three thousand miles of salt water that turned Franklin into a god, served only to tarnish the glitter of Napoleon's reputation, and it is not the "law-giver", but the law that Brackenridge respects. He considers the question, which apparently had popular currency, Why can't have the law "in a pocket-book, and let every man be his own lawyer"? He answers that "The law of nations forms a part of the *municipal law of this state*. This law is of great extent, and to be collected from many books. The common law, before the revolution, made a part of our law; and by an act of our legislature . . . it is recognized and established to be a part of our law, and *such of the statute laws of England as have heretofore been in force*. This law must be collected from commentaries, and decisions. It is of an immense extent. Because the relations of men, and the contracts of parties are of an infinite variety" (p. 446).

Again, we see both Brackenridge's conservatism and pragmatism. Since the law which has been accumulated through history serves a useful and constructive purpose, it would be folly to

[8] Quoted from Bernard Fay, *The Revolutionary Spirit in France and America* (New York, 1927), p. 290.
[9] Friedrich Nietzsche, *Thus Spake Zarathustra* (New York, 1928), p. 15.

discard it. Yet, there is no insistence on the sanctity of law itself, but on the reasonableness of preserving it in order to maintain sanity and equity in human relations.

The reasonableness in this instance happens to be Brackenridge's. But it is the same quality that informs the character of Captain Farrago, and it is this quality that enables him to perceive the imperfections in democratic society. When he happens, on one occasion, to return to his home village on a visit, he observes "that little attention had been paid, for some time, to public works; the pavements were neglected, and the ways and watercourses suffered to fill up. An aqueduct, begun, to bring a spring from the hill, was left unfinished" (p. 357). On inquiry, the Captain finds that the cause of all this neglect is that the elected officials do not want to antagonize the people by raising the taxes which would supply the revenue necessary to complete these highly important projects.

And does this please the people, said the Captain.

No said the citizen who had taken upon him to reply; they have turned out one set for doing too much; and they will turn out the other next for doing nothing.

But why not hit a medium, said the Captain.

A difficulty occurs, continued the speaker. In the works projected, the people insist that no man shall be consulted in his own occupation. The mason shall make out the bills of scantling; and the carpenter determine the arches of a stone bridge . . . . It is better to appeal to persons that know nothing about the matter, and trust them. (pp. 357-58)

The Captain immediately announces that such foolishness is "republicanism run mad". But this is not to say that he condemns republicanism itself. When the citizen who has been his informant laments that "the sovereign people never had a good head upon their shoulders . . .", the Captain replies, "You are an aristocrat. . . . I shall not go so far as that. The sovereign people act wisely, they act madly, just like other people". When the citizen then suggests that the people "might act wisely . . . were it not for political divisions", the Captain refuses to accept that either. "Political divisions", he retorts, "will always exist. It is inseparable from the nature of a community. And it is not in the nature of things that the power can be long on one side. *The duration depends upon the judgment of using it.* The people will revolt from themselves when they find they have done wrong, and that side which was now the weakest will become the strongest" (p. 358).

Brackenridge's italics are significant, for they emphasize Farrago's belief that the essence of democracy lies in the capacity to combine universal suffrage with intelligent, informed judgment, and the exercise of power with rational restraint. As a consequence of this belief, Farrago is a staunch defender of both thought and learning. When the citizen alluded to in the previously cited scene concedes that "these matters I do not much understand. . . . You have the advantage of having seen more", the Captain rejoins, "I may have seen a little, but I have thought more . . ."

As to higher learning, the Captain deplores the low esteem in which it is held in the new country. When a wild mob tries to burn down a college, he risks his life trying to divert them. He tells them that what they are about to do is useless. Since learning is already so despised, burning the college would be a mere superfluity. Moreover, the building may yet serve a useful purpose, adds the Captain: "Politicians say; we have it from their own mouths on some occasions, that though they have no learning, they feel no want of it. Is it to be supposed that a workman does not know whether he wants tools? . . . When learning and law are put down, trial by battle must regulate society. We shall then want barracks and hospitals. This building will accommodate invalids" (p. 368).

In another scene, the Captain, a lawyer, and a Latin schoolmaster "were . . . entering the Lack-Learning settlement, where a great uproar had been made on account of their coming. It had been given out that the company consisted of *Scholars and Lawyers*. . . . A multitude had got together, with sticks and stones, to obstruct the march into their country" (p. 523). The Captain meets the mob's hostility by protesting that there are not really any scholars present. But then he goes on to inquire,

After all, what harm could learning do you, provided that you did not learn yourselves? . . . The raccoons, and the squirrels can crack nuts, maugre all our education and refinement. . . . If you do not find your account, or your amusement in literary studies, what matters it if others do? Learning is not a thing that will grow upon you all at once. . . . The boy feels the birch on his backside, to make him learned. The man gets a headache, poring over books. In fact, it requires some resolution, and much perseverance to become learned. I acknowledge that men were at first like the beasts of the wood, and the fowls of the air, without grammars or dictionaries; and it took a great deal to bring them out of that state, and give them what is called education. At the revival of letters in Europe, after the dark ages, it was thought a great matter to get to be a scholar. Peculiar privileges were attached. Hence what is called 'the benefit of clergy.' (pp. 523-24)

But though he is ready to defend learning and its right to exist unmolested, the Captain does not demand the transference from Europe of the "benefit of clergy". We have seen that he does not hold with "vain philosophers". At one point he goes so far as to insist that "a mere philosopher is but a fool, in matters of business. Even in speculation, he sometimes imagines nonsense" (p. 414). But this occurs only when "there is too much vision mixed with the fact. Want of information of what has been; the not examining the fitness and congruity of things, leads to this" (p. 414). It is not that thought and vision in themselves are undesirable, but they must be combined with a respect for fact and practical necessity. In his own voice, Brackenridge asserts that "it is not the want of learning that I consider as a defect; but the *contempt* of it" (p. 447).

The tendency, then, of the Captain's thought and personality is always toward the pragmatic. It is for this reason, perhaps, that he can conceive of power and intellect going hand in hand. Jacques Barzun, in *The House of Intellect*, expresses the fear that "the greatest danger to a democratic state is probably the contamination of its politics by Intellect. . . . Where . . . is the menace? It lies in the possibility that, for him [the intellectual] and others, ideas will come to seem more important than public service and social peace. The scrimmage of politics is for the purpose of determining who shall transact the government's business. If in the struggle the desire to accomplish one's purpose turns into a desire to annihilate one's opponent, the outcome is civil war. Historically, this desire to annihilate finds its support and justification in Intellect, in ideas, for ideas are clear-cut and divided. Material interests can be compromised, principles cannot".[10]

Barzun's statement is right in so far as it applies to the romantic, messianic intellectual, who is driven by the obsession to impose his will on those benighted souls who do not share his own illumination. The same danger need not exist, however, in the case of the pragmatically oriented man of learning. Where there is no faith in the possibility of achieving the absolute, even absolute earthly perfection, there is not likely to be a strong drive for absolute power. So, while Farrago would not have the intellectual dominate politics, neither would he exclude him from them completely. "There are but two characters", he asserts, "that can be respectable as representatives of the people. A plain man of good sense, whether farmer, mechanic, or merchant; or a man of education and literary talents" (p. 296).

The Captain, then, possesses common sense, a faculty which he applies to the clarification of social and political problems. As a fictional portrait he is not powerful but, then, he is not intended to be. Brackenridge comments at one point that the characters are intended to be caricatures. But the book, perhaps fortunately, is not exactly what Brackenridge intended it to be.

Brackenridge's concept of the novel form is puzzling, but for this very reason, also illuminating. He admired Swift, Smollett, and Fielding, though he was unable to match their achievement. He was also familiar with *Don Quixote*, but he considered it to be largely entertainment: it "contains a great deal of excellent moral sentiment. But, at the same time, has much that can serve only to amuse. Even in health, and with a flow of spirits, from prosperous affairs, it diversifies enjoyments, and adds to that happiness of which the mind is capable" (p. 406).

Yet, Brackenridge started his own book, apparently, in emulation of the picaresque form, and especially *Don Quixote*. He

---

[10] (New York, 1960), p. 146.

finally came to conceive the work as a means of promulgating ideas by presenting them, as much as possible, as entertainment – the old sugar-coated pill:

The vehicle which I have chosen of supposed travels, and conversations, affords great scope, and much freedom, and furnishes an opportunity to enliven with incident. Doubtless it is of the same nature, with many things in the novel way, written by philosophic men, who chose that form of writing, for the purpose merely of conveying sentiments, which in a didactic work, under the head of tract or dissertation, could not so easily gain attention, or procure readers. (p. 630)

But while Brackenridge was hardly a great craftsman, he was a conscious one. Working within the form developed by Cervantes, Fielding, and Smollett, he was bound to be influenced by their stylistic techniques. He was, of course, also influenced by his wide classical background. Both these influences may account for his concept of "high" and "low" styles. We see this classical and neo-classical influence especially in his attempt to manipulate "low" characters. He discusses the problem directly in one of the many asides (so similar to Fielding's in *Tom Jones*) that appear in the book:

It has been asked, why ... have I taken my clown, *from the Irish nation*? The character of the English clown, I did not well understand; nor could I imitate the manner of speaking. That of the Scotch I have tried, as may be seen, in the character of Duncan. But I found it, in my hands, rather insipid. The character of the Irish clown, to use the language of Rousseau, 'has more stuff in it.' He will attempt anything.

The American has in fact, yet, no character; neither the clown, nor the gentleman. So that I could not take one from our own country; which I would much rather have done, as the scene lay here. But the midland states of America, and the western parts in general, being half Ireland, the character of the Irish clown, will not be wholly misunderstood. It is true the clown is taken from the aboriginal Irish; a character not so well known in the North of that country; nevertheless, it is still so much known, even there, and amongst the emigrants here, or their descendants, that it will not be wholly thrown away.

On the Irish stage, it is a standing character; and on the theatre in Britain it is also introduced. I have not been able to do it justice, being but half an Irishman, myself, and not so well acquainted with

the reversions and idiom, of the genuine Thady, as I could wish. However, the imitation at a distance from the original, will better pass than
if it had been written, and read, nearer home. Foreigners will not so
readily distinguish the incongruities; or, as it is the best we can produce for the present, will more indulgently consider them. (p. 405)

It is interesting to watch Brackenridge fluctuate. On the one
hand, he apologizes for the lack of verisimilitude between his
character and one living, thus showing the influence of English
eighteenth-century "realism". On the other hand he states quite
candidly that he is borrowing a literary stock character because
such a character fits his purposes. And yet he is afraid that only
Irishmen will be able to appreciate the character, though real
Irishmen, he fears, will see that the character is incongruous. He
is not sure whether the higher fidelity is to literary models or to
actuality.

In another aside, he asserts that "the characters which we have
introduced, are many of them low. That gives the greater relief
to the mind. . . . Shakespeare has his Bardolph, Nymn, and Pistol,
and the dialogue of these is a relief to the drama of the principal
personages. It is so in nature; and why should it not be so represented in the images of her works. We have the sage and the fool,
interspersed in society, and the fool gives occasion for the wise
man to make his reflections. So in our book" (p. 630).

The insight is admirable, but in spite of it, Brackenridge failed
in the execution. His own characters are never delineated with
sufficient clarity. Especially Farrago, who is surely the "wise
man" in *Modern Chivalry*, wavers back and forth between the
serious and the comic, between the ludicrous and the sensible.
Brackenridge seems to have recognized this, for Farrago finally
asserts, "I cannot but acknowledge . . . that I have resembled Don
Quixote . . . , but I hope I shall not be considered as resembling
that Spaniard in taking a wind-mill for a giant; a common stone
for a magnet that can attract, or transmute metals. It is you that
are the Don Quixotes in this respect, madcaps, and some of you
from the madcap settlement . . ." (p. 783). As a result of this
wavering, the contrast between the "high" and "low" characters
is never quite clear.

Brackenridge's failure in this respect may stem partly from an ideological problem. At several points in the book, Brackenridge affirms his belief in democracy, and in equality of opportunity, though not in equality itself. The difficulty this would present is patent. The English novelist was able to use class differences with the greatest ease. The techniques for using such differences in literature had been established by long tradition – in Chaucer, Elizabethan drama, and the comedies of manners of the Restoration. Moreover, English writers could accept class distinctions as a fact, a natural phenomenon in a world in which every man was expected to know his place. Class differences were not as easily recognized and accepted in the colonies, and certainly not in the western Pennsylvania of Brackenridge's time. But this is not quite the point that Lionel Trilling makes when he says that "In this country the real basis of the novel has never existed – that is, the tension between a middle class and an aristocracy which brings manners into observable relief as the living representation of ideals and the living comment on ideas." [11]

For Brackenridge did not contest the fact that class differences and a perennial tension between classes did exist; though he did, however, deplore the suggestion that such differences should be inherited and perpetuated through rigidified social and political forms. As a matter of fact, a fortune teller advises Farrago that "there is in every government a patrician class, against whom the spirit of the multitude naturally militates: and hence, a perpetual war; the aristocrats endeavoring to detrude the people, and the people contending to obtrude themselves. And it is right that this should be so; for by this fermentation, the spirit of democracy is kept alive" (p. 19).

What made it impossible for Brackenridge to fully exploit "low" characters as a literary device was not that classes did not exist, but that they were not supposed to exist in theory. If every man carried the seed of nobility within him, then a "low" character could not be conceived of as being one in the nature of things. He was low only because of lack of opportunity. And,

[11] Trilling, *The Liberal Imagination*, pp. 249-50.

conversely, a man with such advantages as education, social conscience, and an awareness of the world around him could aspire
to "nobility" in spite of accidents of birth. A Mr. Partridge or a
Parson Adams, both of whom Farrago resembles to some extent,
could not remain a comic figure living in the shadow of a man
who is his better only by an accident of birth.

At the same time, Brackenridge was sufficiently steeped in
Anglo-Saxon and classical tradition to be incapable of treating
"low" characters seriously. Although he, like Fielding, was a
great admirer of Cervantes he did not fully understand him.[12] He
did not have that vision which Gili Gaya attributes to the six-
teenth- and seventeenth-century picaresque novelists: "It is truly
said that this type of novel [the picaresque] is genuinely Spanish.
This does not mean that the life of vagabonds, beggars, and
toughs is a theme exclusive to our literature. . . . [But] what in
the foreigner was cause only for laughter, here inspired deep human compassion".[13]

But if Brackenridge cannot approach the common man with
this deep compassion, still he treats him with a touch of genuine
humility and respect. His position is beautifully summed up by
the editor of the 1846 edition of *Modern Chivalry*: [14]

An enlightened democracy was looked upon by him as the true
nobility. He considered the true democrat as the true gentleman, who
ought to feel a stain on his fair reputation, 'as a wound.' He maintained 'that democracy is not in its nature coarse, and vulgar, or
destitute of high integrity and honor.' The aim and end of his writings
was to raise the standard of democracy, and to elevate 'the noble of
nature' to the same level with any other noble, in those qualities which
constitute true nobility. The noble of nature, in his opinion, ought not
to yield to the noble of aristocracy or monarchy, in strict integrity, in
liberal and benevolent feelings, in propriety of manners and general
intelligence.

It is this kind of character, the liberal gentleman, an enlight-

---

[12]   For a discussion of Fielding's misunderstanding of Cervantes, see A. A.
Parker, "Fielding and the Structure of *Don Quixote*", *Bulletin of Hispanic
Studies*, XXXIII (1956), 1-16.
[13]   Samuel Gili Gaya, "La Picaresca", *Diccionaria de Literatura Espanola*
(Madrid, 1953), p. 563. (Translation mine.)
[14]   (Philadelphia, 1846), p. iii.

ened natural aristocrat, that Farrago became in Brackenridge's hands. And as the author's alter ego, he seems to embody the description that Parrington applies to Brackenridge himself: He "was no truckler either to King George or to his neighbors. Living in the midst of a coonskin democracy, he refused to believe that there was any particular virtue in coonskin. It is not the cap but what is under it that signifies. He was a vigorous individualist, a confirmed democrat, a friend of all honest liberalisms, a man who honored his own counsels and went his own way".[15] His intellectual position was always reasonable if not always logical. Never messianic, a thoroughgoing pragmatist, he avoided, whenever necessary, pushing logic to a destructive extreme. He tried to maintain a constant tension between the preservation of a viable tradition and the movement toward desirable social and intellectual goals.

[15] Vernon L. Parrington, *Main Currents in American Thought* (Harvest Books, New York, 1954), I, 400.

IV

BROWN: IDEAS AND IDEOLOGIES

Bernard Fay observes "a curious phenomenon" in serious American literature of the late eighteenth century. "French writers roused American minds and created original reactions in them at a time when English writers were less interesting and stimulating, but afforded examples that could easily be utilized and imitated. French culture in America was a means of liberation, not a model to be copied. Indeed its great role seems to have been to aid hardy and simple minds, who might have lacked enterprise or imagination, to find themselves and adopt a new spirit that should lead them to create a new form for themselves".[1] This "curious phenomenon" of turning to France for ideas and to England for form was not, as we have seen, entirely applicable to Brackenridge, who, though familiar with the English authors, was perhaps even more familiar with their models. And while he explicitly commended Smollett and Swift for style, he also paid tribute to Cervantes for form. Moreover, in the matter of ideas, he was neither completely taken with "French ideas" when they were at the peak of their popularity in the 80's, nor was he utterly repelled by them when they were under heaviest attack in the 90's. In this, as in all things, Brackenridge remained his own man, seeking a balance between the excesses of new democratic ideas and the abuses of entrenched interests. He wanted order, but never at the expense of individual rights. In temperament and thought, he was thoroughly a liberal intellectual of the enlightenment, and this is reflected in his alter ego, Captain Farrago.

[1] *The Revolutionary Spirit in France and America* (New York, 1927), p. 465.

To Charles Brockden Brown, born in the year that Bracken-ridge was graduated from Princeton (1771), Fay's comment is more applicable. Reared in Philadelphia, "the cultural capital of, ... and least provincial spot in America, ...",[2] during the 1770's and 1780's, Brown "was exposed to all currents of thought, Euro-pean and American, that were molding a new country and a new people".[3]

No less than Brackenridge, Brown was a man of ideas. David Lee Clark describes the variety of his intellectual interests (litera-ture, geography, history, architecture, utopian thought), and adds that he was sufficiently committed to ideas that "even his novels bear witness to Brown's deep concern about the issues facing the new nation".[4]

But Brown differed from Brackenridge in at least one very important particular. Brown, though familiar with the classics, was not educated in them with the same thoroughness as Bracken-ridge. Like the early English Romantics (Brown was born a year after Wordsworth), Brown was soon caught in the tide of French ideas. Clark states that "young Brown was an eager reader of French philosophy ...", especially Montesquieu, Helvetius and Holbach.[5] This was intensified through association with French émigrés who apparently became quite numerous in Philadelphia in the 90's. Brown actually became the tutor of the daughter of one of them, and in a letter written while he was thus employed, he defended French ideas vigorously.

The situation confronting Brown, as an incipient novelist, was similar to that which had faced Brackenridge. Possessed of ideas, Brown was anxious to find some way to promulgate them and get them on the market-place. He tried a series of philosophical essays significantly called "The Rhapsodist", but these evidently were little read. As a result, it must have become quite obvious to Brown that as a writer of philosophical essays he had little

[2] Vernon L. Parrington, *Main Currents in American Thought* (Harvest Books, New York, 1954), II, 177.
[3] David Lee Clark, *Charles Brockden Brown, Pioneer Voice of America* (Durham, 1952), p. 11.
[4] *Ibid.*, p. 6.
[5] *Ibid.*

hope either of bringing his ideas to a large audience or of becoming a professional man of letters. Nevertheless, there was a
possibility of achieving both these goals at one stroke, and that
was by writing novels. More sensitive to public taste than Brackenridge, Brown chose to spread his ideas through the two forms
which had proved their ability to captivate the American and
English reading publics – the sentimental novel of seduction and
the gothic romance.

The inspiration to write a novel was in Brown's mind by at
least 1793. Clark states that Brown "had no notion before 1793
of undertaking a work of fiction. That he entertained such a
notion in the summer of 1793 while in Hartford and New York
may be seen in an unpublished letter to his brother James, dated
October 25, 1796, from New York".[6] The pertinent passage of
the letter reads:

> I was talking of the yellow fever, or rather of that plague. . . . When
> I mentioned to you my treatment [of it] at Hartford in ninety-three,
> I was half disposed to instruct myself, and possibly amuse you, by
> recalling and putting [it] on the paper before me, during a residence
> of two or three days there.

"The important fact which this letter affirms", says Clark, "is
that as early as 1793 Brown's mind was busied with plans for
works of fiction, and that the subject then uppermost in his mind
was the yellow fever . . ."[7]

Actually, Brown may have started experimenting with the novel
even before 1793. In his Journal there is a series of letters addressed to a "Henrietta G." Clark insists that the letters are
autobiographical, but there remains, nonetheless, a good possibility that they represent an early attempt to write an epistolary
novel.[8]

Whatever the answer to the Henrietta riddle, it is certain that
by 1797, Brown's notion of embodying ideas in the form of romance had jelled. He states in a journal entry of that year: "I

---

[6]   *Ibid.*, p. 155.
[7]   *Ibid.*, p. 157.
[8]   *Ibid.*, pp. 54 ff. See Eleanor Tilton, "The Sorrows of Charles Brockden
Brown", *PMLA*, LXIX (1954), 1304-1305.

commenced something in the form of a Romance. I had at first no definite conceptions of my design".[9] The romance Brown had commenced was *Skywalk*, the advertisement to which is highly illuminating:

> To the story-telling moralist, the United States is a new and untrodden field. He who shall examine objects with his own eyes, who shall employ the European models merely for the improvement of his taste, and adapt his fiction to all that is genuine and peculiar in the scene before him, will be entitled at least to the praise of originality.
>
> · · · · · · · · · · · · · · ·
>
> The value of such works lies without doubt in their moral tendency. The popular tales have merit, but there is one thing in which they are deficient. They are generally adapted to one class of readers only. By a string of well-connected incidents, they amuse the idle and thoughtless; but are spurned at by those who are satisfied with nothing but strains of lofty eloquence, the exhibition of powerful motives, and a sort of audaciousness of character. The world is governed not by the simpleton, but by the man of soaring passions and intellectual energy. By the display of such only can we hope to enchain the attention and ravish the souls of those who study and reflect. To gain their homage it is not needful to forego the approbation of those whose circumstances have hindered them from making the same progress. A contexture of facts capable of suspending the faculties of every soul in curiosity may be joined with depth of views into human nature and all the subtleties of reasoning.[10]

Brown, in this preface, already perceives that while the novelist may work from European models, he must eventually shape these models to the exigencies of native materials. More striking, however, is the fact that, like Hawthorne and Melville after him, Brown deliberately plans to "hoodwink" the common reader by writing a fiction that will excite the passions of all men, but that will have an especial appeal to the mind of the intellectual. He will somehow revitalize moribund forms by transfusing them with the blood of new ideas. The sop to the common reader is "a string of well-connected incidents . . .", in a word, narrative. The

[9] *Ibid.*, p. 158.
[10] Charles Brockden Brown, *The Rhapsodist and Other Uncollected Writings*, ed. Harry Warfel (New York, 1943), pp. 135-36.

main dish is the display of the hero with "soaring passions and intellectual energy". He will present ideas and speculation by presenting characters who are obsessed by ideas; characters who themselves are interested in speculation.

By 1798, when, in a fantastic burst of creative energy, he wrote his four important novels, Brown had essentially abandoned the notion of an epistolary romance. Both *Wieland* and *Ormond*, it is true, come to the reader in the form of an epistle. But both narratives are told in one long letter, rather than a series of letters written by different people. Brown, by this time, had also abandoned the notion of the typical sentimental novel of seduction. He had, instead, settled on a combination of this and the gothic romance.

Richard Chase takes this decision as a sign of the congenital inability of American authors to write "novels" rather than "romances", while Leslie Fiedler takes it as a manifestation of "the failure of love in our fiction".[11] It is also possible, however, that Brown was grasping at a ready-to-hand form that would insure a certain amount of popular acceptance and at the same time provide a vehicle for his ideas, thereby establishing him as both a literary man and a philosopher. As the newest and most daring form, one which Godwin had used so successfully for didactic, if not speculative ends, the gothic novel would seem to have been the most natural choice. Fiedler intimates this:

> To promulgate notions of social justice and to write novels, to revolutionize American life and to achieve literary fame: this double ambition he came to feel as a single impulse, not unlike certain young radical writers in the United States of the 1930's. The literary form which eminently suited both such political allegiances, and such literary aspirations was at the moment he began to write (the 1790's were almost gone) the 'new novel,' which is to say, the gothic romance in its doctrinaire Godwinian form. 'To equal Caleb Williams' was the best Brown could hope for himself.[12]

Brown apparently felt that some combination of the novel of seduction and the gothic romance would provide the best salable

[11] *Love and Death in the American Novel* (New York, 1960), p. 126.
[12] *Ibid.*, p. 132.

vehicle for both his ideas and the hero of "soaring passions and intellectual energy". But once committed to this mixture, Brown found himself unable to fuse the individual elements into a new, whole, and significant substance. And it is this that partly explains the chaos of his novels. Having adopted the structure of the gothic, and the devices of the sentimental novel, Brown found himself stuck with their rhetoric as well, and he never did figure out quite what to do with it.

Brown's confusion is apparent in *Wieland*, his first important published work of fiction. Clark says of the preface to the novel that "Here Brown clearly goes beyond his formula as stated in the preface to *Skywalk*; he denounces the puerile Gothic novels, and the sentimental stories of love and seduction fathered by Richardson, and adopts the principles of the Novel of Purpose, made prominent by Holcroft, Bage, and Godwin. Henceforth he will lay bare the hidden motives of men of soaring passions and raging wills; he will choose for his characters men and women who are under some horrid mental or moral delusions, some obsession or perversion of the mind".[13] But far as Brown may go, he never manages to go far enough to break the shackles of the sentimental novel and its language. So, although Wieland is intended as the man of "soaring passions, etc.", he is instead cast inevitably into the mold reserved for characters in sentimental fiction, as is evident in the narrator's description of him:

His deportment was grave, considerate, and thoughtful. I will not say whether he was indebted to sublimer views for this disposition. Human life, in his opinion, was made up of changeable elements, and the principles of duty were not easily unfolded. The future, either as anterior or subsequent to death, was a scene that required some preparation and provision to be made for it. These positions we could not deny; but what distinguished him was a propensity to ruminate on these truths. The images that visited us were blithesome and gay, but those with which he was most familiar were of an opposite hue. They did not generate affliction and fear, but they diffused over his behaviour a certain air of forethought and sobriety. The principal effect of this temper was visible in his features and tones. These, in general, bespoke a sort of thrilling melancholy. I scarcely ever knew him to

[13] Pages 164-65.

laugh. He never accompanied the lawless mirth of his companions with more than a smile, but his conduct was the same as ours.[14]

In his gravity, pensiveness, and melancholy Wieland is a bona fide hero of the gothic romance. But there is a significant difference between him and his forebears. Wieland's melancholy is not motivated, as in most seduction novels, by thwarted love or lust, but by an excessive preoccupation with the general problem of human mortality. Wieland, like Brown himself, *would* ruminate on the great truths of death and mortality, but the verbal structure of which he is composed will not permit him to.

It is interesting to note what Richard Chase has to say on this point:

In *Wieland* emotions are conventionalized.... The language too is highly formalized and often stilted. But whereas there is some sense in the complaint that Brown writes 'he had not escaped the amorous contagion' instead of 'he fell in love,' this is really to miss the point. A stately and elevated language, like the measures of a classic ballet, is as useful in the aesthetic economy of the book as is the tireless rationalism of the conversation. The related complaint that Brown's characters are not realistic may also becloud the fact that the melodramatic method demands characters of a somewhat abstract and conventionalized sort, so that in the extremities of the action they become less human beings than *loci* of the clash of ideas and forces.[15]

That Chase begs the question is quite obvious. To be sure, no one will deny that "stately and elevated language" *can* be of use in the "aesthetic economy" of a novel. The question is whether it is so in *Wieland* and Brown's other novels. The answer is by no means simple, but there is sufficient reason to believe that the diction of eighteenth-century novels became a straitjacket which strangled Brown almost completely.

Brown's description of Wieland is one case in point. Another is his description of the situation of Constantia Dudley, the hero-

[14]   Charles Brockden Brown, *Wieland, or the Transformation* (Philadelphia, 1887), pp. 425-43. Page references in the text are to this edition. In his article, "A Reading of *Wieland*", *PMLA*, LXXVII (March, 1962), Larzer Ziff argues that Brown is contending against the conventions of sentimental fiction.
[15]   *The American Novel and its Tradition* (Anchor Books, New York, 1957), pp. 38-39.

ine of *Ormond*. Harry Warfel comments about her that "Emotions of normal love are alien to her nature, and there seems to be a homosexual tendency in her conduct".[16] What Brown intended was to portray the "new" woman – strong in will, character, and intellect, and capable of entering into intellectual relationship with other women equally strong in these qualities. To some extent, Brown has succeeded in his intention. But at times he fails miserably, and when he does, it is generally because he cannot avoid the excesses of what he conceives to be "high style" in the diction of the novel.[17]

In the passage which follows, Constantia is thinking about Martinette, a woman still a stranger to her. Martinette had bought Mr. Dudley's lute when Constantia was forced to pawn it, and on finding out (through the pawnbroker) that Constantia now wants to buy the lute back, Martinette offers it (again through the pawnbroker) as a gift.

These transactions were reflected on by Constantia with considerable earnestness. The conduct of the stranger, her affluent and lonely state, her conjectural relationship to the actors in the great theatre of Europe, were mingled together in the fancy of Constantia, and embellished with the conceptions of her beauty, derived from their casual meeting at Roseveldt's. She forgot not their similitude in age and sex, and delighted to prolong the dream of future confidence and friendship to take place between them. Her heart sighed for a companion, fitted to partake in all her sympathies.

This strain, by being connected with the image of a being like herself, [Sophia, the narrator,] who had grown up with her from childhood, who had been entwined with her earliest affections, but from whom she has been severed from the period at which her father's misfortunes commenced, and of whose present condition she was wholly ignorant, was productive of the deepest melancholy. It filled her with excruciating, and for a time irremediable sadness. It formed a kind of paroxysm, which like some febrile affections, approached and retired without warning, and against the most vehement struggles.

In this mood her fancy was thronged with recollections of scenes, in which her friend had sustained a part. Their last interview was

---

[16]   *Charles Brockden Brown, American Gothic Novelist* (Gainesville, Florida, 1949), p. 130.
[17]   Two years later, Wordsworth, in the preface to the 1800 edition of the *Lyrical Ballads*, was to attack some of these excesses in the diction of eighteenth-century poetry.

commonly revived in her remembrance so forcibly, as almost to produce a lunatic conception of its reality. A ditty which they sung
together on that occasion, flowed to her lips. If ever human tones were
qualified to convey the whole soul, they were those of Constantia
when she sung; –

> The breeze awakes, the bark prepares,
> To waft me to a distant shore;
> But far beyond this world of cares,
> We meet again to part no more.

These fits were accustomed to approach and to vanish by degrees.
They were transitory but not infrequent, and were pregnant with such
agonizing tenderness, such heart-breaking sighs, and a flow of such
bitter yet delicious tears, that it were not easily decided whether the
pleasure or the pain surmounted. When symptoms of their coming
were felt, she hastened into solitude, that the progress of her feelings
might endure no restraint.[18]

It is no wonder that Warfel, even taking into account the fact
that we live in an age obsessed by Freud, should find a "homosexual tendency" in Constantia's conduct. The language which
describes Constantia's mental state is that which was generally
used to describe lovesick swains or maidens. She is a victim
of "deepest melancholy" and "irremediable sadness". Pleasure
mingles with pain; bitter tears are also sweet. At several points
the lushness of the diction borders on eroticism: paroxysms
"which like some febrile affections, approached and retired . . .",
remembrances which "produce a lunatic conception of reality",
"fits . . . accustomed to approach and vanish by degrees", "pregnant with . . . agonizing tenderness", "heart-breaking sighs". It is
not, one must emphasize, a matter of whether "elevated style" is
good or bad, but of whether it effectively and meaningfully
develops or grows out of character and situation in the novel. In
Brown's novels it too often does not. Instead, it is largely re-
sponsible for the difficulty in creating character which Brown
was never to overcome.

But if Brown was never able to break out of the language and
stereotypes of sentimental and gothic fiction, he nevertheless,

---

[18] *Ormond, or the Secret Witness*, ed. Ernest Marchand (New York, 1937),
pp. 154-55. Page references in my text are to this edition.

tried manfully, and it is the effort, albeit only partly successful, that is significant.

Brown's debt to Godwin for the "philosophical novel" was recognized as early as 1830 in an article in the *American Quarterly Review*. But Godwin, for all the radicalism of his social and political theories, was fairly conventional as a novelist. He wrote *Caleb Williams* (1794) in order to dramatize some of the views he had promulgated a year earlier in *Political Justice* (1793). But he did not project his utopian speculations into his fiction. Instead, he exposed existing evils of society through characters who were not novel or extraordinary. Certainly, the oppressed servant was not new to the English novel (after all, Pamela was one, and so was Joseph Andrews). But Godwin was able to use the situation to emphasize the fact that oppression comes not only from an occasional mean master but from a society which sets a higher value on a man with property than on one without it.

No more unusual than the oppressed servant in the English novel is the cruel squire. But here again Godwin very skillfully and beautifully played a slight variation on an old theme. Falkland, Caleb's oppressor, turns out to be as much a victim of the social order as is his servant, since society has imbued him with the false sense of honor that, ironically, leads to his most dishonorable acts and eventually to his destruction. Godwin criticized the institutions that made a Squire Western, a Squire Allworthy, and a Tom Jones by showing that the same institutions could also make a Barnabas Tyrell, a Falkland, and a Caleb Williams. There was no need for Godwin to experiment in character. All that was necessary was to show the old stock characters in a new light.

Charles Brockden Brown's road was a little rougher. To begin with, many of the evils that Godwin had set out to criticize in the light of new equalitarian ideas had already been abolished, at least theoretically, in this country. There was no monarchy and no legally recognized hereditary aristocracy. In theory, all men were recognized as equal. But since, in actuality, men had still not progressed sufficiently to live by the rule of Reason, revolutionary ideas still seemed to be valid, and Brown found them still stimu-

lating. He picked up where Godwin had left off, proceeding in
some respects to push beyond the master, and in others merely to
confuse his teachings. Whereas Godwin had saved most of his
speculation for *Political Justice*, contenting himself in *Caleb
Williams* with exposing present evils, Brown, in his fiction, was
at least as interested in the problematic nature of good and evil
as in the evils that flourished before his eyes. The revolutionary
ideas that for Godwin grew out of, and were intended to remedy,
an immediate situation, for Brown always remained largely speculative. The acute *American Quarterly Review* critic of 1830 had
recognized this. Explaining the public hostility to Brown, he
asked, "To what end did philosophizing ever come? Who can set
bounds to speculation; or limit the wandering of his thoughts
when he has fairly embarked amidst the perplexing wilds and
interminable labyrinths of metaphysics? It is this unfortunate
propensity to prolixity in the philosophical novelist, together with
his frequent and inevitable lapse into mysticism and obscurity,
which renders his productions ... less readable, and ... less
popular than those of the describer in fiction ...".[19]

It is not merely that Brown philosophizes while Godwin does
not, but that Brown adds to Godwin's eighteenth-century rationalism an interest in the problematic and transcendental that in-
volves him in the "interminable labyrinths of metaphysics", in
"lapses into ... obscurity". It is in just such labyrinths that
Brown becomes involved in *Wieland*. In it, he tries to test the
possibilities of a kind of intellectual aristocracy whose members
live a life of reason. So, Wieland, whose grandfather spent his
life "in the composition of sonatas and dramatic pieces", which
were "not unpopular, but merely afforded him scanty subsistence"
(p. 26), and whose father was a fanatic who built his own temple
on the Schuylkill, sets up his own little intellectual community,
consisting of himself, his sister, his wife, and his brother-in-law,
Henry Pleyel. The entire arrangement resembles a Godwinian
Utopia in which the life of reason is finally realized. But the first
thing that becomes evident is that the life of at least one member

[19] "Brown's Novels", *American Quarterly Review*, VIII (1830), 318.

of the community is not founded on reason. This member is Wieland himself, who inherits not only his grandfather's interest in literature and his father's fanaticism, but also his father's sense of some sort of ineffable and undefinable guilt. Wieland père believed that "a command had been laid upon him, which he had delayed to perform. He felt as if a certain period of hesitation and reluctance had been allowed him, but that this period was passed. He was no longer permitted to obey. The duty assigned to him was transferred, in consequence of his disobedience, to another, and all that remained was to endure the penalty" (p. 32). A similar sense of guilt became a crucial factor in his son's later behavior.

Wieland's inordinate gravity and concern with man's mortality has already been described. His sister elaborates further; stressing the relationship between his gravity and his father's fanaticism:

In his studies, he pursued an austere ... and ... arduous path. He was much conversant with the history of religious opinions, and took pains to ascertain their validity. He deemed it indispensable to examine the ground of his belief, to settle the relation between motives and actions, the criterion of merit, and the kinds and properties of evidence.

There was an obvious resemblance between him and my father in their conceptions of the importance of certain topics, and in the light in which the vicissitudes of human life were accustomed to be viewed. Their characters were similar; but the mind of the son was enriched by science and embellished with literature. (p. 43)

The melancholy and fanaticism are further combined with an obsessive desire to plumb the depths of the human mind. "I said, this man is of an ardent and melancholy character. Those ideas which, in others, are casual or obscure, which are entertained in moments of abstraction and solitude and easily escape when the scene is changed have obtained an immovable hold upon his mind. . . . All his actions and practical sentiments are linked with long and abstruse deductions from the system of divine government and the laws of our intellectual constitution. He is in some respects an enthusiast, but is fortified in his belief by innumerable arguments and subtleties" (p. 55).

But strangely enough, in spite of his "enthusiasm", Wieland

is strongly influenced by the Ciceronian image of the gentleman. To adorn his father's temple he purchases a bust of Cicero, and though he is "an indefatigable student ... well versed in many authors, the chief object of his veneration was Cicero. He was never tired of coming and rehearsing his productions.... Not contented with this, he was diligent in settling and restoring the purity of the text. For this end, he collected all the editions and commentaries that could be procured, and employed months of severe study in exploring and comparing them. He never betrayed more satisfaction than when he made a discovery of this kind" (p. 44). All in all, Wieland is a baffling mixture of types: the religious fanatic, the man of science, the Ciceronian gentleman, the litterateur and dilettante.

The foil set against him is Henry Pleyel. They are alike in their admiration for Latin authors: "It was not till the addition of Henry Pleyel ... to our society that this [Wieland's] passion for Roman eloquence was countenanced and fostered by a sympathy of tastes" (p. 44). And, too, Pleyel "was not behind his friend in his knowledge of the history and metaphysics of religion" (p. 45). But here the resemblance ends, for Pleyel does not usually (though he can when necessary) match the lugubriousness of Wieland. Pleyel's "conversation abounded with novelty. His gayety was almost boisterous, but was capable of yielding to a grave deportment when the occasion required it. His discernment was acute; but he was prone to view every object merely as supplying materials for mirth. His conceptions were ardent but ludicrous, and his memory, aided ... by his invention, was an inexhaustible fund of entertainment" (pp. 44-45).

The difference in temperaments results in a difference in belief:

Their creeds ... were in many respects opposite. Where one discovered only confirmations of his faith, the other could find nothing but reasons for doubt. Moral necessity and Calvinistic inspiration were the props on which my brother thought proper to repose. Pleyel was the champion of intellectual liberty, and rejected all guidance but that of his reason. Their discussions were frequent, but, being managed with candour as well as with skill, they were always listened to by us with avidity and benefit. (p. 45)

Pleyel, then, is more the Godwinian, although precisely how much of a Godwinian is never made quite clear, since his discussions with Wieland are never dramatized. And as things turn out, Pleyel eventually finds happiness, while Wieland, spurred on by his fanaticism, plunges with great gusto to his destruction. Eventually another member is added to this intellectual group. Carwin appears from out of nowhere and for no particular reason. In appearance he is totally outlandish:

His pace was a careless and lingering one, and had none of that gracefulness and ease which distinguish a person with certain advantages of education from a clown. His gait was rustic and awkward. His form was ungainly and disproportioned. Shoulders broad and square, breast sunken, his head drooping, his body of uniform breadth, supported by long and lank legs, were the ingredients of his frame. His garb was not ill adapted to such a figure. A slouched hat, tarnished by the weather, a coat of thick gray cloth cut and wrought, as it seemed, by a country tailor, blue worsted stockings, and shoes fastened by thongs and deeply discoloured by dust, which brush had never disturbed, constituted his dress. (p. 72)

But this initial impression is misleading for "his forehead, his eyes lustrously black, and possessing, in the midst of haggardness, a radiance inexpressibly serene and potent, and something in the rest of his features which it would be in vain to describe, but which served to betoken a mind of the highest order, were essential ingredients in the portrait" (p. 73).

Carwin turns out to be "sparing in discourse . . .". But "notwithstanding the uncouthness of his garb, his manners were not unpolished. All topics were handled by him with skill, and without pedantry or affectation. . . . His observations denoted a mind alive to every generous and heroic feeling. They were . . . accompanied with that degree of earnestness which indicates sincerity" (p. 90).

Because of his "indisputably great . . . intellectual endowments", Carwin is soon completely accepted by the group, though his past remains cloudy. Pleyel provides some enlightenment on this score. Some years before the action of the novel takes place, Pleyel had met Carwin in Spain, where the latter "had embraced the Catholic religion, and adopted a Spanish name instead of his own, which was CARWIN, and devoted himself to the literature and religion of his new country. He pursued no profession, but subsisted on remittances from England" (p. 87).

Carwin's function in the book is somewhat puzzling. On the one hand, it seems as if Brown intended him as a diabolic character, as is indicated by his grotesque appearance, by the horror with which the narrator recalls his name, and finally by the fact that his sinister (and yet scientifically explainable) ability to project his voice, working on Wieland's fanaticism, initiates the series of actions that culminates in Wieland's total ruin. On the other hand, Carwin's diabolism is unwitting. Moreover, he is not totally evil. The narrator, as has been pointed out, admires his generous and heroic mind, and her attraction to him seems to imply that high minds are attracted to each other in spite of physical impediments. This inference is further encouraged when Pleyel, who is soft on Clara, becomes jealous of Carwin.

It is perhaps fitting that both the romantic contenders for Clara's affection should have European backgrounds. The fact that Pleyel has vague, mysterious ties in Germany, and Carwin in Spain, seems, in a sense, to anticipate the two veins of romanticism that Washington Irving was to exploit some twenty years later.

At any rate, these male characters (Pleyel, Carwin, and Wieland) form an interesting triumvirate. Pleyel is a man of reason and learning who is on the whole ineffectual. He thinks of himself as a moralist, and is indeed pompously self-righteous, but he seldom does anything which even remotely resembles a contribution to the good of mankind. He is, in the last analysis, a weak character who is dominated by women, but who eventually marries the right one, the heroine, and in so doing supplies the one pleasant note in an otherwise sordid situation.

Carwin is essentially amoral, but his amorality ends in unintended diabolism. He uses his talent of ventriloquism to benefit himself, but his unthinking egocentricity initiates a series of bloody events. As he rather lamentably confesses to Clara (the narrator), he never meant to harm anybody. He just did not foresee the consequences of his actions. It is not difficult to see operating in him the machinations of the modern technological mind.

Wieland in his ardor, though not in his faith, resembles the new intellectual emerging out of the French Revolution. He is, in the fullest eighteenth-century meaning of the word, "an enthusiast". So possessed does he become by his ideas that he kills his wife and children, and later tries to murder his sister. Wieland's confession is excessively verbose and lengthy, but it is also very revealing. He admits that he has done the killing, and then goes on:

It is needless to say that God is the object of my supreme passion. I have cherished in his presence a single and upright heart. I have thirsted for the knowledge of his will. I have burnt with ardour to approve my faith and my obedience.

My days have been spent in searching for the revelation of that will; but my days have been mournful, because my search failed. I solicited direction; I turned on every side where glimmerings of light could be discovered. I have not been wholly uninformed; but my knowledge has always stopped short of certainty. Dissatisfaction has insinuated itself into all my thoughts. My purposes have been pure, my wishes indefatigable; but not till lately were these purposes thoroughly accomplished and these wishes fully gratified.

I thank thee, my Father, for thy bounty; that thou didst not ask a less sacrifice than this; that thou placedst me in a condition to testify my submission to thy will. What have I withheld which it was thy pleasure to exact? Now may I, with dauntless and erect eye, claim my reward, since I have given thee the treasure of my soul. (p. 184)

Wieland's is the absolutist mind. He demands certainty, and he demands it passionately. He demands it even at the cost of his own destruction. In this he is like Melville's Ahab, who must run down the white whale, no matter what the consequences. But ironically, when Wieland does find certainty he has only found a delusion, after all.

Wieland describes his state of mind immediately preceding the murders by saying that it "was contemplative and calm . . .". His contemplations, he says, "soared above earth and its inhabitants . . .". He wanted "the supreme delight of knowing [God's] will and of performing it". His ardor is finally rewarded with a vision of "heaven", all "luminous and glowing". And then he hears "a shrill voice from behind. . . . As it spoke, the accents thrilled my heart: – 'Thy prayers are heard. In proof of thy faith, render me thy wife!' . . .". The request is not an easy one, even for a fanatic. "'Substitute some other victim.'" he begs. "'My own blood is cheap. This will I pour out before thee with a willing heart . . .'". This is the Abrahamic dilemma descended from the sublime to the melodramatic.

Then, recounting his emotions following the murder of his wife and children, he asserts,

This was a moment of triumph. Thus had I successfully subdued the stubbornness of human passions: the victim which had been demanded was given; the deed was done past recall. . . . I imagined I had set myself forever beyond the reach of selfishness.

You [the jury] say I am guilty. Impious and rash! thus to usurp the prerogatives of your Maker! to set up your bounded views and halting reason as the measure of truth! (pp. 194-95)

There are many ironies here, and many questions raised, but one is never sure whether Brown was aware of them. To begin with, Wieland seems to think that he has acted very reasonably. He has subdued his human passions to perform a difficult task that was required of him. He somehow imagines that he has made a sacrifice to benefit the human race. And except for its violence, his act would appear to be in accord with Godwin's philosophy. Godwin had concluded that a reasonable man who had the choice between saving Archbishop Fenelon or Fenelon's butler should choose to save the Archbishop because of his greater value to mankind. Then Godwin added that it would be immaterial if the butler happened to be the brother or father of the individual who had to make the choice. Thus, for Wieland, an act of madness becomes an act of reason.

The questions raised by the situation are myriad. How is it possible to choose between natural affection and the demands of faith? Moreover, when does an act of faith become an act of madness, and who is capable of judging between the two? Where does one draw the line between faith and fanaticism? More disturbing yet, where does one draw the line between fanaticism and reason?

Brown does not push the questions or the ironies, but their presence, even by implication, tends to cast an air of uncertainty over all human actions, an uncertainty that Brown could not have gotten directly from his preceptor. Godwin had great confidence in man's ability to act constructively, and he believed "Human inventions susceptible of perpetual improvement".[20] Godwin was firmly convinced that through Reason, which in itself was not problematic, man could define benevolence, and then proceed to act benevolently.

But Wieland's situation casts doubt on both the capacity of human Reason and the efficacy of human benevolence. Wieland is convinced that his violent act was the very epitome of unselfishness, the very summit of benevolence. His own Reason, he feels, transcends the "halting" reason of ordinary men. And yet, in the eyes of other men, his behavior has been monstrous.

The full ambiguity of human action, however, occurs after Wieland, through the agency of Carwin's ventriloquism, is awakened from his state of delusion. Clara describes the scene:

> Fallen from his lofty and heroic station; now finally restored to the perception of truth; weighed to earth by the recollection of his own deeds; consoled no longer by a consciousness of rectitude for the loss of offspring and wife, – a loss for which he was indebted to his own misguided hand, – Wieland was transformed at once into the *man of sorrows!*
>
> He reflected not that credit should be as reasonably denied to the last [the voice he has just heard] as to any former intimation [the visionary voices]; that one might as justly be ascribed to erring or diseased senses as the other. He saw not that this discovery in no degree affected the integrity of his conduct; that his motives had lost none of their claims to the homage of mankind; that the preference of supreme good, and the boundless energy of duty, were undiminished in his bosom. (p. 249)

Clara's attitude is somewhat peculiar. She shrewdly points out that there is no reason why Wieland should not consider the

[20] William Godwin, *Political Justice* (Toronto, 1946), Bk. II, ch. I, p. 109.

ventriloquized voice as illusory and continue to believe the hal-
lucinated voice which had originally told him to make the sacrifice. But then she comes to the surprising conclusion that even if
he had been deluded and has committed horrible crimes as a
result of his delusion, his conduct is still noble, for in any case
he has acted with the intention of benefiting mankind.

In his portrait of Wieland, and in the narrator's judgment of
him, Brown seems to be moving toward the concept of the secu-
larized revolutionary intellectuals, who, in their religious passion
to establish the Just State as they see it, are willing to offer any
number of sacrifices on the altar of absolute righteousness. It is
true that Wieland shows no political awareness whatever, but
Brown's next hero, Ormond, is steeped in the political upheavals
of the eighteenth century.

Like Wieland, Ormond occupies himself with "ultimate" questions, and, also like Wieland, he is an "enthusiast". But while
Wieland's meditations confirm him as a religious enthusiast, Ormond's meditations intensify his religious skepticism.

His disbelief was at once unchangeable and strenuous. The universe was to him a series of events connected by an undesigning and
inscrutable necessity, and an assemblage of forms to which no beginning or end can be conceived. Instead of transient views and vague
ideas, his meditations, on religious points, had been intense. Enthusiasm was added to disbelief, and he not only dissented but ab-
horred.[21]

As is typical of the revolutionary intellectual, Ormond fills the
emotional hiatus left by the absence of religious belief with his
fervid political involvement. "His political projects", the reader
is informed, "are likely to possess an extensive influence on the
future condition of this Western World" (p. 92). The political
projects seem to be rooted principally in revolutionary activity,
in which Ormond has become engaged at a young age.

He had embraced, when almost a child, the trade of arms; ... had
found service and promotion in the armies of Potemkin and Roman-
zow; ... had executed secret and diplomatic functions at Constanti-
nople and Berlin; ... in the latter city ... had met with schemers and

[21]   *Ormond*, p. 149.

reasoners who aimed at the new-modeling of the world, and the subversion of all that has hitherto been conceived elementary and fundamental in the constitution of man and of government . . . . Some of
these reformers had secretly united to break down the military and
monarchical fabric of German policy. . . . Others, more wisely, had
devoted their secret efforts, not to overturn, but to build, . . . and for
this end . . . embraced an exploring and colonizing project. [Ormond]
. . . had allied himself to these, and for the promotion of their projects
had spent six years of his life in journeys by sea and land, in tracts
unfrequented till then by any European.

What were the moral or political maxims which this adventurous
and visionary sect had adopted, and what was the seat of their new-
born empire – whether on the shore of an *austral* continent, or in the
heart of desert America – he carefully concealed. (pp. 208-209)

The secret society to which Ormond allied himself was apparently
the Illuminati, a sect founded in Bavaria by Theodore Haupt-
mann, a renegade Jesuit, in 1776. At the time *Ormond* was published the sect was under heavy attack from conservative clergy
as a fountainhead of world conspiracy. Though Ormond has
managed to conceal from the narrator the maxims of the society,
nevertheless she is able to "explain the maxims by which he was
accustomed to regulate his private deportment" (p. 92), and these
give us at least some insight into Ormond's political beliefs and
their influence on his actions.

No one could entertain loftier conceptions of human capacity than
Ormond. But he carefully distinguished between men in the abstract,
and men as they are. The former were beings to be impelled, by the
breath of accident, in a right or a wrong road; but whatever direction
they should receive, it was the property of their nature to persist in
it. Now, this impulse had been given. No single being could rectify
the error. It was the business of the wise man to form a just estimate
of things, but not to attempt, by individual efforts, so chimerical an
enterprise as that of promoting the happiness of mankind. Their condition was out of the reach of a member of a corrupt society to control.
A mortal poison pervaded the whole system, by means of which everything received was converted into bane and purulence. Efforts designed to ameliorate the condition of an individual were sure of answering a contrary purpose. The principles of the social machine must
be rectified, before men can be beneficially active. Our motives may
be neutral or beneficent, but our actions tend merely to the production
of evil. (pp. 92-93)

This initial set of tenets, apparently the result of a misunderstanding of Godwin's then revolutionary theory of ethics, puts man in an impossible position. Man (as he is) cannot improve his lot without first rectifying "the principles of the social machine". But as a product of the machine and a part of it, there is little he can do to rectify it. Wieland had experienced, to his sorrow, the knowledge that actions performed out of the noblest motivation could have not only disastrous but meaningless results. Ormond has already perceived this intellectually, and so he has reached the conclusion that man is faced with a horrible paradox: all human action, motives notwithstanding, ultimately produces evil.

But this is not the worst of the paradox, for man cannot rely on inaction either. As far as Ormond is concerned,

The idea of total forbearance was not less delusive. Man could not be otherwise than a cause of perpetual operation and efficacy. He was part of a machine, and as such had not power to withhold his agency. Contiguousness to other parts – that is, to other men – was all that was necessary to render him a powerful concurrent. (p. 93)

Still, Ormond unaccountably continues to believe that "a man may reasonably hope to accomplish this end, when he proposes nothing but his own good. Any other point is inaccessible". Oddly enough, Ormond also believes that a man "must not part with benevolent desire; this is a constituent of happiness .... A wise man will relinquish the pursuit of general benefit, but not the desire of that benefit, or the perception of that in which this benefit consists, because these are among the ingredients of virtue and the sources of his happiness" (p. 93).

Ormond's ethics seem to resolve as follows: All human action eventually produces evil, and yet all men must act. Since a man can achieve happiness only for himself, he must live selfishly. But in pursuing happiness for himself, he must also retain a sense of universal benevolence. This universal benevolence a man must continue to desire as a goal even though he must refrain from trying to achieve it, and even though it is not quite clear what the desire is intended to accomplish.[22]

[22] To say that there is an ethic here is probably an overstatement. Rather, the entire passage seems to be a botching of Godwin's implicit utilitarianism.

In the face of this belief in the futility of all individual action, it is not surprising that Ormond uses his wealth principally to gratify his own pleasures rather than to promote the betterment of man.

He thought himself entitled to all the splendor and ease which it [his wealth] would purchase, but his taste was elaborate and correct. He gratified his love of the beautiful, because the sensations it afforded were pleasing, but made no sacrifices to the love of distinction. (p. 94)

To spend his money for philanthropic ends would, of course, have been ridiculous, since "The use of money was a science, like every other branch of benevolence, not reducible to any fixed principles. No man, in the disbursement of money, could say whether he was conferring a benefit or injury. The visible and immediate effects might be good, but evil was its ultimate and general tendency" (p. 110).

Neither, however, does Ormond squander his money on the trappings of aristocracy. Though a man of "elaborate and correct" taste, in dress, manners, equipage, and human relationships he is a democrat.

Pompous equipage and retinue were modes of appropriating the esteem of mankind which he held in profound contempt. The garb of his attendants was fashioned after the model suggested by his imagination, and not in compliance with the dictates of custom.

He treated with systematic negligence the etiquette that regulates the intercourse of persons of a certain class. He everywhere acted, in this respect, as if he were alone, or among familiar associates. The very appellations of Sir, and Madam, and Mister, were, in his apprehension, servile and ridiculous; and as custom or law had annexed no penalty to the neglect of these, he conformed to his own opinions. It was easier for him to reduce his notions of equality to practice than for most others. (p. 94)

But in spite of his democratic manners and in spite of his belief in the futility of individual human action, Ormond never overcomes the drive to violence which characterized his early revolutionary career. In order to expedite his seduction of the heroine of the novel, Constantia Dudley, he kills her father. For the same reason he kills a character named Craig. And finally, when the fortress of Constantia's virtue turns out to be invulnerable to deception, he tries to rape her. By this time, however, he has degenerated into a madman. It has been part of his creed that "Love, in itself, was ... of little worth, and only of importance as the source of the most terrible of intellectual maladies. Sexual sensations associating themselves, in a certain way, with our ideas, beget a disease which has, indeed, found no place in the catalogue, but is a case of more entire subversion and confusion of mind than any other" (p. 132). He himself contracts the malady, and it does indeed prove fatal.

Ormond is not the only intellectual on the scene. In this novel as in *Wieland*, Brown tries to experiment with the possibilities of a group of intellectuals. Constantia herself is the most intellectual of women. She is "thoroughly conversant with Tacitus and Milton", and familiar with Newton and Hartley. Her father has "unveiled to her the mathematical properties of light and sound, taught her, as a metaphysician and anatomist, the structure and power of the senses, and discussed with her the principles and progress of human society" (p. 128). She has "always been solicitous for mental improvement" (p. 146), and her beauty is "animated by ... intelligence" (p. 131). It is largely her mind that attracts Ormond: "Her discourse tended to rouse him from his lethargy, to furnish him with powerful excitements, and the time spent in her company seemed like a doubling of existence" (p. 131). Likewise, it is to Ormond's mind that Constantia is attracted. "The conversation of Ormond was an inexhaustible fund. By the variety of topics and the excitements to reflection it supplied, a more plenteous influx of knowledge was produced than could have flowed from any other source. There was no end to the detailing of facts, and the canvassing of theories" (p. 146). Furthermore, "The novelty and grandeur of his schemes could not fail to transport a mind ardent and capacious as that of Constantia" (p. 147).

This introduction to revolutionary ideas is supplemented by an introduction to revolutionary actualities when Constantia meets Martinette de Beauvais. Martinette is also an intellectual woman, and though her education has been similar to Constantia's, her life has been richer and more varied. Born in the middle eastern city of Aleppo, she has been exposed to a broad slice of life.

> My father [she informs a wide-eyed Constantia] talked to me in Scla-
> vonic. My mother and her maids talked to me in Greek. My neigh-
> bors talked to me in a medley of Arabic, Syriac, and Turkish. My
> father's secretary was a scholar. He was as well versed in Lysias and
> Xenophon as any of their contemporaries. He labored for ten years
> to enable me to read a language essentially the same with that I used
> daily to my nurse and mother. . . . To have refrained from learning
> was impossible. Suppose a girl, prompt, diligent, inquisitive, to spend
> ten years of her life partly in Spain, partly in Tuscany, partly in
> France, and partly in England . . . . Would it be possible for her to
> remain ignorant of each of these languages? (p. 159)

Martinette's chief attraction is not the quality and breadth of her formal education, but

> a knowledge of political and military transactions in Europe during
> the present age, which implied the possession of better means of in-
> formation than books. She depicted scenes and characters with the
> accuracy of one who had partaken and witnessed them herself.
>   Constantia's attention had been chiefly occupied by personal con-
> cerns. Her youth had passed in contention with misfortune, or in
> the quietudes of study. She could not be unapprised of contemporary
> revolutions and wars, but her ideas respecting them were indefinite
> and vague. Her views and her inferences on this head were general
> and speculative. Her acquaintance with history was exact and circum-
> stantial in proportion as she retired backward from her own age. She
> knew more of the siege of Mutina than of that of Lille; more of the
> machinations of Catiline and the tumults of Clodius, than of the pros-
> tration of the Bastile and the proscriptions of Marat.
>   She listened, therefore, with unspeakable eagerness to this reciter,
> who detailed to her, as the occasion suggested, the progress of action
> and opinion on the theater of France and Poland. . . .
>   But, while this historian described the features, personal deport-
> ment, and domestic character of Antoinette, Mirabeau, and Robes-
> pierre, an impenetrable veil was drawn over her own condition.
> (pp. 157-158)

Indeed, as it turns out, Martinette has been an intimate participant in the events of the French Revolution, and has been motivated by true revolutionary zeal. When Constantia, at one point, naïvely asks, "Does not your heart shrink from the view of a scene of massacre and tumult, such as Paris has lately exhibited and will probably continue to exhibit?" Martinette coolly answers:

'Thou talkest, Constantia, in a way scarcely worthy of thy good sense. Have I not been three years in a camp? What are bleeding wounds and mangled corpses, when accustomed to the daily sight of them for years? Am I not a lover of liberty? and must I not exult in the fall of tyrants, and regret only that my hand had no share in their destruction?' (p. 171)

And exult in the sight of blood she does. When "she communicated the tidings of the fall of the sanguinary tyranny of Robespierre, her eyes sparkled, and every feature was pregnant with delight, while she unfolded, with her accustomed energy, the particulars of this tremendous revolution. The blood which it occasioned to flow was mentioned without any symptoms of disgust or horror" (p. 170).

It is only natural that in her wide experience Martinette should have encountered other intellectuals and revolutionaries. One is a priest whose "passion for science", Martinette tells Constantia, "was at least equal to that which he entertained for me, and both these passions combined to make him a sedulous instructor. He was a disciple of the newest doctrines respecting matter and mind. He denied the impenetrability of the first, and the immateriality of the second. These he endeavored to inculcate upon me, as well as to subvert my religious tenets . . ." (p. 162). It is on these startling ideas that Martinette has been nurtured.

But she is initiated into first-hand revolutionary activity through love of a young, idealistic Englishman named Wentworth, who is remarkably anticipatory of the Byronic hero, and actually of Byron himself. He changes the entire orientation of Martinette's previous education: "From the computation of eclipses I now betook myself to the study of man. . . . Instead of adulation and gallantry, I was engaged in watching the conduct of states and revolving the theories of politicians" (p. 166). Wentworth himself, in his youth, "proposed no other end of his existence than the acquisition of virtue and knowledge" (p. 164). He is a member of the nobility, and his character is one "not frequently met with in the world. He was a political enthusiast, who esteemed nothing more graceful or glorious than to die for the liberties of mankind. He had traversed Greece with an imagination full of the exploits of ancient times, and derived from contemplating Thermopylae and Marathon, an enthusiasm that bordered upon frenzy" (pp. 166-67). In search of a cause, he joins the Colonists in the American Revolutionary War. He is wounded in the fighting, and eventually his wounds prove fatal.

These vignettes of subordinate characters are typical of Brown's method. But at least in *Ormond* they are understandable. Brown seems to be trying to encompass the character of the new intellectual, but he is never in sufficient command of his material to achieve his end within the dramatic framework of the novel.

This weakness in development of character extends into his attempts to deal with ideas. Never does he appear able to control ideas within the context of the materials and language of fiction. He sets out to portray men and women of ideas, who are apparently supposed to be eloquent, but they wind up mute. When they do speak, it is in the conventions of the heroes and heroines of sentimental and gothic fiction. Brown plunges courageously into Godwinian and French ideas only to become hopelessly entangled in them. Without reason or motivation characters contradict themselves, and frequently their actions seem to contradict their ideas. In many cases, moreover, the very ability to articulate ideas, which was ostensibly intended to make them heroes, turns them into incorrigible villains.

And yet Brown's very confusion is revealing. Like many an American author after him, he wanted the approval of both the public and the intelligentsia. He had said as much in the "Advertisement" to *Skywalk*. Nor was it an accident that he sent a copy of *Wieland* to one of the outstanding intellectuals of the day, Thomas Jefferson, in the hope that "an artful display of incidents, the powerful delineation of characters and the train of eloquent and judicious reasoning which may be combined in a fictitious work, will be regarded by Thomas Jefferson with as much respect as they are regarded by me".[23]

---

[23]   Clark, p. 163.

But there is no evidence that Jefferson was impressed. To satisfy the public, Brown had to provide entertainment in accepted fashion and at the same time avoid the open expression of unpopular ideas; to satisfy "those who study and reflect" he had to provide intellectual substance. He succeeded in satisfying neither.

Perhaps Jefferson's silence is as meaningful as anything he could have said. Most likely, he was baffled. For though many of Brown's insights were sound, he never seemed fully able to comprehend them intellectually, nor to articulate them meaningfully. He sensed the situation of the new intellectual – his derivation from the reasonable Ciceronian gentleman, his unreasoning impassioned elevation of reason into a goddess, his fatal political zeal – but he lacked the intellect or imagination that would have fused these elements into a consciously significant work of art. Probably Brown's most penetrating insight into his thinking characters was his having conceived their violence against a European background, even though the main setting of the action is always American. Wieland, for example, is deeply involved in his Saxon ancestry. Ormond's past is mysterious, but he has been engaged in European revolutionary intrigue since boyhood. Martinette was born in Aleppo, has lived all over the continent, and has been involved in all the major revolutions of the late eighteenth century. Pleyel, when he arrives on the scene, has just returned from Europe. Achsa Fielding (in *Arthur Mervyn*) is a Jewess born and raised in England. Carwin was born in England and has lived a great deal on the Continent. Two lesser Falkland-like villains, Welbeck (in *Arthur Mervyn*) and Ludlow (in *Carwin the Biloquist*), are both of European origin. But Brown himself never brought his own insight fully under control. Had he done so he might have been something more than an historical curiosity.

V

COOPER: IDEAS AND LESSONS

Like Hugh Henry Brackenridge before him, James Fenimore Cooper was generally more interested in discursive ideas than in the aesthetic possibilities of fiction. This concern of Cooper's was noticed by his own contemporaries, who attacked him for corrupting his fiction by introducing ideas into it. The *New Yorker* wrote that "No man has been a greater favorite with his countrymen than Mr. Cooper so long as he condescended to amuse them; but the moment he placed himself in the ungrateful light of an instructor his interest in their affections began to diminish . . .".[1]

More recently, students of Cooper have taken a more positive attitude toward his concern with ideas. D. E. S. Maxwell writes that "Cooper, most instinctively, is a novelist of ideas, specifically of the ideas on which his society subsisted".[2] James Grossman feels about Cooper that ". . . in his own lifetime it was the novel of ideas that undid him". And he adds that in *The Spy* "Cooper mastered a technique of composing novels that was to stand him in good stead throughout his career. Essentially, he had learned how to dramatize his ideas – to make them come alive through the action of his tale".[3] Writing about "Cooper's Americans", Kay House asserts that Cooper's ". . . real interest lay in the ideas that formed the thematic construction of the novel".[4] Donald Ringe finds that "What Cooper did throughout his career was to

[1] Quoted in Richard Abcarian, "Cooper's Critics and the Realistic Novel", *Texas Studies in Literature & Language*, VIII (1966), 33-41, *New Yorker*, VIII (March 14, 1840), 413.
[2] *American Fiction: The Intellectual Background* (London, 1963), p. 159.
[3] *James Fenimore Cooper* (New York, 1949), p. 5.
[4] *Cooper's Americans* (Columbus, Ohio, 1965), p. 13.

refine his ideas about God, man, and society in the light of his increasing experience; to express different elements of his view at different times; and eventually, in his best work, to unite the major streams of his thought into the well-planned books that artistically express his ideas".[5] And Marius Bewley, who attempts to define the "great tradition" of the American novel as a continuation of the same tradition in the English novel, gives Cooper a prominent position as a necessary antecedent, and artistic peer, of Hawthorne, Melville, and Henry James. In the course of placing Cooper in the Leavis tradition of the English novel, Bewley asserts that in his European political novels "Cooper presents a strikingly original analysis of history and of his own times, the brilliance of which has never received any recognition".[6]

But in spite of the widespread commendation of Cooper's ideas and of the admirability of his trying to work with ideas, opinion about the aesthetic effectiveness of the ideas that Cooper introduces into his novels is by no means unanimously favorable. D. E. S. Maxwell maintains that ". . . Cooper never wholly succeeded in cultivating a form congenial to his ideas. He conformed too willingly to the fashions of the romance . . .".[7] Robert E. Spiller focuses more precisely on the problem presented by Cooper's handling of ideas, pointing out that ". . . when ideas take over the center of interest, as they do in many of the . . . later novels, the result is an inner aesthetic conflict between art and didacticism, and didacticism usually wins".[8] What can be seen emerging from Cooper's novels, then, is less a concern with ideas than a desire to instruct the reader. Working within the traditions of neoclassical aesthetics, Cooper attempts to please while he instructs, and the question that arises is whether his instruction is still meaningful and relevant in the twentieth century. It is not a matter of whether didacticism is good or bad in itself but whether Cooper's specific lessons can be taken seriously by the modern reader.

5   *James Fenimore Cooper* (New York, 1962), p. 23.
6   *The Eccentric Design* (New York, 1963), p. 47.
7   *American Fiction*, p. 139.
8   *James Fenimore Cooper* (Minneapolis, Minnesota, 1965), p. 33.

Marius Bewley makes a heroic attempt to arouse the modern reader's interest in, and respect for, Cooper's ideas by presenting him as an acute economic and political analyst. He finds that "the brilliance of Cooper's analysis of the American political situation as he focused it in his European novels exists in the fullness of his economic recognitions. He believed that the shifting of economic power in the United States into the hands of a small moneyed class might mean a radical reshaping of government under the Constitution".[9] Bewley's dilemma, though, is that he can find viable ideas only in Cooper's lesser known and, it is generally agreed, less meritorious works – the European novels and the Littlepage trilogy. When he comes to the Leatherstocking tales he seems to be at a loss to deal with them. His judgment that *"The Deerslayer* is probably the best thing Cooper ever wrote . . ." has not, to my knowledge, been seconded by any reputable Cooper scholar. Moreover, what Bewley seems to find praiseworthy in *The Deerslayer* seems to be less the ideas he finds in the book than its moral soundness. "The whole action", he writes, "is animated by Deerslayer's vision. It takes firm control of the action, elevating it above plot mechanics into the realm of life and moral form".[10]

What Bewley's dilemma would seem to suggest is that there is a split between Cooper's most powerful ideas and his most successful fiction. For ideas discursively developed it is necessary to look to the minor fiction. The major work, on the other hand, is rich, not in ideas but in moral vision. Some further illumination in this regard is provided by Richard Poirier's *A World Elsewhere*, in which he calls Leatherstocking "one of the great creations of American fiction", but then makes a somewhat startling distinction between the character and the words he utters. Deerslayer, according to Poirier,

is in the truest sense a mythic character, and he deserves to be, not for his mouthings of virtue and of ideas that belong to the history of ideas, but for his being the incarnation of the American 'beau ideal'; silent, marvelously alert, capable of irresistible mechanical proficiency

9   *The Eccentric Design*, p. 51.
10 *Ibid.*, p. 98.

without explanatory claptrap, the servant of principles the more eloquent for being vaguely defined, and with a will undisrupted by
muddled personal feeling of sexual love or the desire for gain. This
is the Deerslayer a contemporary could find interesting, not the
Sunday School prize essayist who emerges from the dialogue.
But the dialogue unfortunately exists.[11]

There is an ambivalence underlying Poirier's strident assertion
of Leatherstocking's mythic chracter, which parallels the problem encountered by Bewley, of not being able to bring Cooper's
major fiction and his major ideas together. How is it possible
to think of Natty as a silent "*beau ideal*" when it is necessary, at
the same time, to acknowledge that his "dialogue unfortunately
exists"? Or how can it come about that this "silent, marvelously
alert . . . *beau ideal*" should also indulge in "mouthings of virtue
and of ideas" that are worthy of nothing better than a "Sunday
School prize essayist"? The acuteness of the problem is readily
apparent when one considers that the subtitle of this book is "The
Place of Style in American Literature". If we are to take at face
value what Poirier says about Cooper, then we must conclude
that style has no place in American literature.

The solution to the dilemma shared by Bewley and Poirier may
lie in something that T. S. Eliot says about the difference between
the English poets of the seventeenth and nineteenth centuries.
"The difference", he writes,

is not a simple difference of degree between poets. It is something
which had happened to the mind of England between the time of
Donne or Lord Herbert of Cherbury and the time of Tennyson and
Browning; it is the difference between the intellectual poet and the
reflective poet. Tennyson and Browning are poets, and they think;
but they do not feel their thought as immediately as the odor of a
rose. A thought to Donne was an experience; it modified his sensibility.[12]

To Cooper, a thought is not an experience, nor is there any evidence that thoughts modified his sensibility. The problem that
Cooper never solved as a novelist was the problem of making his

11   (New York, 1966), p. 72.
12   "The Metaphysical Poets", *Selected Essays* (New York, 1932), p. 247.

ideas an integral part of the novel, making them dramatized fictions instead of moral tracts that intrude into the action, invariably bringing it to an abrupt halt.

For Cooper, the characteristic form for the expression of ideas is the sermon, lengthy set speeches that come from such characters as Leatherstocking, Judge Temple, and the Effinghams, among others. While these speeches may present a multitude of ideas, they never present thoughts feelingly, and while they demonstrate that Cooper is an intellectual novelist, that is, a novelist who thinks, they also demonstrate that he is not a reflective novelist, that is, one who feels his thought "as immediately as the odor of a rose". It is true that Cooper manages to inject into the middle of his adventurous and romantic plots passages that deal with ideas, but he rarely manages to make the adventure and romance interact with the ideas. Leatherstocking's many hair-raising adventures and narrow escapes from death, for example, do not invite the reader to meditate on the quality and brevity of life or on the marvels of a destiny that permits Leatherstocking to prevail in the teeth of hostile forces. An adventure always remains an adventure; a speech is rarely more than a set piece. Neither Leatherstocking's adventures nor his speeches become explorations into the unknown inner depths of man or world. Neither are we encouraged to ponder the more immediate wonder that so simple and "uneducated" a man as Natty should be such a repository of wisdom.

One might, perhaps, translate Eliot's terminology into that of Cooper's later contemporary, Ralph Waldo Emerson, to say that Cooper portrays men who think but never man thinking. Cooper's characters have ideas, but they are never transformed by ideas. We never see them in the process of discovering or creating ideas that change the quality of their existence. Although Cooper writes romances of the forest in which he creates a "mythic" character who is intended to embody certain ideals and give expression to certain ideas, the character and the ideas never quite fuse. Rather, Deerslayer the myth stands aside from his own thoughts, a true neoclassicist. Leatherstocking the myth is speechless, while Natty the speaker ceases to be mythic. It is generally true of Cooper's fiction that ideas are set apart from the characters. They are loose thoughts that do not spring spontaneously from the inner necessities of those who speak them.

Perhaps the nature of this dissociation between character and language can best be demonstrated by examining closely the novel that has been widely received as Cooper's masterpiece, *The Prairie*. It is the novel that combines most effectively Cooper's favorite subject matter and novelistic methods on the one hand, with his most characteristic themes and intellectual preoccupations on the other. Ringe writes of this book that of the three early Leatherstocking tales it ". . . is probably the richest thematically and the most complex intellectually".[13] Henry Nash Smith calls *The Prairie* ". . . a rich and complex book",[14] and D. E. S. Maxwell finds that ". . . the action of this novel carries the ideas with considerable success".[15]

Before coming to Cooper's ideas as such, however, it may be useful to glance at the action and plot of this novel. The former retains many of the formulas that Cooper had used successfully in the two previous Leatherstocking tales: Indian ambushes, capture and escape, heroic single combat between well-matched antagonists. But the plot of *The Prairie* has caused critics some concern. Ringe calls *The Prairie* "the weakest of the early Leatherstocking tales on the plot level – the kidnapping of Inez and the transporting of her to the trans-Mississippi west are most implausible . . .".[16] Smith asserts that "From the standpoint of the 'realism' that came to dominate American fiction later in the century, the plot of *The Prairie* is absurd". But he then goes on to argue that ". . . it is a mistake to analyze *The Prairie* in these terms. A generation that has witnessed a revolt against realism need not begrudge Cooper the privilege of grouping his characters to achieve certain effects without bothering too much over external details of motivation".[17]

13 *James Fenimore Cooper*, p. 45.
14 *The Prairie* (New York, 1960), Introduction, p. v.
15 *American Fiction*, p. 134.
16 *James Fenimore Cooper*, p. 45.
17 *The Prairie*, pp. viii, ix.

Smith is right, of course, in insisting that we should not be limited by false standards of "realism" that are, at any rate, questionable. I think, however, that it may be somewhat misguided to try to overlook the problems presented by Cooper's plot. As in the case of Cooper's language, the critic's task is not to sweep problems under the rug but to see what can be learned from them. If we focus on Cooper's plot it becomes evident that the difficulties do not arise solely from the critic's application of later nineteenth-century standards of realism but from Cooper's own novelistic method and the underlying beliefs which make themselves felt in the novel. The element in the plot that appears to vex the critics is the manner in which Cooper gets his characters on stage and moves them about once they are there. Smith states the nature of the problem succinctly:

He wants four groups of characters brought into contact with one another in the West and he puts them there with a kind of imaginative arbitrariness. Furthermore, he treats the portion of the Plains in which the action takes place as if it were an Elizabethan stage, a neutral space where any character may be brought at a moment's notice without arousing in the audience a desire to have the entrance accounted for.[18]

I think, however, that the problem is just the opposite of what Smith says it is. It is not that Cooper thinks he can bring characters on stage "at a moment's notice without arousing in the audience a desire to have the entrance accounted for", but precisely that he thinks he must account for everything. We would not, I believe, "begrudge Cooper the privilege of grouping his characters to achieve certain effects without bothering too much over external details of motivation", except that it is Cooper himself who raises the questions of motivation.

The particular aspect of the plot that Cooper has difficulty in explaining is the abduction and transportation of Inez. Having kidnapped her to extort a royal ransom from her husband, the Bush clan adopts an itinerary designed to make collection of the ransom impossible. By common sense standards this is a problem.

[18] *Ibid.*, p. ix.

But the problem and our questionings are not raised simply by a common-sense reader, but by Cooper himself, who sets aside a chapter for the telling of the long melodramatic story of the misadventures of Middleton and Inez. Cooper introduces this melodrama in the following way:

> It is proper that the course of the narrative should be stayed, while we revert to those causes which have brought in their train of consequences, the singular contest just related. The interruption must necessarily be as brief as we hope it may prove satisfactory to that class of readers, who require that no gap should be left by those who assume the office of historians, for their own fertile imaginations to fill.[19]

It is Cooper who suggests that there is a set of causes that has led to a "train of consequences". It is Cooper, also, who puts himself in the position of "historian" whose task it is to fill all causal and logical gaps in the narrative. But having put himself in that position he comes up with an explanation that is inadequate. He comes up, that is, with a wholly conventional late eighteenth-century sentimental narrative. Both Cervantes and Fielding had made skillful use of the device of the novelist as historian by making the historian an ironic device, Cervantes creating the mysterious Arab Cid Hamete de Benengeli, and Fielding an "implied narrator". In both instances, the author undermines any clear-cut preconceived distinctions between story and history that the reader might bring to the work, and as a consequence, common-sense notions of cause and effect become inoperative. That is, in a skeptical age, the writer of fiction can overcome the reader's skepticism by introducing a narrator who poses as a greater skeptic than the reader himself, and who keeps the reader off balance by undermining his own narrative.

Cooper, however, does not give his narrator a character that would enable him to cope with the problem of the reader's skepticism. Rather, the narrator suggests that he can supply the information necessary to establish a plausible continuum of causes and effects. On the one hand, Cooper follows his urge to create

---

[19]   *Ibid.*, p. 178. Hereafter references to the novel will be cited in the text.

a mythic narrative, and on the other he succumbs to the temptation to rationalize and explain all levels of experience so as to eliminate any dimension of the mysterious or the unknown. To be sure, there is a lame gesture in the direction of irony with the clause, "that class of readers, who require that no gap should be left by those who assume the office of historians, for their own fertile imaginations to fill", but the irony is unfocused, and one cannot tell whether it is directed against the literalists or those with "fertile imaginations".

The plot difficulties Cooper encountered, then, may be seen as one sign of the problems he faced as an intelligent post-Enlightenment writer attempting to use mythic motifs. In spite of his insistence that the events being narrated are held together by a chain of causes and effects, Cooper does not give his narrative a cohesive linear structure, but rather organizes the novel spatially. As Smith asserts, "an analysis of the structure of *The Prairie* reveals that Cooper works from one to another of a series of sharp visual images conceived as if they were paintings lacking the dimension of time. These moments of stasis are interlarded with spurts of violent action ... and with long debates between Leatherstocking and Obed Bat, or among the parliamentary orators of the Sioux council".[20]

It is not that the moments of stasis are objectionable in themselves, but that they point to an unresolved difficulty that pervades Cooper's novel. Although the action of the novel is organized in terms of a journey, and though the reader is led to expect a journey, yet the journey can never quite get underway. For one thing, the scene keeps shifting from one group of characters to another. Secondly, the action must constantly pause to allow for the introduction of discursive ideas, either by the narrator directly or in the course of lengthy conversations. And to add to the difficulties of travel, the action itself makes the journey impossible: Ishmael ensconces himself in a cozy natural fortress, a move that foreshadows his future immobility; when his horses are stolen, his immobility is assured. The trapper's ability to move

[20] *Ibid.*, p. ix.

is inhibited by the entourage he accumulates and by the Indians, who keep capturing him.

This inability on Cooper's part to choose between a linear and a spatial development manifests itself also in the development of the character of the trapper. Poirier writes that Leatherstocking is a mythic character and also a *beau ideal*, but it is not clear that the two are compatible. Mircea Eliade has written that "the myth is assumed by man in as much as he is a whole being; it is not addressed to his intelligence or his imagination only. When no longer assumed to be a revelation of the 'mysteries' the myth becomes 'decadent', obscured; it turns into a tale or a legend".[21] Just such a "decadent" myth is Leatherstocking. Cooper starts to create a mythic character and then it turns out he does not believe in him. He cannot decide whether Leatherstocking is to be a myth ("a revelation of the 'mysteries'") or a rational ideal (the embodiment of a set of logically arrived at exemplary behavioral characteristics).

It is clear, for example, that in his initial presentation of Natty in *The Prairie*, Cooper wants him to appear larger than life. The passage in which Cooper introduces the trapper has been justly praised for the effectiveness with which it outlines the old man's mythic dimensions:

> The sun had fallen below the crest of the nearest wave of the prairie, leaving the usual rich and glowing train on its track. In the centre of this flood of fiery light a human form appeared, drawn against the gilded background as distinctly, and seemingly as palpable, as though it would come within the grasp of any extended hand. The figure was colossal; the attitude musing and melancholy; and the situation directly in the route of the travellers. But imbedded, as it was, in its setting of garish light, it was impossible to distinguish its just proportions or true character.
>
> The effect of such a spectacle was instantaneous and powerful. The man in front of the emigrants came to a stand, and remained gazing at the mysterious object with a dull interest, that soon quickened into superstitious awe. His sons, so soon as the first emotions of surprise had a little abated, drew slowly around him, and as they who governed the teams gradually followed their example, the whole party was soon

21   *Myths, Dreams, and Mysteries* (New York & Evanston, 1960), p. 16.

condensed in one silent and wondering group. Notwithstanding the impression of a supernatural agency was very general among the travellers, the ticking of gunlocks was heard, and one or two of the bolder youths cast their rifles forward, in readiness for service. (p. 8)

Students of Cooper have commented frequently on the mythic dimensions in which the trapper is introduced. But it should be noted that the dimensions, here, are not only mythic but also a manifestation of the Burkean sublime. In *A Philosophical Enquiry into the Origin of our Ideas of the Sublime and Beautiful* Edmund Burke had defined the sublime as that which ". . . is productive of the strongest emotion which the mind is capable of feeling".[22] In Burke's view, that would be anything capable of causing an observer to feel astonishment, especially an astonishment associated with terror. "No passion", Burke had maintained, "so effectually robs the mind of all its powers of acting and reasoning as *fear*. For fear being an apprehension of pain or death, it operates in a manner that resembles actual pain. Whatever therefore is terrible, with regard to sight, is sublime too, whether this cause of terror be endued with greatness of dimension or not . . .".[23] One other element, Burke holds, contributes to the sublime, and that is obscurity: "To make anything very terrible, obscurity seems in general to be necessary".[24]

All of these elements are present in Cooper's description, which focuses not simply on the figure of Natty but on the effect that the figure has on the minds of the Bush family. Their primary emotion is, as it should be in experiencing the sublime, astonishment. The silhouetted figure itself gives the illusion of vastness and obscurity, and in doing so, inspires an awe and wonder that linger on the threshold of terror. So much so, that the stolid Bush family, not much given to flights of imagination, is even ready to entertain thoughts of a "supernatural agency". But no sooner is the supernatural contemplated than it is removed by the readied rifles of the more aggressive members of the Bush clan.

It is not long, either, before Natty himself diminishes, shrinking

---

[22] *Burke's Works* (London, 1869), I, 74.
[23] *Ibid.*, p. 88.
[24] *Ibid.*, p. 89.

from the awesome figure outlined against the sunset to the shrivelled old man he is: "In place of the brightness which had dazzled
the eye, a grey and more sober light had succeeded, and as the
setting lost its brilliancy, the proportions of the fanciful form
became less exaggerated, and finally distinct" (p. 9). What is of
interest in the fluctation between the sublime and the lowly is
the ease with which the mythic stature of Leatherstocking is
dissipated. What is apparent is that it is all too possible for Cooper
to impose the qualities of sublimity on Leatherstocking. His sublime appearance is all facade; he does not achieve sublimity
through struggle, either within himself or with the powers of a
hostile universe. And what is true of his sublimity is true, as well,
of his mythic stature. Myth, according to Eliade is a way of
understanding reality, but the reality inherent in Natty as a myth
disintegrates as quickly as his sublimity. Just as he attempts to
impose sublime stature upon Natty, so Cooper tries to graft a
mythic reality onto him. But since the mythic reality, like the
dimension of the sublime, is not organic and does not develop out
of the old trapper's personality, it does not hold up.

Another manifestation of this alternation between the sublime
and the lowly is Leatherstocking's dialogue. When Ishmael Bush
first questions the Old Trapper about the lay of the land, he
answers in the following terms:

'You may travel weeks and you will see it the same. I often think
the Lord has placed this barren belt of prairie behind the States, to
warn men to what their folly may yet bring the land! Ay, weeks, if
not months, may you journey in these open fields, in which there is
neither dwelling nor habitation for man or beast. Even the savage
animals travel miles on miles to seek their dens; and yet the wind
seldom blows from the east, but I conceit the sound of axes, and the
crash of falling trees, are in my ears.' (p. 19)

In this speech Natty is clearly expressing an idea with which
Cooper was preoccupied: the despoliation of the virgin land, the
march of civilization which is, unfortunately, destructive of Nature, the encroachment of corrupt man on the purity of the nonhuman Creation. But in order to give expression to such serious
matters, Natty's speech must rise to the level of the sublime,

which accounts for the utterance of such phrases as, "this barren belt of prairie", "to what their folly may yet bring the land!" "months, may you journey", "neither dwelling nor habitation for man or beast", "I conceit the sound of axes". Again, I must emphasize that my purpose is not to deny that wisdom may be uttered by untutored men in simple language, but to demonstrate that it is Cooper who seems to be denying this. Before Cooper can permit Natty to say anything profound, he must find a high style for him that will be suitable for conveying elevated thoughts. Great wisdom cannot be uttered in lowly language.

When Natty turns from speaking deep thoughts, however, his language suffers a rapid decline. Later in this same scene, Natty has reason to speak as a participant in the action, and not as a pure moralizer:

'What now, dog?' he said, looking down at his companion, as if he addressed a being of an intelligence equal to his own, and speaking in a voice of great affection. 'What is it, pup? ha! Hector; what is it nosing, now? It won't do, dog; it won't do; the very fa'ns play in open view of us, without minding so worn out curs, as you and I. Instinct is their gift, Hector; and they have found out how little we are to be feared, they have!' (p. 21)

The diminution in language is equivalent to the diminution in stature that the Old Trapper had undergone earlier.

Similar problems are also to be found in the language of the narrator of the novel. His most thorough statement of the complex of ideas underlying the action and plot occurs in the opening section of the sixth chapter. Smith writes of this passage that

the novelist attempts to state this theory [about the necessary outcome of frontier conditions] in Chapter VI of *The Prairie*. The two pages devoted to the effort are among the cloudiest and most pretentious he ever wrote, but the ideas he is trying to formulate are so important both for his work and for American intellectual history in general that the reader is obliged to make the effort required to follow Cooper's meaning. (pp xii-xiii)

Cooper's theory, as Smith outlines it, is that the westward movement of the frontier has reversed the historical process of the evolution of societies from the primitive to the refined. But, as

Smith goes on to point out, once he has established the theory, Cooper cannot choose between the values of primitivism and those of society. Cooper presumably solves this dilemma by embodying in Leatherstocking the best of both worlds: the stoicism, courage, purity, and innocence of the noble savage tempered by the humanistic Christianity of the Moravians and the exercise of Lockean common sense.

Nevertheless, this mixture of elements in Leatherstocking does not make itself felt in his character or in his psychological make-up. Surprisingly, for a character who embodies the qualities of two opposed cultures, Natty does not reflect any self doubts or internal stress. He is remarkably free of the torments one would expect to find in a man of total sincerity and commitment who finds himself torn between two ways of life, one pagan the other Christian, one primitive, the other civilized, one living by the brutal code of an eye for an eye and the other professing a universal law of Love. This is not to say that he does not consciously recognize these conflicts but that the conflicts do not penetrate the inner depths of his soul.

The famous death scene, which is a graphic inversion of the trapper's advent, may serve to demonstrate this singular lack of inner conflict. Too feeble, now, to do much more than occupy "... a rude seat, which had been made, with studied care, to support his frame in an upright and easy attitude", the trapper waits patiently and unperturbedly for the call from the Angel of Death. Having commenced his activities in the novel with the setting sun at his back, he now sits with "his body ... placed so as to let the light of the setting sun fall full upon the solemn features" (p. 445). Where earlier the setting sun had magnified the trapper's proportions to such an extent as to terrify the hostile Bush clan, now the dying trapper, confronting the fading fount of earthly life, is first perceived by his old Christian friends, Middleton and Paul, who constitute a much more benign point of view than the Bush clan.

The death itself is an odd mixture of pagan, Biblical, and sentimental attitudes. The old trapper is in the position of a patriarch who must offer solace to those he is leaving behind, two sets of descendants with two opposite sets of values. As the scene commences, the primitive and pagan values seem to be uppermost. Hard-Heart, his adopted Indian son, is the trapper's principal caretaker and his closest human communicant. The relationship between them is touching in its openness and simplicity; it is, as a matter of fact, the clearest and most powerful love relationship in the novel, one that offers an alternative to the destructive oedipal relationships that pervade the Bush family.[25] In the trapper's request that he be buried as a Christian and without benefit of pagan ritual, echoes of Beowulf's funeral pyre abound. And his insistence that Middleton deliver his "rifle, pouch, and horn ... to the person whose name is graven on the plates of the stock", is reminiscent of the magic weapons that adorn medieval adventures.

When the trapper decides to bless Hard-Heart, he is returning to a still more primitive condition, the condition of the Biblical patriarchs, although he couches the phenomenon in terms of the customs of his people as opposed to those of Hard-Heart:

'Pawnee,' continued the old man, always changing his language to suit the person he addressed, and not unfrequently according to the ideas he expressed, 'it is a custom of my people for the father to leave his blessing with the son, before he shuts his eyes forever. This blessing I give to you; take it; for the prayers of a Christian man will never make the path of a just warrior to the blessed prairies either longer or more tangled. May the God of a white man look on your deeds with friendly eyes, and may you never commit an act that shall cause him to darken his face. I know not whether we shall ever meet again. There are many traditions concerning the place of Good Spirits. It is not for one like me, old and experienced though I am, to set up my opinions against a nation's. You believe in the blessed prairies, and I have faith in the sayings of my fathers. If both are true our parting will be final; but if it should prove that the same meaning is hid under different words, we shall yet stand together, Pawnee, before the face of your Wahcondah, who will then be no other than my God. There is much to be said in favor of both religions, for each seems suited to its own people, and no doubt it was so intended. (pp. 448-449)

[25] For a penetrating analysis of those relationships see William Wasserstrom, "Cooper, Freud, and the Origins of Culture", *American Imago*, XVII (Winter, 1960), 423-437. Reprinted in Warren S. Walker, *Leatherstocking and the Critics* (Chicago, 1965), pp. 104-113.

This verbose blessing in an elongated death scene is typical of Leatherstocking, who is, at this weighty moment, far from the silent and marvelously alert *beau ideal* described by Poirier. In this scene, the elevated Natty and the colloquial Natty exist, if not fused, at least in close proximity. The approach of mysterious, obscure, inscrutable death, with all that it portends, once again raises the action to the level of the sublime. The sublimity is sustained, further, by the echoes of ancient epic traditions. But it reaches its peak in the paternal blessing, which is so reminiscent of Isaac's blessing Jacob in Genesis, 27:27-29. And yet, what a sharp contrast between Isaac's brief and powerful statement and the rambling musings of Natty. What a difference, too, between the blessings themselves. Natty's blessing, like his mind, is amorphous: "May the God of a white man look on your deeds with friendly eyes, and may you never commit an act that shall cause him to darken his face."

What does such a blessing mean? Isaac, though the least impressive of the patriarchs, is nevertheless, still a man of faith, a man who must remain ever conscious of the fact that for the sake of a blessing he was nearly sacrificed by his father. When Isaac blesses his son he believes in the potency of what he is doing; the text makes it abundantly clear that the actors in the events being described believe that the events in which they participate are deeply involved with the whole of human history and will ultimately affect the furthest reaches of human destiny. As a consequence, all that takes place pulsates with significance. A recent commentator on Genesis observes that "the scene between Isaac and Esau [after Jacob has taken the blessing], both so shaken and helpless, could scarcely be surpassed for pathos. Most poignant of all is the stark fact that the deed cannot be undone. For all the actors in this piece are but the tools of fate which – purposeful though it must be – can itself be neither deciphered nor side-stepped by man".[26]

Leatherstocking, however, despite his assurances that he received his early training from Moravian missionaries, and despite

[26] *The Anchor Bible*, ed. E. A. Speiser (Garden City, New York, 1964), p. 213.

his constant moralizing, has at no time been portrayed as a man of faith. Why, then, does he feel empowered to bless? What can a blessing mean to him? What efficacy can he expect a blessing to have? Not much, apparently, as Natty himself seems to recognize, when he says that "the prayers of a Christian man will never make the path of a just warrior to the blessed prairies longer or more tangled". That is, the blessing, as far as the trapper is concerned, may not do any good but neither can it do any harm. such candor is what the reader has come to expect of Natty, and such naiveté, it may be added, is not uncharacteristic of his creator. If one considers for a moment the blessing of Isaac upon Jacob, it is apparent that what a blessing does is to make the paths pursued by humans tangled and thorny indeed. In the power that the blessing has over the consciousness of the participants lies the immensely moving effectiveness of the Isaac-Rebekah-Jacob-Esau episode. Jacob, who receives the blessing, must immediately flee into exile; he must sojourn in a strange land and labor for uncertain wages. Esau, who is denied the primary blessing, sees his life abruptly and irrevocably channeled into a new and unexpected course. Exactly what the blessing does is to make life more entangled. The blessing puts man under a burden that is nearly intolerable, a burden that is tolerable, as a matter of fact, only to the man of faith. In the Biblical encounter, the blessing sets wife against husband, son against father, brother against brother. But whereas the Biblical blessing puts the greatest imaginable strain on the blessed, Leatherstocking's blessing is nothing if not innocuous.

So little store does the trapper put in the efficacy of his blessing that he immediately continues with a discussion, worthy of an Enlightenment man, of the comparative values of different religious systems. The Biblical patriarch blesses because he has a kingdom to dispose of, a visionary or spiritual kingdom, as well as a historical and physical one. But Leatherstocking has nothing to pass on to posterity. The most he can offer is some rambling speculation, in which he himself seems to put little store, that perhaps he and his adopted son will meet in a vague hereafter ruled by a Wahcondah who may also be identical with a rather

nebulous "my God" who may be the mechanistic deity of the
deists or a non-denominational Christian God or perhaps the God
of the Moravians.

In some ways, of course, the scene is conventionally sentimental, having much in common with the graveyard school of
eighteenth-century poetry and the Gothic novel. But its sentimentality lies, I think, not in the powerful overflow of emotion
but in Cooper's unwillingness or inability to ground these strong
emotions in the ideational context of the novel. As Eliot writes,
in his essay on Phillip Massinger, "The debility of romantic
drama . . . consists in an internal incoherence of feelings, a concatenation of emotions which signifies nothing".[27] Just such a
concatenation occurs in the scene under discussion. The ideas
that are given fleeting expression by Cooper are never permitted
to feed back into the novel. We may describe Natty's religious
position in his speech to Hard-Heart as "pragmatic". The white
man's religion is functional, and therefore good, for him; similarly,
the red man's religion is valuable for the red man because it has
provided him with a viable life style. But there is also a tacit
claim for the absoluteness of his God in Natty's speech, and no
attempt is made to reconcile these positions. Neither is there any
attempt made to clarify the contours of Leatherstocking's God.

What may be observed in this speech is that Natty's mind, as
an instrument of thought, has, so to speak, the consistency of felt
rather than the consistency of a woven fabric. His mind does not
consist of strands of ideas that weave in and out, that cross each
other, that pass over and under, in and out, and form themselves
into a texture that is rich and complex. Rather, ideas appear as
solid blocks of abstraction. Natty's "God of a white man" does
not have any historical or theological substance. He does not
grow out of meditations on Biblical texts; He is not bodied forth
in specific Mosaic commandments or New Testament modifica-
tions of those commandments; He is not the God of Abraham
and neither is he the God of Socrates; He is not the God of
Church theologians, or of Luther, or of Calvin, or of A. G. Span-

[27] *Selected Essays* (New York, 1932), p. 190.

genberg. He is, rather, a vague concept lacking any detailed definition, something like the tulip that Dr. Johnson would have had the neo-classic artist paint, one whose stripes are not numbered.

The same absence of subtlety characterizes Cooper's attempt, as Smith puts it, to deal with

the intellectual issues emerging from the scientific rationalism of the Enlightenment. This is the valid reason for including Dr. Bat, whose supposedly comic pedantry and cowardice are so painful that readers are likely to miss the point of his overlong debates with Leatherstocking. Cooper's characterization of Bat expresses one of the most profoundly conservative facets of his mind. His attitude toward science is substantially that of Swift in the description of Gulliver's voyage to Laputa. In every conceivable fashion the novelist derides the misunderstanding of nature resulting from the scientist's cocksure reliance on reason and his craze for classification, in contrast with the illiterate trapper's direct, intuitive grasp of nature.[28]

The modern reader, I suspect, would no longer agree with Smith that an antipathy to "scientific rationalism" and "cocksure reliance on reason and [a] craze for classification" are inherently "conservative", unless conservative is defined in terms of a specific historical context. The fact is that many of the great artists of the nineteenth (and twentieth) century were distrustful of science, and it is just as easy to think of such artists now, in an age of mass genocide, atomic holocausts, and germ warfare, as prophetic rather than conservative. But again, it is not Cooper's specific position on the matter that is important. It hardly seems to matter very much whether he was for science or against it, whether he was for the white man or the red man, the Federalists or the Whigs. What is important, is that whatever side Cooper was on, the fabric of ideas he presents in dealing with "the intellectual issues emerging from . . . scientific rationalism" is, as always, a fabric lacking in texture. We may take as further example a passage singled out by Smith:

Dr. Bat's version of the doctrine of man's perfectibility ('. . . nay, I know not, if time and opportunity were given him, but he might become the master of all learning, and consequently equal to the great moving principle') is solemnly rebuked by Leatherstocking: 'Say, you

[28] *The Prairie*, xix.

who think it so easy to climb into the judgment-seat above, can you tell me anything of the beginning and the end? Nay, you're a dealer in ailings and cures: what is life, and what is death?' And the trapper demonstrates that his dog Hector has a better insight into the actual world than the Doctor can achieve with all his scientific deductions.[29]

It must be granted, I think, that Dr. Bat's version of the doctrine of perfectibility is not so much a legitimate version of the doctrine as a caricature of it. Smith says that Natty's answer is given with solemnity, a very apt word, and one that expresses with nice precision just what is wrong with Cooper's expression of ideas. This rather crude device of presenting ideas one does not like in caricature, while presenting their opposite with solemnity is self-defeating. For although Natty's speech is supposed to contain an inherent dignity that flows from the trapper's saintly purity, advanced age, and his knowledge of natural lore accumulated through a long lifetime of careful devotion to nature and Creation, the proximity of the caricature undermines this intended majesty. In the part of Leatherstocking's speech that Smith cites, echoes of Job and Psalms are clearly to be heard. Elsewhere in the same speech there are echoes of Ecclesiastes: "This is neither more nor less than mortal wickedness! Here have I been a dweller on the earth for fourscore and six changes of the seasons, and all that time have I look'd at the growing and the dying trees, and yet do I not know the reasons why the bud starts under the summer sun, or the leaf falls when it is pinch'd by the frosts. Your l'arning, though it is man's boast, is folly in the eyes of Him who sits in the clouds, and looks down in sorrow at the pride and vanity of his creatures" (pp. 206-207). But the allusions do not enhance the meaning of the sources. There is no attempt to meditate on the texts themselves, or to relate them to the characters in the novel. Ecclesiastes laments the futility of all activity, human and nonhuman, but Cooper seems to suggest that Natty's activities are more meaningful than Dr. Bat's. The discussion is abruptly ended by an Indian adventure which in no way modifies or relates to the discussion of ideas that has preceded it.

[29] *Ibid.*

VI

HAWTHORNE: THE INTELLECTUAL AS OUTSIDER

1

Charles Brockden Brown wanted to combine morality, philosophy, and art so as to write novels with deep meaning and universal significance. But the time was not ripe, and his mind was not powerful enough to overcome the problems raised by his ambitions. Between the forces of eighteenth-century rationalism and nineteenth-century romanticism he could never quite choose. Alone he could not assimilate French ideas, English forms, and American experience. When he tried to create intellectual characters they turned out either sentimental heroes or melodramatic villains. Too often he never got off the ground, and when he did, he found, like Icarus, that his wings were not substantial enough to carry him very high without disastrous consequences.

James Fenimore Cooper found himself in a similar quandary. He wanted to combine morality, philosophy, and story-telling in such a way as to provide his countrymen with a maximum of pleasure and edification. But he, too, found himself caught between eighteenth-century rationalism and nineteenth-century romanticism. The success that eluded Brown and Cooper, Hawthorne managed to grasp, but only after almost a quarter of a century's apprenticeship at his craft, and only after Ralph Waldo Emerson had "made the first full examination of . . . [the] potentialities"[1] of our literature. Hawthorne's first novel, *Fanshawe,* which was published anonymously in 1828, he quickly renounced. The following years he spent perfecting his art, achieving an unquestionable mastery of the short story by 1837. In 1849, after a twenty-one year hiatus, he returned to the novel. A year later,

[1]   F. O. Matthiessen, *American Renaissance* (New York, 1946), p. xii.

The Scarlet Letter was published, and "with that . . . novel, New World fiction arrived at its first fulfillment, and Hawthorne at his".[2] In it Hawthorne managed to fuse all the elements that for Brown had always remained hopelessly disparate. Just how, is not yet quite clear. Perhaps it is inevitable that a touch of mystery should always hover over the "how" of a great work of art.

But if mystery remains, it is not for any lack of attempts to solve it. Matthiessen writes, "Why Hawthorne came nearest to achieving [the] wholeness [of imaginative composition] in *The Scarlet Letter* may be accounted for in various ways".[3] Trollope, according to Matthiessen, thought that "here Hawthorne had developed his most coherent plot". Matthiessen himself adds that "Hawthorne has also managed here his utmost approach to the inseparability of elements that James insisted on when he said that 'character, in any sense in which we can get at it, is action, and action is plot.' Of his four romances, this one grows most organically out of the interactions between the characters. . . . Furthermore, his integrity of effect is due in part to the incisive contrasts among the human types he is presenting".[4] More recently, R. H. Fogle has said that "The intensity of *The Scarlet Letter*, at which Hawthorne himself was dismayed, comes from the concentration, selection, and dramatic irony".[5] And Hyatt H. Waggoner demonstrates convincingly that the greatness of the book is owing to Hawthorne's brilliant handling of symbols and images to develop both plot and theme.[6]

Since great works of art can never be reduced to one simple formula, there is no need to attempt to deny any of the foregoing explanations of the greatness of *The Scarlet Letter*. However, I would like to explore an avenue which Matthiessen opens but does not fully investigate. He adds to what I have already quoted from *American Renaissance* that "beyond any interest in ordering of plot or in lucid discrimination between characters, Hawthorne's

[2] R. W. B. Lewis, *The American Adam* (Chicago, 1955), p. 111.
[3] *American Renaissance*, p. 275.
[4] *Ibid.*
[5] *Hawthorne's Fiction: The Light and the Dark* (Norman, Oklahoma, 1952), p. 110.
[6] *Hawthorne, A Critical Study* (Cambridge, 1955), pp. 117-150.

imaginative energy seems to have been called out to the full here by the continual correspondences that his theme allowed him to make between external events and inner significances".[7] What Matthiessen has in mind is Hawthorne's use of such phenomena as the "A" that Dimmesdale sees blazoned in the sky, out of which Hawthorne "developed one of his most fertile resources, the device of multiple choice ...".[8] That is, the reader can take the "A" in the sky as a supernatural portent or as a symptom of the disease in the "eye and heart" of Dimmesdale. Hence, the external event – a meteor "burning to waste" – becomes another means of probing the mind and heart of the minister.

In the section of his book called "Hawthorne and Milton", Matthiessen extends this idea of "continual correspondences ... between external events and inner significances" to the correspondence between a character's inner being and his physical attributes, maintaining that the physical qualities and actions become emblematic of the psychic core. "Hawthorne's most valuable inheritance from the seventeenth century tradition", he asserts, "lay in his comprehension of the dependence of the body on the mind, especially of the power with which the ego can warp man's physical constitution to its own savage bent. In the degree of objective equivalence that he could devise to give external form to these inner workings, he was indebted to the greatest masters of allegory ...".[9]

Matthiessen develops this idea with reference to Hawthorne's drawing upon Milton for his portrait of Chillingworth. "The physician's transformation", states Matthiessen,

is handled with strictest accord to the Puritans' belief in how an erring mind could become so divorced from God that it lapsed into a state of diabolic possession.
* *
However, the portrayal of Chillingworth's behavior at the moment of his discovery of the mark on the sleeping minister's breast draws upon a profounder moralist than any of the Mathers. His face is distorted with a mixed 'look of wonder, joy, and horror. With what a

[7] Page 276.
[8] *Ibid.*
[9] Page 305.

ghastly rapture, as it were, too mighty to be expressed only by the eye and features, and therefore bursting forth through the whole ugliness of his figure, and making itself even riotously manifest by the extravagant gestures with which he threw up his arms towards the ceiling, and stamped his foot upon the floor! Had a man seen old Roger Chillingworth, at that moment of his ecstasy, he would have had no need to ask how Satan comports himself when a precious human soul is lost to heaven, and won into his kingdom'.

How integrally Hawthorne accepted Milton's analysis of the way the passions operate can be suggested by the passage where Uriel looked down upon the sudden unrestraint of Satan, and

> Saw him disfigured, more than could befall
> Spirit of happy sort; his gestures fierce
> He mark'd, and mad demeanour, then alone,
> As he supposed, all unobserved, unseen.[10]

In all this Matthiessen seems to be saying that in characterizing Chillingworth Hawthorne discovered a set of recognizable, conventional behavioral patterns, already a respectable part of the literary tradition, which served as a kind of "objective correlative" to reveal the innermost depths of Chillingworth's soul. What I wish to demonstrate at this point is that Hawthorne did almost the same thing in his characterization of Dimmesdale, but much more originally and brilliantly than with Chillingworth. Infusing new life into a worn but still useful set of literary clichés, Hawthorne created a character whose guilt-ridden existence forces the reader to ponder the meaning of man's relation to himself, his fellow mortals, and his God.

Hawthorne's method in creating his character is to start with the metaphor of adultery. *The Scarlet Letter* is a novel about adultery, and it is also a novel that focuses most painfully and acutely on the problem of human sin and guilt,[11] the ineffable and not easily measurable concomitants of what apparently was

[10]   Pages 306-307.
[11]   In his chapter on this novel in *Sins of the Fathers: Hawthorne's Psychological Themes* (New York, 1966), Frederick C. Crews writes about Hawthorne's concern with guilt. Crews, however, unlike such earlier critics as Q. D. Leavis, Hyatt H. Waggoner, and Roy Male (*Hawthorne's Tragic Vision* [Austin, Texas, 1957]), attempts to dissociate psychological guilt entirely from theological sin, a rather imprudent polarization to make when dealing with a writer like Hawthorne. See also, Ernest Sandeen, "*The Scarlet Letter* as a Love Story", *PMLA*, LXXVII (September 1962), 425-435.

in Hawthorne's time a much graver transgression than it is in the second half of the twentieth century. Nevertheless, it is through the act of adultery that the novel focuses on the problems of sin and guilt, and it is partly because Hawthorne found here a literary convention embodying a human act to objectify his moral and philosophical speculation that *The Scarlet Letter* is the first great American novel.

The great literature of adultery (and chastity), is, of course, preserved in the medieval romances of courtly love. How familiar Hawthorne was with the courtly-love tradition is not clear. A connection between Hawthorne and the courtly-love romances does not, however, seem far-fetched if we bear in mind two important facts: (1) that he consciously labeled his own works romances while many of his contemporaries called theirs "tales of truth", and (2) that he thought of himself as an allegorist. The intricate relationship between the romances and allegory, the way in which one developed into the other, has been traced by C. S. Lewis in his *Allegory of Love*. It does not seem likely that Haw-thorne could have been aware of the fact that he was working in both these modes and yet have been totally unacquainted with the literature from which they had evolved. But even if this were the case, he would certainly have been familiar with elements of the courtly-love tradition through one of his favorite poets, Edmund Spenser.[12]

Now, one of the most pervasive developments of the courtly-love romance, one reflected to some extent in Spenser's Red Cross Knight and Sir Guyon, was the lover both licentious and chaste: licentious in so far as he had to make love to a woman he could not hope to marry, and chaste in so far as he was expected to be

---

[12]   Matthiessen, p. 200 n., writes: "Hawthorne's final opinion on the sub-ject of poetry was expressed in a letter to Longfellow in 1864: 'I take vast satisfaction in your poetry, and take very little in most other men's, except it be the grand old strains that have been sounding all through my life'. These great exceptions were Spenser, Milton, and Shakespeare". I have not been able to check Hawthorne's reading, except for his borrowings from the Essex Athenaeum. However, by the 1840's, the medieval romances were certainly accessible. Between 1810 and 1855, at least eight collections of romances were published.

faithful to the object of his love. The code of courtly love, and the ideal of behavior of the lover had been described in the twelfth century by Andreas Capellanus.

In *The Art of Courtly Love*, Andreas lays down thirty-one rules for lovers. Of these, five describe physical manifestations of the psychological condition of the lover. These are:

XV   Every lover turns pale in the presence of his beloved.

XVI   When a lover suddenly catches sight of his beloved his heart palpitates.

XX   A man in love is always apprehensive.

XXX   A true lover is constantly and without intermission possessed by the thought of love.

XXIII He whom the thought of love vexes, eats and sleeps very little.[13]

The physical condition described by these symptoms indicates a state of extreme neurasthenia. The lover is alternately pale and flushed. He trembles in constant fear and apprehension. His mental state is one of constant abstraction, his physical state, one of gradual atrophy. In addition, a phenomenon Andreas does not mention, the lover is much given to sighing.

But there is also another rule which would seem to make it quite difficult to keep all those that have been mentioned so far. That is the thirteenth, which declares that "When made public love rarely endures". So, though the lover is "sick", though he must endure the pains of love, and show the physical symptoms of his malady, yet, at the same time, he must somehow contrive to conceal them from society, and especially must he conceal the identity of his beloved.

In English literature there is no more consummate courtly lover than Chaucer's Troilus, who was probably known to Hawthorne. He shows all the symptoms. When he first sees Criseyde in the temple "his herte gan to sprede and rise,/ and softe sighed, lest men myghte him here,/ and caughte ayeyn his firste pleyinge chere".[14] From this moment on, Troilus isolates himself so that

---

[13] Trans. J. J. Parry, ed. F. W. Locke (New York, 1957), pp. 42-43.

[14] *Troilus and Criseyde*, ed. R. K. Root (Princeton, 1926), Bk. I, ll. 278-80.

he may suffer secretly. His health declines, and his misery eventually becomes so intense as to endanger his very life. Troilus's courtship, conquest, and betrayal is a long story containing, it is true, a few moments of joy, but essentially it is a tale of woe.

But the courtly lover refuses to die with the Middle Ages or even with the courtly-love romance. Even that foundling of eighteenth-century "realism", Tom Jones (with whom Hawthorne was certainly acquainted[15]) is not immune to the dread disease. When Tom first realizes that he loves Sophia, he knows, also, that he cannot have her. As an honorable English gentleman, he must repress his passion; consequently, he finds himself in a dilemma:

It may, perhaps, be a question, whether the art which he used to conceal his passion, or the means which honest nature employed to reveal it, betrayed him most: for while art made him more than ever reserved to Sophia, and forbad him to address any of his discourse to her, nay, to avoid meeting her eyes, with the utmost caution; nature was no less busy in counter-plotting him. Hence, at the approach of the young lady he grew pale; and if this was sudden, started. If his eyes accidentally met hers the blood rushed into his cheeks, and his countenance became all over scarlet. If common civility ever obliged him to speak to her, as to drink her health at table, his tongue was sure to falter. If he touched her, his hand, nay, his whole frame, trembled. And if any discourse tended, however, remotely, to raise the idea of love, an involuntary sigh seldom failed to steal from his bosom. Most of which accidents nature was wonderfully industrious to throw daily in his way.[16]

The symptoms that identify Troilus and Tom as courtly lovers also identify Arthur Dimmesdale, but whether as a conventional courtly lover we shall see. He is first introduced to us as "a pale young man".[17] It is true that Chillingworth is also introduced as pale. But his is a mustier kind of pallor, that of "a man stricken in years, a pale, thin, scholar-like visage, with eyes dim and bleared by the lamp-light that had served them to pore over many

---

[15]   Randall Stewart, *Nathaniel Hawthorne, A Biography* (New Haven, 1948), p. 8.
[16]   Henry Fielding, *Tom Jones*, ed. George Sherburn (New York, 1950), p. 183.
[17]   Nathaniel Hawthorne, *The Scarlet Letter*, ed. Harry Levin (Boston, 1960), p. 66. Page references in my text are to this edition.

ponderous books" (p. 60). Dimmesdale's pallor is much more romantic and much more neurotic.

He was a person of very striking aspect, with a white, lofty, and impending brow, large, brown, melancholy eyes, and a mouth which unless when he forcible compressed it, was apt to be tremulous, expressing both nervous sensibility and a vast power of self-restraint. Notwithstanding his high native gifts and scholar-like attainments, there was an air about this young minister, – an apprehensive, a startled, a half-frightened look, – as of a being who felt himself quite astray and at a loss in the pathway of human existence, and could only be at ease in some seclusion of his own. Therefore, so far as his duties would permit, he trod in the shadowy by-paths, and thus kept himself simple and childlike; coming forth, when occasion was, with a freshness, and fragrance, and dewy purity of thought, which, as many people said, affected them like the speech of an angel. (p. 67)

Dimmesdale's pallor is owing not to scholarly seclusion but to "nervous sensibility". "The trying nature of his position drove the blood from his cheek, and made his lips tremulous" (p. 67). The blood has not been drained from his cheeks, as in the case of Chillingworth, it has been driven from them. When Dimmesdale must exhort Hester to confess the name of her lover, he cannot speak. And when he does, "The young pastor's voice was tremulously sweet, rich, deep, and broken" (p. 68). When she resolutely refuses to confess, Dimmesdale reacts as follows: "'She will not speak', murmured Mr. Dimmesdale, who, leaning over the balcony, with his hand upon his heart, had awaited the result of his appeal. He now drew back, with a long respiration. 'Wondrous strength and generosity of a woman's heart. She will not speak!'" (p. 69). These symptoms – sighing, pallor, flushes, pain – are elaborated at great length, and intertwined with indications of a general physical decline. When Hester appeals to him to prevent the authorities from taking Pearl from her, "the young minister at once came forward, pale, and holding his hand over his heart, as was his custom whenever his peculiarly nervous temperament was thrown into agitation. He looked now more careworn and emaciated than as we described him at the scene of Hester's public ignominy; and whether it were his failing health, or whatever the cause be, his large dark eyes had a world of pain in their melancholy depth" (pp. 112-13). After defending Hester, he is "tremulous with the vehemence of his appeal" (p. 114).

As Dimmesdale continues to decline, his parishioners look for an explanation. "By those best acquainted with his habits, the paleness of the young minister's cheek was accounted for by his too earnest devotion to study, his scrupulous fulfilment of parochial duty, and, more than all, by the fasts and vigils of which he made a frequent practice, in order to keep the grossness of his earthly state from clogging and obscuring his spiritual lamp" (p. 119). The irony is that all the phenomena cited as causes for his paleness are themselves part and parcel of it. Ultimately, his vigils and fasts and discipline are effects of the same thing that is causing his pallor and general physical decline. At one point, Hawthorne, with an almost Beethoven-like touch, draws all these themes together: the emaciation, the sweet voice, the melancholy, the paleness, the apprehensiveness, the hand-over-heart, the pain.

With all this difference of opinion as to the cause of his decline, there could be no question of the fact. His form grew emaciated; his voice, though still rich and sweet, had a certain melancholy prophecy of decay in it; he was often observed, on any slight alarm or other sudden accident, to put his hand over his heart, with first a flush and then a paleness, indicative of pain. (p. 119)

But the physical trait that receives the fullest development is Dimmesdale's compulsive covering of his heart. When Hester asks Pearl if she knows why her mother wears the scarlet letter, Pearl answers, "It is for the same reason that the minister keeps his hand over his heart" (p. 177). And then, a little later, Pearl asks, "Why does the minister keep his hand over his heart?" (p. 178). Several moments later, she repeats the question (p. 180). When Pearl and Hester first see the minister in the forest, he has his hand over his heart. Pearl now asks if he keeps his hand over his heart "because . . . the Black Man [Chillingworth] set his mark in that place" (p. 186). Dimmesdale has been declining physically, but "to Hester's eye, the Reverend Mr. Dimmesdale exhibited no symptom of positive and vivacious suffering, except that . . . he kept his hand over his heart" (p. 187). It is not necessary to list every instance of Dimmesdale's performing this act (I have counted thirteen). What becomes apparent, however, in these instances, is that the act has two purposes. First, it marks Dimmesdale's attempt to conceal his guilt from the world, just as the courtly lover would conceal his love. And secondly, it is a way of both assuaging and savoring the ache of his guilt, in the same way that a man with a nagging pain in some part of his anatomy will perform the one physical act most likely to remind him of his pain.

Two objections may be made at this point. One is that Dimmesdale is no longer in love, that his foray into adultery is past, and that he is now merely paying for his sin. The other is that any guilty man might have acted the same way as Dimmesdale. The minister himself seems to rebut this second objection when he tells Hester, "Were I an atheist, – a man devoid of conscience, – a wretch with coarse and brutal instincts, – I might have found peace, long ere now. Nay, I never should have lost it! But, as matters stand with my soul, whatever of good capacity there originally was in me, all of God's gifts that were the choicest have become the ministers of spiritual torment" (p. 190). Obviously, Dimmesdale's is a special guilt that requires a special set of symptoms.

Dimmesdale's sense of his special guilt may provide an answer to the first objection as well. It is true that Dimmesdale's situation is in many ways far from that of the courtly lover. My point, however, is not that Dimmesdale *is* the courtly lover, but that in the conventions of courtly love Hawthorne's genius found an objective correlative to communicate Dimmesdale's guilt. Q. D. Leavis, in a most incisive article on Hawthorne in the *Sewanee Review*, asserts that "Hawthorne has imaginatively recreated for the reader that Calvinist sense of sin, that theory which did in actuality shape the early social and spiritual history of New England. But in Hawthorne, by a wonderful feat of transmutation, it has no religious significance, it is as a psychological state that it is explored".[18] It is an exaggeration to say that the "sense of sin" Hawthorne recreated has "no religious significance", but at any

18   "Hawthorne as Poet", LIX (Spring, 1951), 197-98.

rate, the process that Mrs. Leavis describes seems to elucidate Hawthorne's art. Hawthorne used the same process in handling the conventions of courtly love. He recreated the courtly lover's capacity for intense suffering as a psychological state, but the sexual significance of the tradition is minimized. He did not merely borrow a set of conventions, he transmuted them, tearing them out of their specifically Pagan and Catholic origins, and using them to portray a psychological condition growing out of a Protestant ethic.

Dimmesdale, "the young divine, whose scholar-like renown still lived in Oxford", is the Puritan embodiment of the courtly lover. He is highly sensitive, gentle, seemingly noble, passionate. But whereas the courtly lover lives only for love, Dimmesdale lives only for guilt. "Love", says Andreas, in the very first sentence of his first chapter, "is a certain inborn suffering derived from the sight of and excessive meditation upon the beauty of the opposite sex . . .".[19] Guilt, for Dimmesdale, is also an inborn suffering, derived, perhaps, from excessive meditation upon the human heart and the self, or perhaps, upon guilt itself.

This is one of the ironies of the courtly love situation, that the object of love becomes secondary, while the lover is transported by love itself. The passion (in the sense of suffering and "intense emotion" as well as lust) that the lover seeks is infinite and hence insatiable, and his love, as Denis de Rougement points out, ultimately becomes an end in itself. "Tristan and Iseult", he says,

do not love one another. They say they don't, and everything goes to prove it. *What they love is love and being in love.* They behave as if aware that whatever obstructs love must ensure and consolidate it in the heart of each and intensify it infinitely in the moment they reach the absolute obstacle, which is death. Tristan loves the awareness that he is loving far more than he loves Iseult the Fair. And Iseult does nothing to hold Tristan. All she needs is her passionate dream. Their need of one another is in order to be aflame, and they do not need one another as they are.[20]

Something of the same element is present in Dimmesdale's guilt

[19]   *The Art of Courtly Love*, p. 2.
[20]   *Love in the Western World* (New York, 1957), p. 31.

and his morbid preoccupation with it. He lives in an ecstasy of guilt that eventually becomes a *raison d'être*. "The only real truth that continued to give Mr. Dimmesdale a real existence on this earth, was the anguish in his inmost soul, and the undissembled expression of it in his aspect. Had he once found power to smile, and wear a face of gayety, there would have been no such man!" (p. 144).

I have said that Dimmesdale lives in an *ecstasy* of guilt. I have chosen the word deliberately. Love is a suffering, and in the lover's suffering is his joy. In the courtly love tradition, suffering is not merely an undesirable by-product of love, it is the essence of love. And the lover's greatest pleasure is the intensity and irremediability of his pain. As de Rougement puts it, "To love love more than the object of love, to love passion for its own sake, has been to love to suffer and to court suffering all the way from Augustine's *amabam amare* down to modern romanticism. Passionate love, the longing for what sears us and annihilates us in its triumph – there is the secret which Europe has never allowed to be given away . . .".[21] Not only does the lover make no effort to avoid pain, he positively invites it. Chretien de Troyes writes, "My malady differs from all others. It delights me: I rejoice at it; my ill is what I want and my suffering is my health. . . . My ill comes to me by my will; . . . but I am so pleased to want this that I suffer agreeably, and have so much joy in my pain that I am sick with delight".[22]

Here is a light on Dimmesdale's character. He does not suffer because he conceals his sin, he conceals his sin partly because he wants to suffer. His suffering, like that of the victim of love, seems to be an absolute delight. In his pain is pleasure. Chase writes that "Dimmesdale is intellect without will. He is passive; he is all eloquence, sensitivity, refinement, and moral scruple. What violence he has has long since been turned inward. He has preyed on himself as Chillingworth preys on him".[23] Chase is not entirely accurate. Dimmesdale is not intellect without will. He is the

---

21   De Rougement, p. 41.
22   Quoted by De Rougement, p. 27.
23   *The American Novel and Its Tradition*, p. 78.

Puritan intellectual with the will to suffer, the Puritan intellectual in love with sin and the blackness of the human psyche. Perry Miller, in *The New England Mind*, points out that one manifestation of the Augustinian piety that dominated the Puritan consciousness was a desire to suffer.[24] In Dimmesdale this desire becomes a monomania, as Hawthorne makes explicit on several occasions. At one point, Dimmesdale hears his illegitimate daughter, Pearl, laughing. He responds with "a thrill of the heart, – but he knew not whether of exquisite pain, or pleasure as acute" (p. 151). It is also revealed that

in Mr. Dimmesdale's secret closet, under lock and key, there was a bloody scourge. Oftentimes, this Protestant and Puritan divine had plied it on his own shoulders; laughing bitterly at himself the while, and smiting so much the more pitilessly, because of that bitter laugh. It was his custom, too, as it has been that of many other pious Puritans to fast, – not, however, like them in order to purify the body and render it the fitter medium of celestial illumination, – but rigorously, and until his knees trembled beneath him, as an act of penance. He kept vigils, likewise, night after night, sometimes with a glimmering lamp. . . . (p. 143)

Is it necessary to comment on the horror of this flagellation, of this picture of a man whipping himself, all the while convulsed by mad laughter, and then beating himself some more to scourge the laughter? Public confession, he knows, will lift his burden. But that would be too easy, so he tortures himself instead by walking the ledge. He teases himself with the soul-balm of confession, but he cannot apply it. "He longed to speak out from his own pulpit, at the full height of his voice, and tell the people what he was" (p. 142). He wants to denounce himself as "utterly a pollution and a lie". He taunts himself with the possibility of ending his suffering: "More than once, Mr. Dimmesdale had gone into the pulpit, with a purpose never to come down its steps, until he should have spoken words . . ." of self-deprecation and confession. But he will not reveal "the black secret of his soul", for keeping it is too delicious. Nevertheless, "he had actually spoken. . . . He had told his hearers that he was altogether vile, a

[24]   (New York, 1939), especially pp. 3, 4, 5, 8, 14.

viler companion of the vilest, the worst of sinners, an abomination, a thing of unimaginable iniquity; and that the only wonder
was, that they did not see his wretched body shrivelled up before
their eyes, by the burning wrath of the Almighty!" (p. 142).

The denunciation is a masterpiece of ministerial rhetoric, but
when Dimmesdale calls himself a viler companion of the vilest
and the worst of sinners, this is not mere rhetoric. He means it.
When he finally does make his public confession, knowing that
he is about to die, he implores the "people of New England" to
behold him, "the one sinner of the world!" (p. 252).

As a matter of fact, nothing will suffice Dimmesdale but to
be recognized as the most loathsome of sinners. "Had I one
friend", he tells Hester, "to whom . . . I could daily betake myself, and be known as the vilest of all sinners, methinks my soul
might keep itself alive thereby" (p. 191). When Hester tells him
that he has atoned for his sin with penitence and good works, and
that his "present life is not the less holy, in very truth, than it
seems in people's eyes", he answers, "'No, Hester, no!' There is
no substance in it [his own penitence]! It is cold and dead, and
can do nothing for me! Of penance I have had enough! Of
penitence there has been none! Else, I should long ago have
thrown off these garments of mock holiness, and have shown
myself to mankind as they will see me at the judgment-seat" (pp.
190-91).

"Sad indeed", to use Hawthorne's own words, "that an introspection so profound and acute as this poor minister's should be
so miserably deceived!" (p. 214). Of neither penance nor penitence will there ever be enough for Dimmesdale. He is determined
to wear sackcloth, if not for committing adultery with Hester,
then surely for something else. There is a remarkable passage in
Jonathan Edward's *Personal Narrative*, in which he describes
what is actually too magnitudinous to be describable – his sense
of his own sinfulness. He writes:

I have had very affecting views of my own sinfulness and vileness;
very frequently to such a degree as to hold me in a kind of loud
weeping, . . . so that I have often been forced to shut myself up. It has
often appeared to me, that if God should mark iniquity against me, I

should appear the very worst of all mankind; ... and I should have by far the lowest place in hell. When others ... have expressed the sense they have had of their own wickedness, ... I thought their expressions seemed exceeding faint and feeble to represent my wickedness.

My wickedness ... has long appeared to me perfectly ineffable.... I know not how to express better what my sins appear to me to be, than by heaping infinite upon infinite and multiplying by infinite.... It appears to me, that were it not for free grace, exalted and raised up to the infinite height of all the fulness and glory of his sovereignty, I should appear sunk down in my sins below hell itself....[25]

Extract that ray of hope, and it is not difficult to imagine Dimmesdale addressing his parishioners. But that minim of hope in Edwards is important. Edwards was still capable of being moved by the thought of "free grace", and by "the fulness and glory of the great Jehovah". It is true that his eye remains fixed fairly steadily on the blackness (He says, at one point, "I knew ... my repentance was nothing to my sin."); nevertheless, it can still register light. And it is to the light that Edwards strives to ascend. He had become reconciled to God's ways through what seems to have been a mystic experience of the pleasantness and sweetness of God. He describes the experience in the *Personal Narrative*:

I remember the time very well, when I seemed to be convinced, and fully satisfied, as to this sovereignty of God, and his justice in thus eternally disposing of men, according to his sovereign pleasure. But never could give an account, how, or by what means, I was thus convinced.... God's absolute sovereignty and justice, with respect to salvation and damnation, is what my mind seems to rest assured of.... But I have often since that first conviction, had quite another kind of sense of God's sovereignty than I had then. I have often since had not only a conviction, but a delightful conviction. The doctrine has very often appeared exceeding pleasant, bright, and sweet.[26]

Edwards, in this passage, seems to have achieved what Evelyn Underhill describes as "the great swing back into sunshine which is the reward of that painful descent into the 'cell of self-knowl-

---

[25] *Works* (New York, 1943), I, 22-23.
[26] *Ibid.*, p. 15.

edge . . .'".[27] It is something that Dimmesdale never does achieve. His vision of God remains one of unrelieved blackness. There is no intimation that to him the doctrine of God's sovereignty has ever appeared pleasant, bright, or sweet. The two most penetrating modern critics of Hawthorne's work, R. H. Fogle and Hyatt Waggoner, both agree on the blackness of the book. Fogle avers that "the more cheerful readings" of *The Scarlet Letter* can be dismissed.[28] Waggoner writes that *"The Scarlet Letter*, . . . like the majority of the best tales, suggests that Hawthorne's vision of death was a good deal stronger and more constant than his vision of life. This is indeed, as Hawthorne calls it, a dark tale. . . . For in it there is perfect charity, and a real, though defective, faith, but almost no hope".[29]

This almost complete hopelessness stems partly from the fact that the purpose of the sum total of all the suffering in the lives of the characters is never really resolved. The promise of salvation through suffering, though not distinctly denied, is nonetheless never made quite explicit. As Fogle puts it:

Without doubt *The Scarlet Letter* pushes *towards* the limit of moral judgment, suggesting many possible conclusions. It is even relentless in its search in the depths of its characters. There is yet, however, a point beyond which Hawthorne will not go; ultimate solutions are not appropriate in the merely human world. His sympathy with Hester and Dimmesdale is clear enough, but he allows them only to escape the irrevocable spiritual ruin which befalls Chillingworth. Figuratively his good wishes pursue them beyond life, but he does not presume himself to absolve them. (p. 107)

But if not salvation, then what? Especially about Dimmesdale, one is tempted to ask why it is that he courts suffering so ardently. De Rougement asks a similar question about Tristan:

Why does he yearn after this particular kind of love [insatiable passion] notwithstanding that its effulgence must coincide with his self-destruction? The answer is that he reaches self-awareness and tests himself only by risking his life — in suffering and on the verge of

[27]   *Mysticism* (New York, 1961), p. 233.
[28]   *Hawthorne's Fiction*, p. 104.
[29]   *Hawthorne*, p. 149.

death. . . . Suffering and understanding are deeply connected; death and self-awareness are in league.[30]

We must ask ourselves if to understand through suffering is not the capital feature as well as the daring element in our most self-conscious *mysticism*.[31]

That the answer to De Rougement's question is at least a qualified yes, is indicated by Evelyn Underhill. Speaking about the mystic's "ecstasy", she asks, "What does the mystic claim that he attains in this abnormal condition – this irresistible trance? The price that he pays is heavy, involving much psychophysical wear and tear. He declares that his rapture or ecstasy includes a moment – often a very short, and always an indescribable moment – in which he enjoys a supreme knowledge of or participation in Divine Reality".[32]

Dimmesdale, like the mystic, seems to seek union with God through his agony. When Chillingworth asks Dimmesdale to lay open his soul, to confess and cast off his burden of guilt, he retorts with violent jealousy: "Who art thou who meddlest in this matter? – that dares thrust himself between the sufferer and his God?" (p. 136). In his mortification, too, Dimmesdale resembles the mystic (Rulman Merswin, for example, who, following a mystic transport, was "seized with a hatred of his body, and inflicted on himself such hard mortifications that he fell ill"),[33] and Hawthorne, in describing Dimmesdale's secret closet and his "bloody scourge", comments that "his inward trouble drove him to practices, more in accordance with the old, corrupted faith of Rome, than with the better light of the church in which he had born and bred" (p. 143).

Finally, Dimmesdale, like the mystic, tries to arrive at self-knowledge, and consequently union with the Divine, by sounding the deepest recesses of his psyche. He sometimes sits "viewing his own face in a looking-glass, by the most powerful light which he could throw upon it. He thus typified the constant introspection

---

[30]   De Rougement, p. 42.
[31]   *Ibid.*, p. 46.
[32]   Page 369.
[33]   Quoted from Underhill, p. 202.

wherewith he tortured, but could not purify himself" (p. 143). The horrible irony, of course, is that for Dimmesdale, the light burns without illuminating. He does not, like Edwards, find a "delightful conviction". Instead, he finds only more blackness. The soul of the "successful" mystic ascends to the Divine radiance. Through purgation and purification, the mystic achieves illumination and finally union with the Absolute, at which point his entire being seems suffused with the light of the "Divine Immanence".[34] Dimmesdale, however, instead of ascending toward the light, tries to purify himself by focusing the light inward into his own blackness. When the "successful" mystic achieves purification "the Self . . . surrenders itself, its individuality, and its will completely. It desires nothing, asks nothing, is utterly passive, and is thus prepared for Union . . .".[35] But Dimmesdale never surrenders Self. And the result is that the blackness eventually envelops the light.

"To the true lover of the Absolute", writes Miss Underhill, "Purgation no less than Illumination is a privilege, a dreadful joy". But Dimmesdale, perhaps because he is not a *true* lover of the absolute, experiences only the Purgation. Dimmesdale, as far as the reader knows, never finds union with God. One is at first tempted to attribute this inability to his Puritan individualism and love of blackness, and certainly this seems to be implied in the novel. Yet, as we have seen, Jonathan Edwards, perhaps the greatest of the Puritans, did manage to achieve the mystic's goal. The answer, then, to Dimmesdale's failure must lie elsewhere as I shall try to show in my conclusion.

If Dimmesdale, though, never finds union with God, he does, nevertheless, find a measure of self-knowledge. It comes to him, however, not while he is sitting in front of his lamp, but after his forest interview with Hester.

Returning to town after his interview with Hester, Dimmesdale meets several people. The first three are one of his own deacons, the "oldest female member of his church", and "the youngest sister of them . . ., a maiden newly won — and won by the Rev-

[34]   See Underhill, pp. 167-75 *et seq.*
[35]   Underhill, p. 170.

erend Mr. Dimmesdale's own sermon, on the Sabbath after his vigil". To the first he can hardly "refrain from uttering certain blasphemous suggestions that rose into his mind, respecting the communion supper" (p. 217). In his encounter with the old woman "Mr. Dimmesdale, as the great enemy of souls would have it, could recall no text of Scripture, nor aught else, except a brief, pithy, and, as it then appeared to him, unanswerable argument against the immortality or the human soul" (pp. 217-18). Then, as the young girl approaches him, "the arch-fiend whispered him to condense into small compass and drop into her tender bosom a germ of evil that would be sure to blossom darkly soon, and bear black fruit betimes" (p. 218). He subsequently fights off a temptation to teach "some very wicked words to a knot of little Puritan children", and another to bandy bawdy jokes with a sailor. Finally, he turns down an invitation from "Mistress Hibbins, the reputed witch lady" (p. 219).

Eventually, he manages to get back to his chamber without any external mishap, but he realizes that "Another man had returned out of the forest; a wiser one; with a knowledge of hidden mysteries which the simplicity of the former never could have reached. A bitter kind of knowledge that!" (p. 222). Precisely what this bitter knowledge is that Dimmesdale has found is never quite clear. Perhaps it is that his entire being has become infected with sin, and not only with sin, but with doubt (even as he is on the scaffold, about to confess, ". . . he trembled, and turned to Hester with an expression of doubt and anxiety in his eyes . . ." [p. 251]). He wants to shake the faith of the old man and woman and plant the seed of evil in the children and the young girl. Perhaps he has at last seen that his obsessive love of the blackest corners of the human soul has finally delivered him into the powers of darkness. Whatever the knowledge, its bitterness is unmistakable. This bitterness is confirmed by Dimmesdale before he dies.

Hester, leaning over him, pleads with him for one word of affirmation.

'Shall we not meet again?' whispered she, bending her face down close to his. 'Shall we not spend our immortal life together? Surely,

surely, we have ransomed one another, with all this woe! Thou lookest far into eternity, with those bright dying eyes! Then tell me what thou seest?'

'Hush, Hester, hush!' said he, with tremulous solemnity. 'The law we broke! – the sin here so awfully revealed! – let these alone be in thy thoughts! I fear! I fear! It may be, that when we forgot our God, – when we violated our reverence each for the other's soul, – it was thenceforth vain to hope that we could meet hereafter, in an ever-lasting and pure reunion.' (p. 254)

That last ray of hope Dimmesdale refuses to grant Hester, per-haps out of honesty. But having dampened her last hope that "we . . . spend our immortal life together", he continues: "'God knows; and He is merciful! He has proved his mercy, most of all, in my afflictions. By giving me this burning torture to bear upon my breast! By sending yonder dark and terrible old man, to keep the torture always at red-heat! By bringing me hither, to die this death of triumphant ignominy before the people! Had either of these agonies been wanting, I had been lost for ever! Praised be his name! His will be done! Farewell.'" (p. 254).

The implication seems to be that he may not be lost forever. But saved or not, Dimmesdale's last address to the world reveals again his unconquerable love of suffering; it betrays, also, his romantic sensibility and ego. God "hath proved his mercy . . . in *my* afflictions!" He has given *me* this "burning torture to bear upon *my* breast!" He has brought *me* hither. And has turned *my* ignominy into triumph. Nor is this egocentricity a new twist in Dimmesdale's character. Not only has he abandoned Hester to face her fate alone, but when he finally meets her in the forest he commences to pour his own burdens on her. When she asks if he has found peace, he answers, "None! – nothing but despair!" (p. 189). And when she asks if his work does not bring him comfort, he replies that it brings "'More misery, Hester! – only the more misery'". Finally, he has the audacity to tell her, "'Happy are you, Hester, that wear the scarlet letter openly upon your bosom! Mine burns in secret!'" (p. 191). Even if it is true, it is not a generous thing to say.

Not a word does Dimmesdale have to say, as he lies on the threshold of death, about the suffering of the others who have been involved. Worse, he assumes that Chillingworth has been expressly sent by God to effect his, Dimmesdale's, salvation. The questions this assumption raises are critical. Dimmesdale has told Hester at one point, "We are not, Hester, the worst sinners in the world. There is one worse than even the polluted priest! That old man's revenge has been blacker than my sin. He has violated, in cold blood, the sanctity of a human heart. Thou and I, Hester, never did so!" (p. 194). The first question concerns the quality of God's mercy. If, as Dimmesdale states, Chillingworth is the blackest of sinners, and if he has been sent to insure Dimmesdale's salvation, then the unavoidable inference must be that God has purposely damned one man to rescue another. Surely this is a dismal kind of mercy. The God of Jonathan Edwards may have been arbitrary, but he was not perverse.

The second question is one of the central problems of the novel and crucial to the destiny of the main characters. Is it possible for good to issue from evil, or evil from good? The conundrum is explored in two beautifully handled scenes, one between Chillingworth and Dimmesdale, and the other between Hester and Dimmesdale.

In the first of these scenes, Chillingworth is shown at his most diabolic. He is examining flowers picked from the graveyard. He explains their ugliness to Dimmesdale, who is watching him, by saying "They grew out of . . . [a dead man's] heart, and typify, it may be, some hideous secret that was buried with him, and which he had done better to confess during his lifetime" (p. 130). After some discussion in which Chillingworth tries to prod Dimmesdale into confessing what is gnawing at him, both men agree that it is best to publish one's sins. Whereupon Chillingworth remarks, "Yet some men bury their secrets . . ." (p. 131).

'True; there are such men,' answered Mr. Dimmesdale. 'But, not to suggest more obvious reasons, it may be that they are kept silent by the very constitution of their nature. Or, – can we not suppose it? – guilty as they may be, retaining, nevertheless, a zeal for God's glory and man's welfare, they shrink from displaying themselves black and filthy in the view of men; because, thenceforward, no good can be achieved by them; no evil of the past be redeemed by better service. So, to their own unutterable torment, they go about among their fellow-creatures, looking pure as new-fallen snow; while their hearts are all speckled and spotted with iniquity of which they cannot rid themselves.'

'These men deceive themselves,' said Roger Chillingworth, with somewhat more emphasis than usual, and making a slight gesture with his forefinger. 'They fear to take up the shame that rightfully belongs to them. Their love for man, their zeal for God's service, – these holy impulses may or may not coexist in their hearts with the evil inmates to which their guilt has unbarred the door, and which must needs propagate a hellish breed within them. But, if they seek to glorify God, let them not lift heavenward their unclean hands! If they would serve their fellow-men, let them do it by making manifest the power and reality of conscience, in constraining them to penitential self-abasement! Wouldst thou have me to believe, O wise and pious friend, that a false show can be better – can be more for God's glory, or man's welfare – than God's own truth? Trust me, such men deceive themselves!'

'It may be so,' said the young clergyman indifferently, as waiving a discussion that he considered irrelevant or unreasonable. (pp. 131-32)

Ironically, all this intellectual wrangling resolves into nothing. On the basis of reason alone, it is impossible to choose between the two arguments, since each takes off from a different premise. Both men know this to be the case. Chillingworth, however, is not particularly interested in arriving at abstract truth or in establishing his sophistic superiority; he is trying to trap Dimmesdale, to find the man who has "wronged" him. The minister, on the other hand, wants to justify himself, to attenuate his own procrastination and unwillingness to confess. It is the latter who finally terminates the discussion as irrelevant. He realizes that, given a certain set of circumstances, he (like Chillingworth, who later tells Hester that all he has done has been "a dark necessity"), acts not by logic but by the "constitution of his nature".

In the second scene, the confrontation with Hester in the forest, Dimmesdale, as is to be expected, is less the logician and more the impetuous lover. He blurts out his despair, and when Hester tries to reason him out of it, he winds up taking the same position that Chillingworth had taken earlier.

'The people reverence thee,' said Hester. 'And surely thou workest good among them! Doth this bring thee no comfort?'

'More misery, Hester! – only the more misery!' answered the clergyman, with a bitter smile. 'As concerns the good which I may appear to do, I have no faith in it. It must needs be a delusion. What can a ruined soul, like mine, effect towards the redemption of other souls? – or a polluted soul towards their purification?' (p. 190)

Hester is unable to move Dimmesdale from this position by rational argument, but when she suggests that he run away, he contradicts his original stand by replying: "Lost as my own soul is, I would still do what I may for other human souls! I dare not quit my post, though an unfaithful sentinel, whose sure reward is death and dishonor, when his dreary watch shall come to an end!" (p. 196).

What should be the last word on the subject occurs after Dimmesdale returns from the forest and is in his study.

Left alone, the minister summoned a servant of the house, and requested food, which being set before him, he ate with ravenous appetite. Then, flinging the already written pages of the Election Sermon into the fire, he forthwith began another, which he wrote with such an impulsive flow of thought and emotion, that he fancied himself inspired; and only wondered that Heaven should see fit to transmit the grand and solemn music of its oracles through so foul an organ-pipe as he. However, leaving that mystery to solve itself, or go unsolved for ever, he drove his task onward, with earnest haste and ecstasy. (pp. 223-24)

The question of how heaven can project good through evil, Dimmesdale decides, is unanswerable. But underlying this is another question which, surprisingly enough for a Puritan minister, he does not raise explicitly, though Hawthorne does, with the phrase "fancied himself inspired". That is, tainted as he is, how can he be sure that his inspiration is coming from above and not below? Perry Miller states, "The Augustinian piety lives by its moments of exaltation; it requires that they who have great moments live afterwards in the memory of them, but no man on his black days can be certain that it was the finger of God which touched him the day before yesterday – particularly, when his minister tells him that Satan can simulate an angel of light and lead men to destruction by giving them false confidence".[36] Un-

---

[36] *The New England Mind*, pp. 53-54.

answerable, then, is not only the question of how good can come out of evil, but of how one can know whether what appears to be good is good.

When Hawthorne, in the conclusion to *The Scarlet Letter*, informs the reader that in the absence of any "more devil's work on earth for him [Chillingworth] to do, it only remained for the unhumanized mortal to betake himself whither his Master would find him tasks enough, and pay him his wages duly" (p. 258), he strikes a false note, especially false since the destinies of both Hester and Dimmesdale have been left (as they must be) so equivocal. It is as false a note as the moral which precedes it: "Be true! Be true! Be true! Show freely to the world, if not your worst, yet some trait whereby the worst may be inferred!" Both the damnation and the moral try to resolve what in the course of the book has proved to be irresolvable: the interrelationship between good and evil, human will and sin, guilt and redemption.

It is true, perhaps, that Dimmesdale himself does not show any capacity for entertaining these questions on a high level of abstraction. That is, he does not seem at any point to concern himself with larger social and cultural issues, but to concentrate with morbid intensity on his own personal problem. But that problem is itself inseparable from larger issues. For in probing his ego, Dimmesdale gropes for the ultimate dividing line between individual responsibility to God and individual responsibility to man. The fact that he is a minister in a Puritan community complicates his situation infinitely, as he himself realizes when he tells Hester that there would be no problem if he were an atheist devoid of conscience.

The problem is crystallized at the moment of Dimmesdale's confession, an act of tantalizing ambiguity. No doubt the confession has a beneficial effect on Dimmesdale himself. It purges him of the corruption he has been carrying in his heart. On the other hand, it is very likely that if his confession were believed by his congregation, it might, as he well realizes, shake their faith irreparably. And if the act does indeed have such an effect, might it not, in the end, be more damning in the eyes of God than keeping silence? Since he has already started on the path of concealment, what ultimate good can it do for him to confess publicly just when he knows he is about to die? Dimmesdale, as we have seen, has weighed the problem intellectually in his conversations with Chillingworth and Hester. He is fully aware that he must make a choice between duty to Man and duty to God. In the final analysis, however, Dimmesdale's act is no more rational in this instance than his previous actions have been. Like Chillingworth, he acts out of a "dark necessity". Just as in life he did not have the strength to confess, so in dying he does not have the strength to resist confessing. This lack of strength allies Dimmesdale to those other productions of the nineteenth-century imagination who are capable of intellectual awareness and activity at the same time that they are incapable of acting rationally. Raskolnikov should have too much sense to slaughter a vicious pawnbroker who probably will not live much longer anyway, but he commits the act just the same. It is both futile and foolhardy for Julien Sorel to murder Madame de Renal; he tries it nevertheless. Charles Swann realizes that he should know better than to get involved with Odette, but still he does.

2.

The failure of reason to help Dimmesdale choose between God and Man, nay, the very need for Dimmesdale to choose, plunges him directly into what Martin Buber considers the crisis of Western man: the inability to overcome "the distance between the sacred and the profane", a crisis, Buber remarks, recognized by Kierkegaard "as an unprecedented shaking of the foundations of man as man".[37] For Hawthorne, with his nineteenth-century sensibility, to conceive imaginatively a seventeenth-century Puritan divine functioning in a theocratic society is exactly to reproduce this "crisis" Buber speaks of. Quite rightly from a socio-historical point of view, all cultural and social issues as far as Dimmesdale

---

[37] *Hasidism and Modern Man*, ed. & trans. Maurice Friedman (New York, 1958), p. 38.

is concerned, finally boil down to what Buber calls the primary word, *I-Thou*, which establishes "the world of relation", as opposed to the world of experience.[38] It is this relation to a living *Thou* that Dimmesdale seeks, rather than mere experience of an *It*. But it is doubtful whether he ever finds it.

In the search for evil in his own soul, and in his attempt to purify himself, Dimmesdale manifests the social consciousness of the intellectual Puritan. But "there is a sterile kind of heart-searching", says Buber, "which leads to nothing but self-torture, despair and still deeper enmeshment".[39] This is the kind of searching that Dimmesdale's turns out to be. His relation to man is contingent on finding his relationship to God; yet he cannot place himself over against God until he has genuinely confronted man. It is a mystery that Buber puts as follows: "If man can become 'humanly holy', i.e., become holy as man, in the measure and in the manner of man, and, indeed, as it is written, 'to Me', i.e., in the face of God, then he, the individual man, can also . . . become one in the sight of God. Man cannot approach the divine by reaching beyond the human; he can approach Him through becoming human".[40] In attempting to reach beyond the human, Dimmesdale, paradoxically, fails to approach the divine.

The relentlessness with which Hawthorne probes this "crisis" is beautifully illustrated in that most perplexing description of the Election Sermon:

His subject, it appeared, had been the relation between the Deity and the communities of mankind, with a special reference to the New England which they were planting in the wilderness. And, as he drew towards the close, a spirit as of prophecy had come upon him, constraining him to its purpose as mightily as the old prophets of Israel were constrained; only with this difference, that, whereas the Jewish seers had denounced judgments and ruin on their country, it was his mission to foretell a high and glorious destiny for the newly gathered people of the Lord. (p. 247)

Coming, as it does, between Dimmesdale's discovery of new

38   *I and Thou*, trans. Ronald Gregor Smith (New York, 1958).
39   *Hasidism and Modern Man*, p. 135.
40   *Ibid.*, pp. 42-43.

knowledge and his confession, the sermon seems to project a ray of light into an otherwise desperate situation. Some critics even take the sermon to be a sign of Dimmesdale's regeneration. And at first sight the description seems to be quite straightforward and relatively innocent. But closer examination shows it to be one of the high points of Hawthorne's ironic method.

To begin with, the narrator, though he seems to be quite candid, actually is not, for he refuses to commit himself on the subject of the sermon. He says that it "appeared" to be on the relation between "the Deity" and New England. It may be objected that this obliqueness is part of Hawthorne's method and style, but this objection would still not eliminate the problem of why Hawthorne should be oblique in this particular way, and introduce a note of doubt at this particular moment. Moreover, the diction itself is suspect, especially the word "Deity", which, of course, would be a perfectly natural word to use if the narrator were describing the subject of a talk by Benjamin Franklin or Thomas Jefferson. But used to describe the subject of a Puritan minister's sermon, the word sounds a distinctly false note. Again, it may be contended that using eighteenth-century diction in this way is part of Hawthorne's narrative technique. True, but such a contention serves only to point up that much of the genius of fiction, especially Hawthorne's fiction, is rooted in the method of narration. This use of the secular, rationalist verbal substitute for the name of the living God to describe the subject of Dimmesdale's sermon emphasizes the unbridgeable hiatus between the sacred and profane that is so much a part of Dimmesdale's (and probably Hawthorne's own) crisis.

Then, the narrator says that towards the close of the sermon a "spirit *as of* prophecy had come upon him". But he immediately undermines the prophetic Dimmesdale with the comparison between Dimmesdale and the "Jewish seers". They, the narrator declares, "had denounced judgments and ruin on their country", while Dimmesdale foretells "a high and glorious destiny" to his flock. And yet, to remove the message of denunciation from the prophets is to remove the prophets. William Foxwell Albright takes the Hebrew word for prophet (*nabhi*) to mean "one who is called" (by God), and continues: "This interpretation of the word suits its meaning exactly; the prophet was a man who felt himself called by God for a special mission, in which his will was subordinated to the will of God, which was communicated to him by direct inspiration. The prophet was thus a charismatic spiritual leader, directly commissioned by Yahweh to warn the people of the perils of sin and to preach reform and revival of true religion and morality".[41]

But Dimmesdale, as far as we know, has shirked this duty of denunciation (unless, of course, he believes the entire community to be completely righteous, a supposition that a minister in a settlement dominated by the Calvinist doctrine of original sin could not conceivably make). Certainly this neglect of his obligation at so crucial a moment must be considered startling. Either he lacks the will to denounce, or (what amounts to much the same thing) his commitment to the "prophetic mission" is not strong enough to make him capable of facing the wrath of the multitudes. Apparently he fears their wrath more than he fears the wrath of God. Nor will it do to say that his optimistic message is a reflection of Christian eschatology. For among the "Jewish seers" to whom he is compared, even the most eschatological of them, Isaiah, is a denouncer of the people to themselves. And this failing in Dimmesdale becomes most striking indeed when we compare his apparently benign Election Sermon with the fiery words that Father Mapple hurls from the pulpit:

... How gladly would I come down from this masthead and sit on the hatches there where you sit, and listen as you listen, while some one of you reads *me* that other and more awful lesson which Jonah teaches to *me* as a pilot of the living God. How being an anointed pilot-prophet, or speaker of true things, and bidden by the Lord to sound those unwelcome truths in the ears of a wicked Nineveh, Jonah, appalled at the hostility he should raise, fled from his mission, and sought to escape his duty and his God by taking ship at Joppa. ...

This, shipmates, this is that other lesson; and woe to that pilot of the living God who slights it. Woe to him whom this world charms from Gospel duty! Woe to him who seeks to pour oil upon the waters

[41] *From the Stone Age to Christianity* (Garden City, New York, 1957), p. 303.

when God has brewed them into a gale! Woe to him who seeks to please rather than to appal.[42]

But precisely what Dimmesdale does is to pour oil on the waters; to please, rather than appal. Instead of sounding unwelcome truths in the ears of his congregation he tells them what they want to hear. He plays to the people, and thereby seems to show himself a false prophet.

When Hawthorne told Horatio Bridge that *The Scarlet Letter* is positively a h[ell-fire]d story . . .",[43] he was much closer to the truth than he was in the concluding chapter of the book. Hawthorne discovered that once the hell-fire had been kindled it was not easily extinguished. To James T. Fields, junior partner in the firm which published *The Scarlet Letter*, Hawthorne wrote, "I find it impossible to relieve the shadows of the story with so much light as I would have thrown in".[44] It should be no surprise, then, to find that the book, as Hyatt Waggoner observes, shocked not only his contemporaries, but "to some degree Hawthorne himself . . .".[45] Recreating a Puritan divine in the light of his own post-eighteenth-century consciousness, Hawthorne engulfed him in problems from which a Dimmesdale could not possibly extricate himself. In so doing, Hawthorne penetrated the most terrifying frontiers of the modern consciousness, and anticipated what has become the continuing crisis of twentieth-century man.

3.

The House of the Seven Gables is not as shocking, not as black, and not as great a work of art as *The Scarlet Letter*. It "represents the beginning of that decline in the quality of Hawthorne's writing which did not end until it had reached the almost com-

[42] Herman Melville, *Moby Dick*, ed. Alfred Kazin (Boston, 1956), pp. 56-57.
[43] Horatio Bridge, *Personal Recollections of Nathaniel Hawthorne* (New York, 1893), p. 112.
[44] Quoted from Stewart, p. 95.
[45] *Hawthorne*, p. 151.

plete failure of creativity of the unfinished romances".[46] Hawthorne, however, considered the later book "more characteristic of my mind, and more proper and natural for me to write".[47] He may have felt this way precisely because *The Scarlet Letter* is so much more relentless and terrifying in its drive to uncover the core of the human psyche and of the human condition in general. It is possibly a revulsion against the burrowing Hawthorne himself had done in the earlier book when he has Phoebe say of Clifford, "When he is cheerful, – when the sun shines into his mind, – then I venture to peep in just as far as the light reaches, but no further. It is holy ground where the shadow falls".[48] But having made his dive into the impenetrable blackness, Hawthorne was ready to come to the surface, to write a book which would accommodate the light that refused to enter *The Scarlet Letter*.

Consequently, from Dimmesdale, the Puritan intellectual, to Holgrave, the secular intellectual, the decline in the depth of characterization is apparent. Of Holgrave, Roy Harvey Pearce writes, "Explicitly, Hawthorne makes . . . [him] out to be a young intellectual, like so many other young intellectuals in nineteenth century America, at once mobile, unstable, rationalistic, disinterested, liberal, and eager for change".[49] He is "the 'new man'", says Fogle, "the democrat at his best, yet possessed of flaws as well as virtues. In his haste he would destroy much that is good along with the evil. . . . His well-meant universal philanthropy would eradicate all human warmth, idiosyncrasies, relationships – all that is represented by the heart, in fact".[50]

Holgrave is a "new man", moreover, not only in his political liberalism, but in his person and associations. He is a natural aristocrat, and whatever he has achieved he has achieved by his own effort. Of plebian Maule stock, as opposed to the aristocratic

[46] *Ibid.*, p. 170.
[47] Bridge, p. 126.
[48] Nathaniel Hawthorne, *The House of the Seven Gables* (New York, 1931), p. 214. Page references in my text are to this edition.
[49] *The House of the Seven Gables*, ed. Roy Harvey Pearce (London, 1954), p. vii.
[50] Fogle, p. 128.

Pyncheons, he is nonetheless recognizable, in both bearing and dress, as a gentleman. He is

a slender young man ... with rather a grave and thoughtful expression for his years, but likewise springy alacrity and vigor. These qualities, were not only perceptible, physically, in his make and motions, but made themselves felt almost immediately in his character. A brown beard, not too silken in its texture, fringed his chin, but as yet without completely hiding it; he wore a short mustache, too, and his dark, high-featured countenance looked all the better for these natural ornaments. As for his dress, it was of the simplest kind. . . . He was chiefly marked as a gentleman – if such, indeed, he made any claim to be – by the rather remarkable whiteness and nicety of his clean line. (p. 61)

The combination of dignity and simplicity in Holgrave's dress and bearing are telling, just as they were for Benjamin Franklin while he was in Paris. He is impressive, but without being a dandy.

The flaws that Fogle speaks of also fall into these two categories of personal and ideological, both intermixing to some extent. Holgrave's personal flaw, already mentioned by Fogle, is congenital in almost all of Hawthorne's intellectual characters. It is the Chillingworth, Ethan Brand, Rappaccini flaw without the obsession: the dessication of the heart by the intellect, and the consequent alienation from the mainstream of humanity. Phoebe, in reflecting on the romantic young man, "scarcely thought him affectionate in his nature. He was too calm and cool an observer. Phoebe felt his eye often; his heart, seldom or never. He took a certain kind of interest in Hepzibah and her brother, and Phoebe herself. He studied them attentively, but never gave any reliable evidence that he loved them better in proportion as he knew them more. In his relations with them, he seemed to be in quest of mental food, not heart-sustenance. Phoebe could not conceive what interested him so much in her friends and herself, intellectually, since he cared nothing for them ... as objects of human affection" (p. 213).

In answer to Phoebe's declaration that she would probe Clifford's mind only "as far as the light reaches", Holgrave asserts, "Had I your opportunities, no scruples would prevent me from fathoming Clifford to the full depth of my plummet line!" (p. 214).

It is Phoebe who rescues Holgrave from the fate of the "lost" intellectuals. His love for her finally shakes him out of his role of observer. "Her thought had scarcely done him justice when it pronounced him cold; or, if so, he had grown warmer now" (p. 218). When she questions his intentions toward the Pyncheon family, he replies, "I do feel an interest in this . . . poverty-stricken old . . . lady, and this . . . shattered gentleman. . . . But you have no conception what a different kind of heart mine is from your own. It is not my impulse . . . either to help or hinder; but to look on, to analyze, to explain matters to myself, and to comprehend the drama. . . . If permitted to witness the close, I doubt not to derive a moral satisfaction from it. . . . But, though Providence sent you hither to help, and sends me only as a privileged and meet spectator, I pledge myself to lend these unfortunate beings whatever aid I can!" (p. 258).

At first, Holgrave conceives himself as merely a spectator in the human drama unfolding around him. He is an analyst, an objective, uninvolved scientist. But under Phoebe's influence, he begins to emerge from his passivity, and assume his human responsibility. When he has Phoebe in a state of near hypnosis, he does not, as his ancestor had done to Alice Pyncheon, take advantage of her. Instead, because of his "reverence for another's individuality" (p. 253), he breaks the spell before it is indissoluble.

Ideologically, Holgrave is an Emersonian. Emerson had attacked the preoccupation with the past in the "Introduction" of *Nature*, asserting that "our age is retrospective. It builds the sepulchres of the fathers. It writes biographies, histories, and criticism". Holgrave asks, "Shall we never get rid of this Past?" And then, in a passage reminiscent of Emerson's *American Scholar*, he goes on to tell Phoebe that "we read in dead men's books! We laugh at dead men's jokes, and cry at dead men's pathos! We are sick of dead men's diseases, physical and moral. . . . We worship the living Deity according to dead men's forms and creeds. Whatever we seek to do, of our own free motion, a dead man's icy hand obstructs us! . . . I ought to have said, too, that we live in dead men's houses; as, for instance, in this of the Seven Gables!" (pp. 219-20). But perhaps the key to the difference between Holgrave and his master lies in the last sentence. Holgrave is not so much an idealist as a pragmatist. Before becoming a daguerreotypist, he had been a schoolmaster, salesman, political editor of a country newspaper, a peddler, a dentist, an official on a packetship, a world traveller, a Fourierist, and a lecturer on Mesmerism. As long as the Pyncheon house does not belong to him, he is anxious to tear it down. With nothing to lose and with no stake in the society he lives in, he can well afford to be a bohemian. When he first takes lodging from Hepzibah,

He had the strangest companions imaginable; men with long beards, and dressed in linen blouses, and other such new-fangled and ill-fitting garments; reformers, temperance lecturers, and all manner of cross-looking philanthropists; community-men, and come-outers, as Hepzibah believed, who acknowledged no law, and ate no solid food, but lived on the scent of other people's cookery, and turned up their noses at the fare. As for the daguerreotypist, she had read a paragraph in a penny paper, the other day, accusing him of making a speech full of wild and disorganizing matter, at a meeting of his banditti-like associates. (p. 108)

But Holgrave's bohemianism, like his ideas, is shallow. He does not really believe in bohemianism any more than he believes in the ideas he has articulated to Phoebe. And he abandons both at the first opportunity. For Holgrave, detestation of the past and its burdens is more a matter of spring fever than of intellectual commitment. Describing Holgrave's state of mind, Hawthorne writes, "Man's own youth is the world's youth; at least, he feels as if it were, and imagines that the earth's granite substance is something not yet hardened, and which he can mould into whatever shape he likes. So it was with Holgrave. He could talk sagely about the world's old age, but never actually believed what he said. . ." (p. 215).

At the first promise of solidity and stability, Holgrave gives up "his crude, wild, and misty philosophy, . . . his magnanimous zeal for man's welfare, and his recklessness of whatever the ages had established in man's behalf . . ." (p. 217). Again it is Phoebe who is the catalyst. Not only does she rescue Holgrave from his intellect, she also rescues him from his political and social radicalism. There is for both of them a moment of danger. Phoebe is frightened by Holgrave, "not by any doubt of his integrity to whatever law he acknowledged, but by a sense that his law differed from her own" (p. 213). But just as Jane Talbot takes William Colden into hand and converts him from Godwinism, so Phoebe straightens out Holgrave. A woman unleashing her feminine charm and moral force is too much for the most politically sophisticated male. In the following dialogue, Phoebe is reacting to a tentative proposal made by Holgrave: "And thee – I am afraid!" continued Phoebe, shrinking towards Holgrave, even while she told him so frankly the doubts with which he affected her. "You will lead me out of my own quiet path. You will make me strive to follow you where it is pathless. I cannot do so. It is not my nature. I shall sink down and perish!" (p. 362).

But Phoebe need have no fear. Through the prism of her female sensibility Holgrave has already seen the error of his ways.

'Ah, Phoebe!' exclaimed Holgrave, with almost a sigh, and a smile that was burdened with thought. 'It will be far otherwise than as you forebode. The world owes all its onward impulses to men ill at ease. The happy man inevitably confines himself within ancient limits. I have a presentiment that, hereafter, it will be my lot to set out trees, to make fences, – perhaps, even in due time, to build a house for another generation, – in a word, to conform myself to laws, and the peaceful practice of society. Your poise will be more powerful than any oscillating tendency of mine.' (p. 363)

Holgrave's presentiment is remarkably accurate. At the death of the old Judge Jaffrey Pyncheon, Clifford Pyncheon "became rich; so did Hepzibah; so did our little village maiden, and, through her, that sworn foe of wealth and all manner of conservatism, – the wild reformer, – Holgrave!" (p. 370). And this, of course, is to say that he has now lost all justification for his former radicalism. Just before the Holgraves and remaining Pyncheons move into "the elegant country-seat of the late Judge Pyncheon," Holgrave comments, "I wonder that the late Judge –

being so opulent, and with a reasonable prospect of transmitting his wealth to descendants of his own – should not have felt the propriety of embodying so excellent a piece of domestic architecture in stone, rather than in wood". In answer to Phoebe's ejaculation of surprise at the inconsistency between Holgrave's recent observation and his former principles, Holgrave says, "Ah, Phoebe, I told you how it should be! ... You find me a conservative already! Little did I think ever to become one. It is especially unpardonable in this dwelling of so much hereditary misfortune, and under the eye of yonder portrait of a model conservative, who, in that very character, rendered himself so long the evil destiny of his race" (p. 373).

"Holgrave," remarks Waggoner, "is an interesting creation, the product of a shrewd analysis".[51] The estimate, is, I think, just. Hawthorne portrays in Holgrave the ubiquitous rebellious dispossessed intellectual who modifies his liberalism and recants his radicalism as soon as he assumes social ties and becomes a respected member of the establishment.

The seeds of corruption that remain dormant in Holgrave flower in Miles Coverdale, who is a Holgrave grown middle-aged without the tempering influence of a Phoebe. In Coverdale, "only a poet, and ... no great affair at that",[52] Holgrave's intellectual objectivity and coolness have crystallized into ice. From the point of view of structure of the novel, of course, Coverdale, as narrator (and a forerunner of the Jamesian central consciousness), must remain to some extent aloof. Nevertheless, he states quite explicitly about himself: "That cold tendency, between instinct and intellect, which made me pry with a speculative interest into people's passions and impulses, appeared to have gone far towards unhumanizing my heart" (p. 151).

Coverdale, describing in Blithedale a Utopian venture in which he has been a participant, avers that he does not regret that he (like Holgrave) "once had a faith and force enough to form generous hopes of the world's destiny, – yes! – and to do what in

---

[51]   Page 171.
[52]   Nathaniel Hawthorne, *The Blithedale Romance* (New York, 1931), p. 3. Page references in my text are to this edition.

me lay for their accomplishment" (pp. 6-7). But that he no longer believes in the improvability of man's lot is also clear, for he says, "I rejoice that I could once think better of the world's improvability than it deserved" (p. 16). The unimprovability of the world is directly related to Coverdale's own basic flaw: spiritual coldness, and an inability to experience and communicate real human affection.

But the flaw is not limited to Coverdale himself, and it is its very ubiquity that makes the attempt at establishing a Utopia at Blithedale, or anywhere else, a dismal failure. The inability to communicate a sense of brotherhood becomes apparent even before the Utopian experiment is well under way. On the night before their departure for Blithedale, four charter members of the group are riding through a heavy snow storm, feeling, as Coverdale describes the scene, a rather gay spirit of anticipation and benevolence.

Sometimes, encountering a traveller, we shouted a friendly greeting; and he, unmuffling his ears to the bluster and the snow-spray, and listening eagerly, appeared to think our courtesy worth less than the trouble which it cost him. The churl! He understood the shrill whistle of the blast, but had no intelligence for our blithe tones of brotherhood. This lack of faith in our cordial sympathy, on the traveller's part, was one among the innumerable tokens how difficult a task we had in hand, for the reformation of the world. (p. 8)

The double irony here is not very subtly concealed. On the one hand, the traveller is incapable of accepting a proffer of love tendered by strangers, while on the other, Coverdale's hostile reference to the "churl" casts doubt on the sincerity of the greeters, and implies that the "churl's" belligerence may indeed be justified.

All reform, as a matter of fact, becomes dangerous principally because it tends to become an end in itself which eventually displaces human values. Hollingsworth, the most zealous of reformers, shows himself to be a warm, tender, solicitous human spirit when he devotedly nurses the ailing Coverdale to health. But even he has joined Blithedale "chiefly because we were estranging ourselves from the world, with which his lonely and exclusive object in life had already put him at odds" (p. 151). And it is not long before Coverdale finds that

> by and by, you missed the tenderness of yesterday, and grew drearily conscious that Hollingsworth had a closer friend than ever you could be; and this friend was the cold, spectral monster which he had himself conjured up, and on which he was wasting all the warmth of his heart, and of which, at last, – as these men of a mighty purpose so invariably do, – he had grown to be the bond-slave. It was his philanthropic theory.
>
> This was a result exceedingly sad to contemplate, considering that it had been mainly brought about by the very ardor and exuberance of his philanthropy. Sad, indeed, but by no means unusual: he had taught his benevolence to pour its warm tide exclusively through one channel; so that there was nothing to spare for other great manifestations of love to man. . . . (p. 51)

Hollingsworth's drive to reform mankind has stultified his natural human warmth and made him into a monster. Like the revolutionary zealot, he is convinced that he must reform the human race whether the race wishes it or not. Coverdale recognizes the disparity between the desire to reform humanity and true human love in a moment of revelation, which comes while he is watching Hollingsworth drive a yoke of oxen:

> The harsh tones of his voice, shouting to the sluggish steers, made me sensible even at such a distance, that he was ill at ease, and that the balked philanthropist had the battle-spirit in his heart.
>
> . . . .
>
> 'Mankind, in Hollingsworth's opinion,' thought I, 'is but another yoke of oxen, as stubborn, stupid, and sluggish as our old Brown and Bright. He vituperates us aloud, and curses us in his heart, and will begin to prick us with the goad-stick, by and by.' (pp. 97-98)

One must remember that the scene is being reflected on by Coverdale's skeptical mind. But the disastrous events which follow (the collapse of Blithedale and the suicide of Zenobia) would tend to indicate that Coverdale cannot be completely wrong.

If Hollingsworth has abandoned himself too monomaniacally to reform, the same is not true of Coverdale. Though the latter says that he "once had faith . . . enough to form generous hopes of the world's destiny", it is obvious that it does not take much to shake that faith. The mere presence of Silas Foster, a shrewd Yankee farmer who still carries part of his farm under his finger-nails, convinces Coverdale of the impossibility of equalitarian brotherhood as an ideal. While the future Blithedale residents are sitting around the fire after dinner, "stout", "practical" Silas re-minds the group that someone will have to "go to Brighton fair, and buy half a dozen pigs" (p. 16). "Pigs!" Coverdale reacts. "Good heavens! had we come out from among the swinish multi-tude for this?" Nor does it take a great deal of Silas's practical plain talk before Coverdale becomes "sensible that, as regarded society at large, we stood in a position of new hostility, rather than new brotherhood" (p. 16).

Coverdale's misgivings as to the efficacy and advisability of smashing the established dividing lines of society turn out to be justified. The intellectual "communitarians" are not, as is to be expected, very efficient farmers. But this is not what bothers Coverdale primarily.

The peril of our new way of life was not lest we should fail in be-coming practical agriculturists, but that we should probably cease to be anything else. While our enterprise lay all in theory, we had pleased ourselves with delectable visions of the spiritualization of labor. It was to be our form of prayer and ceremonial of worship. Each stroke of the hoe was to uncover some aromatic root of wisdom, heretofore hidden from the sun. Pausing in the field, to let the wind exhale the moisture from our foreheads, we were to look upward, and catch glimpses into the far-off soul of truth. In this point of view, matters did not turn out quite so well as we had anticipated. . . . The clods of earth, which we so constantly belabored and turned over, were never etherealized into thought. Our thoughts, on the contrary, were fast becoming cloddish. . . . Intellectual activity is incompatible with any large amount of bodily exercise. The yeoman and the scholar – the yeoman and the man of finest moral culture . . . are two distinct individuals, and can never be melted or welded into one substance. (p. 62)

Clearly, Coverdale is convinced that without an intellectual "class" there can be no intellectual artifacts. By the very nature of his cold personality he is separated from the rest of humanity, but he also believes in the separation theoretically. It is as ridicu-

lous for Coverdale to belabor clods of earth as it is for Silas
Foster to discuss books.

Emerson had tried to impress on the mind of the American
scholar that "Man is not a farmer, or a professor, or an engineer,
but he is all. Man is priest, and scholar, and statesman, and
producer, and soldier." [53] He had advised that "The first in time
and the first in importance of the influences upon the mind is
that of nature. Every day, the sun; and, after sunset, Night and
her stars. Ever the winds blow; ever the grass grows. Every day,
men and women, conversing – beholding and beholden. The
scholar is he of all men whom this spectacle most engages".[54]
But the grass and the wind, the sun and the stars are not avenues
of truth for Coverdale. Emerson had also said, "There goes in
the world a notion that the scholar should be a recluse . . .".[55]
At least Coverdale seems to have found that notion correct. In
the midst of his farm labor he cannot make poetry. The earth
thickens his fist and the sun bakes his brain. Involved in the
everyday labor of the communitarian enterprise, he loses his
poetic inspiration.

What Coverdale finds at Blithedale is not "Man", the Emersonian ideal, but the ugliness of the multitude and the drudgery
of toil. When Hollingsworth asks Coverdale to join him, therefore, it is not surprising that the latter sees "in his scheme of
philanthropy nothing but what was odious. A loathesomeness that
was to be forever in my daily work! A great black ugliness of
sin, which he proposed to collect out of a thousand human hearts,
and that we should spend our lives in an experiment of trans-
muting it into virtue!" (p. 131).

Coverdale is constitutionally incapable of egalitarian democracy. The masses he finds repulsive, both in actuality and in the
abstract. His coldness, which colors the tone of the entire book,
and his revulsion from the proletariat, end in a sense of complete
enervation and malaise. He confesses, "As regards human prog-

[53] *Selections from Ralph Waldo Emerson*, ed. Stephen E. Whicher (Cambridge, 1957), p. 64.
[54] *Ibid*., p. 65.
[55] *Ibid*., pp. 69-70.

ress . . ., let them believe in it who can, and aid in it who choose. If I could earnestly do either, it might be all the better for my comfort. As Hollingsworth once told me, I lack a purpose. How strange! He was ruined, morally, by an overplus of the very same ingredient, the want of which, I occasionally suspect, has rendered my own life all an emptiness" (p. 243).

Hollingsworth is destroyed by his devotion to reform as an abstraction. Coverdale cannot devote himself to either man or abstract ideals. Even his poetry, which he eventually gives up, is not enough to fill the vacuum left by his lack of human compassion. He has rejected just about everything but his study and his comfort, and yet, from his study, the best he has been able to do is "a pretty little volume". And the enervation of his intellect is underlined by the presence of Zenobia's powerful mind and will.

Roy Male feels that "We sympathize with Coverdale partly because he resembles the modern intellectual cut off from ancient certitudes, longing to submerge himself in a group yet fearful that in doing so he will lose his individuality".[56] Waggoner, however, writes, "Surely the chief difficulty, in the way of a greater enjoyment of the novel is created by Coverdale. He is . . . a very Jamesian character. . . . But whereas James manages to make us feel sympathy for his characters, Hawthorne makes us feel little or none for Coverdale. Perhaps the basic reason is that Hawthorne disliked the Coverdale in himself too much, so that he was not in sympathy with his own central creation".[57]

I would tend to agree with Waggoner that it is difficult to sympathize with Coverdale. His morbid fear of losing his individuality, his intense egocentricity, his aesthete's aloofness and snobbishness, his inability either to project or to accept any human warmth, all make him one of the least admirable of Hawthorne's characters.

If Coverdale has a saving grace, it is that he never quite gives in completely to his weaknesses. In spite of his natural coolness, he manages to fall in love with Priscilla, though he remains too ashamed to express his love till the very last line of the book.

[56] *Hawthorne's Tragic Vision* (Austin, Texas, 1957), p. 153.
[57] Page 194.

And much as he seems to prefer an emasculated existence, still he feels, "were there any cause, in this whole chaos of human struggle, worth a sane man's dying for, and which my death would benefit, then – provided, however, the effort did not involve an unreasonable amount of trouble – methinks I might be bold to offer up my life" (p. 243).

Kenyon, the sculptor in *The Marble Faun*, is a moralizing extension of Coverdale. As Male puts it, "If he is more substantial than Miles Coverdale, he is also much more stuffy. Hawthorne undoubtedly intended to portray the rigidity of the refined intellectual, but surely he did not mean Kenyon to be as insufferable as the modern reader finds him".[58]

Kenyon retains the cold aloofness of Coverdale, but adds to it an insufferable pomposity that is his own. He is more of an aesthete than Coverdale, but also more of a moralizer. Meditating over Trajan's Forum, he says, "Dead emperors have very little delight in their columns, I am afraid. . . . All that rich sculpture of Trajan's bloody warfare, twining from the base of the pillar to its capital, may be but an ugly spectacle for his ghostly eyes, if he considers that this huge, storied shaft must be laid before the judgment-seat, as a piece of the evidence of what he did in the flesh" (p. 180). Such self-righteous outbursts are what Kenyon is made of.

When Miriam, after Kenyon has showed some reluctance to listen to her troubles, says to him, "You are as cold and pitiless as your own marble" (p. 155), she is probably right. What she should have added, perhaps, is that he is also maddeningly complacent and smug. Dimmesdale is more than redeemed by his agony; Holgrave is redeemed by his love of Phoebe; and Coverdale by his ability to view himself ironically. Kenyon has none of these qualities. He is too pleased with himself to undergo any sort of agony comparable to Dimmesdale's. He does not so much love Hilda as worship her angelic goodness. Finally, he takes himself too seriously to recognize his own pomposity.

But it is certainly difficult for anyone else to take seriously the man who can say to the simple Hilda: "Were you my guide, my counsellor, my inmost friend, with that white wisdom which clothes you as a celestial garment, all would go well. O Hilda, guide me home!" (p. 520).

The most verbose of Hawthorne's intellectual characters, Kenyon is also the shallowest. Immediately preceding his proposal, Hilda had rebuked Kenyon for advocating the heresy of the Fortunate Fall. Be that as it may, there is nothing at all fortunate about the fall from the sublime agony of Dimmesdale to the ridiculous transport of Kenyon.

VII

ISHMAEL AND MELVILLE: THE DEMOCRAT
AS MAN THINKING AND MAN CREATING

1

Hawthorne's intellectuals feel constantly threatened by the danger
that the mind will dominate the heart. In the "sunny" novels
(*The House of the Seven Gables* and *The Marble Faun*) heart
and head combine (Holgrave and Phoebe, Kenyon and Hilda) to
bring to the intellectual salvation and happiness. In the dark
novels, the intellectual remains incarcerated in the dungeon of his
own mind. But in all cases there is a tendency in the intellectual
to retreat from the world, or to approach it coldly and distrust-
fully – to dread exposure, and to prefer the role of observer
(Dimmesdale turns the observation inward) to that of participant.

Hawthorne's intellectuals, then, much as they may hover on
the threshold of democracy, always retreat eventually. Out of a
congenital dread of the masses they turn from a lukewarm, shallow liberalism to a quiet, secure, isolated, and equally shallow
conservatism. Always their coldness stands between them and the
turbulent flux of common humanity. Holgrave shifts from investigator in the Pyncheon household to custodian of Pyncheon
aristocracy. Coverdale, even in the midst of an experiment in
communal life, finds himself a secret tree hermitage from which
he can observe the inhabitants of Blithedale without being seen.
And Kenyon becomes a calm spectator of the doom of Donatello
and Miriam.

This inability of Hawthorne's intellectuals to immerse themselves in the stream of humanity, and to experience the feeling
of Utopian optimism, prevents them from ever sliding into a
complete rejection of the past and of established societal and
class structures.

A very different sort of intellectual is Ishmael, who sails before the mast of the Pequod in Melville's *Moby-Dick*. The most profound of all fictional American intellectuals, he is also the most dedicated democrat, and it is not surprising that he narrates the great democratic epic. In some ways he resembles Holgrave. Both are self-educated. Both have engaged in numerous occupations, and both have been, among other things, schoolteachers. Aside from an occasional denunciation of the past, however, Holgrave does not show any signs of deep thought, and one rather tends to agree with the narrator's estimation of him: "He considered himself a thinker, and was certainly of a thoughtful turn, but, with his own path to discover, had perhaps hardly yet reached the point where an educated man begins to think".[1]

In this he is not at all like Ishmael, who thinks furiously in all directions. As Alfred Kazin points out,

Ishmael is . . . the single mind, from whose endlessly turning spool of thought the whole story is unwound. It is Ishmael's contemplativeness, his *dreaming*, that articulates the wonder of the seas and the fabulousness of the whale and the terrors of the deep. All that can be meditated and summed up and hinted at, as the reflective essence of the story itself, is given us by Ishmael. . . . It is Ishmael who tries to sum up the whole creation in a single book. . . . It is Ishmael's gift for speculation that explains the terror we come to feel. . . . It is Ishmael who . . . embodies for us man as a thinker, whose reveries transcend space and time. . .[2]

And yet, in good American fashion, Ishmael points out that "perhaps, to be true philosophers, we mortals should not be conscious of so living or so striving. So soon as I hear that such or such a man gives himself out for a philosopher, I conclude that, like the dyspeptic old woman, he must have 'broken his digester'".[3] Unlike Holgrave, Ishmael refuses the title of philosopher. He refuses it, moreover, at the very moment that he is philosophizing, and shows his disdain for the title-minded man by ending in a flourish

---

[1] Hawthorne, *The House of the Seven Gables*, p. 216.
[2] Herman Melville, *Moby-Dick*, ed. Alfred Kazin (Cambridge, 1956), p. vi.
[3] *Ibid.*, p. 59. Page references in my text are to this edition. Thoreau had recorded, in his *Journal*, "What is religion? That which is never spoken" (Entry for August 18, 1858).

of colloquialism. Here is the realization *par excellence* of Emerson's distinction between the 'mere thinker' and *Man Thinking*.

Ishmael, too, does not suffer from the congenital reserve of Holgrave, Coverdale, and Kenyon. As a result, he falls much more easily into his democratic pose, and is much less self-deprecating about it. As H. P. Vincent points out in *The Trying-out of Moby Dick*, Ishmael is a kind of Everyman.[4] And yet, what an Everyman he is: an Everyman who is a walking encyclopedia, stuffed to overbrimming with cetological facts; an Everyman who speculates on the deepest human problems; an Everyman who can warn the unwary to avoid the honey-head of Plato, and to beware of the opposing philosophies of Kant and Locke. And withal, he is a democrat; not an apologetic democrat, either, but a democrat with swagger. He brags that he does not go to sea as a passenger, "for to go as a passenger you must needs have a purse . . ." (p. 24). "Nor" he adds,

though I am something of a salt, do I ever go to sea as a Commodore, or a Captain, or a Cook. I abandon the glory and distinction of such offices to those who like them. For my part, I abominate all honorable respectable toils, trials, and tribulations of every kind whatsoever. It is quite as much as I can do to take care of myself, without taking care of ships, barques, brigs, schooners, and what not. And as for going as cook – though I confess there is considerable glory in that, a cook being a sort of officer on shipboard – yet, somehow, I never fancied broiling fowls; . . .

No, when I go to sea, I go as a simple sailor, right before the mast, plumb down into the forecastle, aloft there to the royal masthead. True, they rather order me about some, and make me jump from spar to spar, like a grasshopper in a May meadow. And at first, this sort of thing is unpleasant enough. It touches one's sense of honor, particularly if you come of an old established family in the land, the Van Rensselaers, or Randolphs, or Hardicanutes. And more than all, if just previous to putting your hand into the tar-pot, you have been lording it as a country schoolmaster, making the tallest boys stand

---

[4] (Boston, 1949), p. 56. Richard Chase, in his superb chapter on *Moby-Dick*, refers to Ishmael as an intellectual (*Herman Melville: A Critical Study* [New York, 1949]). The general view of Ishmael that I express here is, at many points, in agreement with the view beautifully expressed by Daniel Hoffman in *Form and Fable in American Fiction* (New York, 1961), a view with which I was not familiar at the time I wrote this section of my chapter.

in awe of you. The transition is a keen one, I assure you, from a schoolmaster to a sailor, and requires a strong decoction of Seneca and the Stoics to enable you to grin and bear it. But even this wears off in time.

What of it, if some old hunks of a sea-captain orders me to get a broom and sweep down the decks? What does that indignity amount to, weighed, I mean, in the scales of the New Testament? Do you think the archangel Gabriel thinks anything the less of me, because I promptly and respectfully obey that old hunks in that particular instance? Who ain't a slave? Tell me that. Well, then, however the old sea-captains may order me about – however they may thump and punch me about, I have the satisfaction of knowing that it is all right; that everybody else is one way or other served in much the same way – either in a physical or metaphysical point of view, that is; and so the universal thump is passed round, and all hands should rub each others shoulder-blades, and be content. (pp. 24-25)

We hear much of the magnificence of Ahab. But who can be more magnificent than Ishmael, revelling so good-humoredly in his hard-knocks, and yet without any of the Panglossian optimism that is so irritating in the philanthropists who were such an abomination to Hawthorne? His acceptance is not grounded on a belief in the best of all possible worlds, but in the belief that from a metaphysical point of view, all men get their knocks in the end. He says, at one point, "There are certain queer times and occasions in this strange mixed affair we call life when a man takes this whole universe for a vast practical joke, though the wit thereof he but dimly discerns, and more than suspects that the joke is at nobody's expense but his own" (p. 186). Amazing, too, in the first quotation, is the movement of Ishmael's mind, of which I will have more to say subsequently. At this juncture, it is sufficient to point out the dexterity with which he moves from description in the first paragraph to reflection on the facts in the second, and finally, to metaphysical speculation in the last paragraph. We get the sense that Ishmael's mind is simultaneously diving into the unknown and expanding toward the infinite. No shallow democrat or reformer is this Ishmael.

And yet, he is a reformer. Charles H. Foster, in a recent reinterpretation of *Moby-Dick* points out, perhaps a little strenuously, but convincingly nonetheless, that in addition to George

Stewart's two *Moby-Dicks* there is a third one, which is "a demo-cratic anti-slavery fable".[5] Foster's case is grounded mainly on external evidence, Melville's relationship with his father-in-law, Judge Lemuel Shaw, and with Hawthorne. "When we appraise Melville in 1850-1851", Foster writes, "we have a writer who despite his relations with the American right had also evinced the attitudes of the American left, and his interests seem a good deal less timeless, and a good deal more engaged than is implied in most accounts of the creation of *Moby-Dick*. There begin to appear some reasons for suspecting that Melville may have been actually as independent of Hawthorne in his social views as in his artistic practice".[6] Furthermore, Foster feels that in his much-quoted June 1851 letter to Hawthorne, Melville "is issuing a warning that there are dangerously democratic things coming in *Moby-Dick* . . .".[7]

It does not, I think, detract from the cogency of Foster's argu-ment to say that Melville was engaged not only on the level of contemporary social issues but on the level of timelessness as well; indeed, his very ability to invest particular issues with eter-nal significance is part of the greatness of the book. We have

---

[5] "Something in Emblems: A Reinterpretation of *Moby-Dick*", *New England Quarterly*, XXXIII (March, 1961), 21. From *Mardi*, Foster quotes the following in support of his thesis: "But sin it is, no less: – a blot, foul as the crater-pool of conscience or no conscience – ere he die – let every master who wrenches bond-babe from mother, that the nipple tear; unwreathes the arms of sisters; or cuts the holy unity in twain; till apart fall man and wife, like one bleeding body cleft: – let that master thrice shrive his soul; take every sacrament; on his bended knees give up the ghost; – yet shall he die despairing; and live again, to die forever damned". Herman Melville, *Mardi: And a Voyage Thither* (New York, 1849), II, 247-48. He might also have used the following passage from *Pierre*: "Some unprofessional gentlemen of the aristocratic South, who happen to own slaves, give those slaves liberty to go and seek work, and every night return with their wages, which con-stitute those idle gentlemen's income . . . . Yet let not such an one be over-confident. Our God is a jealous God; he wills not that any man should permanently possess the least shadow of his own self-sufficient attributes". *Pierre: or the Ambiguities* (London, 1923), p. 364.
[6] *Ibid.*, p. 8.
[7] *Ibid.*, p. 10. One of the key citations from the letter: "When you hear of my ruthless democracy on all sides, you may possibly feel a touch of a shrink".

already seen this tendency operating in the mind of Ishmael as he shifts from the question of his own lowly position in society to the universal question of man's place in the Cosmos. This same process of expansiveness occurs in the abolition theme.

When Foster moves from external evidence to the novel itself, he sees the abolition theme working out principally in the relationship between Ahab and Pip. And surely some element of it is there. But once one acknowledges that the theme is in the book at all, it certainly seems most obvious in the relationship between Ishmael and Queequeg. If Ishmael is an abolitionist, however, he is not the abolitionist who was roundly denounced by Emerson in "Self-Reliance":

If an angry bigot assumes this bountiful cause of Abolition, and comes to me with his last news from Barbadoes, why should I not say to him, 'Go love thy infant; love thy wood-chopper; be good natured and modest; have that grace; and never varnish your hard and un-charitable ambition with this incredible tenderness for black folk a thousand miles off. Thy love afar is spite at home.' Rough and grace-less would be such greeting, but truth is handsomer than the affec-tation of love. Your goodness must have some edge to it, – else it is none.[8]

Ishmael's abolitionism is firmly rooted in brotherly, if not Christian love, and as a consequence, the contemporary social issue of American slavery is merged with the timelessness of the question of universal human interdependence. And the miracle of *Moby-Dick* is that the contemporaneity and timelessness are fused into a majestic whole. Melville, to borrow a phrase from Thoreau, "Legislated for all time". But it is, of course, precisely Melville's ability to saturate human relationships (in this case that of Ishmael and Queequeg) with meaning that makes *Moby-Dick* such a hard book to write about. If we consider for just a moment the barriers that are broken by those cozy bedfellows, Ishmael and Queequeg, we have a hint of an idea of the com-plexity woven into the book. The two men (and their manhood is about the only thing they do seem to have in common) are

---

[8]   Riverside, p. 150.

separated by differences in color, nationality, culture, manners, morals, religion, and finally class.

Nevertheless, all differences vanish when man confronts man, and color, especially, is abolished, not by law but by love. Ishmael is surprised to see some "boobies" and "bumpkins" marvelling "that two fellow beings should be so companionable" as he and Queequeg, "as though a white man were anything more dignified than a white-washed negro" (p. 65). True, the relationship between Ishmael and Queequeg begins ominously enough. When Ishmael first sees the tattooed skin of the man who is going to share his bed (still unaware, however, that he is not a white man) he is terrified. On second thought, he reflects: "What is it . . . after all! It's only his outside; a man can be honest in any sort of skin" (p. 37). But when he sees Queequeg's blackness, his former terror returns. He realizes "that he must be some abominable savage or other shipped aboard of a whaleman in the South Seas, and so landed in this Christian country" (p. 38). After a little bedroom farce, which is peacefully resolved by the landlord, Queequeg and Ishmael are finally reconciled:

'You gettee in,' he added, motioning to me with his tomahawk, and throwing the clothes to one side. He really did this in not only a civil but a really kind and charitable way. I stood looking at him a moment. For all his tattooings he was on the whole a clean, comely looking cannibal. What's all this fuss I have been making about, thought I to myself – the man's a human being just as I am: he has just as much reason to fear me, as I have to be afraid of him. Better sleep with a sober cannibal than a drunken Christian.

'Landlord,' said I, 'tell him to stash his tomahawk there, or pipe, or whatever you call it; tell him to stop smoking in short, and I will turn in with him. But I don't fancy having a man smoking in bed with me. It's dangerous. Besides, I ain't insured.'

This being told to Queequeg, he at once complied, and again politely motioned me to get into bed – rolling over to one side as much as to say – I won't touch a leg of ye.

'Good night, landlord,' said I, 'you may go.'

I turned in, and never slept better in my life. (p. 40)

There may or may not be an irony in Ishmael's saying that Queequeg has as much reason to fear him as he Queequeg. After all, it is not Queequeg's people who are enslaving Ishmael's. Then too, Ishmael recognizes the common bond of humanity that unites him and his prospective bedmate. His objection to Queequeg's smoking is a reflection of his continuing white man's fastidiousness, a touch, perhaps, of Coverdale's coldness. But unlike Coverdale, who can warm himself only in front of an artificial fire, Ishmael discovers his own inner human warmth.

When on the next night, Queequeg wants to smoke in bed, Ishmael does not object at all: "Be it said, that though I had felt such a strong repugnance to his smoking in the bed the night before, yet see how elastic our stiff prejudices grow when love once comes to bend them. For now I liked nothing better than to have Queequeg smoking by me, even in bed, because he seemed to be full of such serene household joy then. I no more felt unduly concerned for the landlord's policy of insurance. I was only alive to the condensed confidential comfortableness of sharing a pipe and blanket with a real friend. With our shaggy jackets drawn about our shoulders, we now passed the Tomahawk from one to the other, till slowly there grew over us a blue hanging tester of smoke, illuminated by the flame of the new-lit lamp" (p. 61).

What a change has already begun in Ishmael. The last icicle has melted from around his heart. With it goes a bit of his "civilized" white man's nicety, and also some of his preposterous property-consciousness. On the first night he is worried about social decorum and, of all things, the landlord's property, but once he can accept and return Queequeg's friendship freely, these things lose their importance for him.

Nor is it only in this matter of the smoking in bed that Ishmael has lost all his qualms. On the first morning after sleeping with Queequeg, Ishmael wakes up to find "Queequeg's arm thrown over me in the most loving and affectionate manner. You had almost thought I had been his wife" (p. 40). His situation recalls to him a "similar circumstance" that befell him in his youth, one that he had found extremely frightening. This time, however, he does not feel fear, but "lay alive only to the comical predicament". His first impulse, a very natural one, is to free himself: "Though I tried to move his arm – unlock his bridegroom clasp

– yet, sleeping as he was, he still hugged me tightly, as though naught but death should part us twain. I now strove to rouse him – Queequeg! – but his only answer was a snore. . . . A pretty pickle, truly, thought I; abed here in a strange house in the broad day, with a cannibal and a tomahawk! 'Queequeg! – in the name of goodness, Queequeg, wake!' At length, by dint of much wriggling, and loud and incessant expostulations upon the unbecomingness of his hugging a fellow male in that matrimonial sort of style, I succeeded in extracting a grunt . . ." (pp. 41-42).

But by the time the second night rolls around, all this is changed. Ishmael's frigidity has left him completely. This time, he and Queequeg "lay . . . in our hearts' honeymoon, . . . – a cosy, loving pair. We had lain thus in bed, chatting and napping at short intervals, and Queequeg now and then affectionately throwing his brown tattooed legs over mine, and then drawing them back; so entirely sociable and free and easy were we . . ." (p. 60). And finally, before going to sleep, "Queequeg embraced me [and] pressed his forehead against mine" (p. 63). To all this display of affection between males, Ishmael voices no objection.

The implications of homosexuality are fairly apparent, but I think, at this point, irrelevant. Matthiessen writes that "Melville's hopes for American democracy, his dread of its lack of human warmth, his apprehension of the actual privations and defeats of the common man, and his depth of compassion for courageous struggle unite in giving fervor to the declaration of his purpose in writing *Moby-Dick*".[9] Ishmael, in his friendship with the pagan Queequeg, rediscovers true human warmth. What is more, he rediscovers it within the possibilities provided by American democratic society. Queequeg and Ishmael can recognize each other as men because the strata of society, while they are there, have not yet become rigidified. So, Ishmael is conscious of Queequeg's manners, which are certainly boorish, even by Ishmael's standards. But the fact that he cannot approve Queequeg's manners does not mean he cannot approve of Queequeg. Describing Queequeg's behavior at breakfast, Ishmael says, "I cannot say much for his breeding. His greatest admirer could not have cor-

[9]   Page 444.

dially justified his bringing his harpoon into breakfast with him, and using it there without ceremony; reaching over the table with it, to the imminent jeopardy of many heads, and grappling the beefsteaks towards him. But *that* was certainly very coolly done by him, and everyone knows that in most people's estimation, to do anything coolly is to do it genteelly" (p. 44).

But in spite of this, Ishmael can recognize Queequeg's truly princely qualities. "Savage though he was, and hideously marred about the face – at least to my taste – his countenance yet had something in it which was by no means disagreeable. You cannot hide the soul. Through all his unearthly tattooings, I thought I saw the traces of a simple honest heart; and in his large, deep eyes, fiery black and bold, there seemed tokens of a spirit that would dare a thousand devils. . . . Queequeg was George Washington cannibalistically developed" (p. 58). Ishmael, at this point, has become quite Rousseauistic. Queequeg, the noble savage, is set against the corruption of society. And indeed, Ishmael has found society disillusioning. Democrats are not democratic, Christians are not Christian, and, in a young country, snobs who substitute civilized frigidity for intrinsic merit are already being heard in the land. In a land of promise, genteel frigidity predominates, and love itself has become the rarest of commodities.

In desperation, Ishmael decides to try a "pagan friend, . . . since Christian kindness has proved but hollow courtesy" (p. 69). Thoreau had opened his lecture, "Walking", by telling the audience, "I wish to speak a word for Nature, for absolute freedom and wildness, as contrasted with a freedom and culture merely civil – to regard man as inhabitant, or a part and parcel of Nature, rather than a member of society".[10] It is the same desire to experience the expansiveness of cosmic democracy that tantalizes Ishmael. But this cosmic democracy has to do with men, not with forms; with love, not with laws.

Ishmael wants to see man face to face, just as Ahab later wants to see God. But civilized men do not have faces, or at least if they do, the faces are well concealed behind the mask of social forms. Sitting with Queequeg, "solitary twain", Ishmael begins

[10]   *The Writings of Henry David Thoreau* (Boston, 1906), V (14 Vols.), 265.

"to be sensible of strange feelings. I felt a melting in me. No more my splintered heart and maddened hand were turned against the wolfish world. This soothing savage had redeemed it. There he sat, his very indifference speaking a nature in which there lurked no civilized hypocrisies and bland deceits" (p. 59). And Queequeg is capable of reciprocating these feelings:

If there yet lurked any ice of indifference towards me in the Pagan's breast, this pleasant, genial smoke we had, soon thawed it out, and left us cronies. He seemed to take to me quite as naturally and unbiddenly as I to him; and when our smoke was over, he pressed his forehead against mine, clasped me round the waist, and said that henceforth we were married; meaning, in his country's phrase, that we were bosom friends; he would gladly die for me, if need should be. In a countryman, this sudden flame of friendship would have seemed far too premature, a thing to be much distrusted; but in this simple savage those old rules would not apply. (p. 59)

It is "rules", social forms, which seem to create distrust, harden hearts, concretize greed, freeze the natural warmth of Ishmael's countrymen. Love alone can melt this ice, as Ishmael perceives when he is squeezing sperm aboard the Pequod:

Squeeze! squeeze! squeeze! all the morning long; I squeezed that sperm till I myself almost melted into it; I squeezed that sperm till a strange sort of insanity came over me; and I found myself unwittingly squeezing my co-laborers' hands in it, mistaking their hands for the gentle globules. Such an abounding, affectionate, friendly, loving feeling did this avocation beget; that at last I was continually squeezing their hands, and looking up into their eyes sentimentally; as much as to say, – Oh! my dear fellow beings, why should we longer cherish any social acerbities, or know the slightest ill-humor or envy! Come; let us squeeze hands all round; nay, let us all squeeze ourselves into each other; let us squeeze ourselves universally into the very milk and sperm of kindness. (p. 323)

Acerbities are social, and it is only love that can dissolve them. But by this time, Ishmael's love has expanded. It is not only love between him and Queequeg that he feels, but love to all men. And yet, it is not the "philanthropist's" cold, dutiful love of man in the abstract. It is a more objectified emotion Ishmael feels, one evoked by a concrete situation. But once evoked, it increases and deepens until it finally becomes so intense as to overwhelm Ishmael and make him desire to encompass all mankind with his love. His benevolence is both spontaneous and organic, rather than artificial and mechanical. Instead of retreating inward as a result of his disillusionment with democracy, as does Coverdale, Ishmael tries to move further outward.

Nor does he, like Holgrave, attempt to retreat into the past. Whatever may be wrong with the democratic present, it is still better than the aristocracies and monarchies that preceded it. For hereditary royalty, Ishmael has only the deepest contempt. About this he is clear and emphatic. "In behalf of the dignity of whaling . . .", Ishmael suggests that kings and queens may be anointed with whale oil. He then continues, "Certain I am, however, that a king's head is solemnly oiled at his coronation, even as a head of salad. Can it be, though, that they anoint it with a view of making its interior run well, as they anoint machinery? Much might be ruminated here, concerning the essential dignity of this regal process, because in common life we esteem but meanly and contemptibly a fellow who anoints his hair, and palpably smells of that anointing. In truth, a mature man who uses hair-oil, unless medicinally, that man has probably got a quoggy spot in him somewhere. As a general rule, he can't amount to much in his totality" (p. 103).

In discussing the law that grants the head of a captured whale to the "King, as Honorary Grand Harpooneer", and the tail to the Queen, Ishmael wonders if the sturgeon, also a royal fish, is divided in the same way, "the King receiving the highly dense and elastic head peculiar to that fish, which symbolically regarded, may possibly be humorously grounded upon some presumed congeniality" (p. 312). Furthermore, any question about the trenchancy and prevalence of these attacks should be dispelled by Robert Shulman's article, "The Serious Functions of Melville's Phallic Jokes", in which he demonstrates beyond cavil that Ishmael's phallic jokes invariably "satirize religion, property, or rank" by juxtaposing the obscene and the sacred.[11]

[11] *American Literature*, XXXIII (May, 1961), 183.

And yet, how does this rancor fit in with Ishmael's universal love? Isn't this prejudice against kings a blemish? It could be. But it must be remembered that Ishmael consorts with royalty as well as commons, for Queequeg, after all, is the son of a king. It is inherited and irrational privilege, not kingliness itself, that Ishmael detests. In his view, being a king is not in itself enough to make a man, but every true man is a king.

The relationship between Ishmael and Queequeg, as I have already indicated, is extremely complex, and through it Melville undermines the foundations of all of Western man's absolutes, except perhaps the absolute of man himself and his ability to accommodate himself to the external world through human love. He accomplishes this subversion of Western man's beliefs not by putting Queequeg's values above Ishmael's, but by putting both sets of values side by side. Ishmael eats with a fork, Queequeg with a harpoon. Ishmael's God is the tetragrammaton, and Queequeg's is Yojo. Finally, Ishmael is a plebian, while Queequeg is a prince. Yet no indication is given that one set of values is more valid than the other. Queequeg makes himself ridiculous in Sag Harbor by putting his trunk in a wheelbarrow and then strapping the wheelbarrow to his back and carrying it. But an American sea captain makes himself equally ridiculous in Rokovoko when he washes his hands in a punch bowl. Manners, color, religion, class are all external and relative, and do not define a man. What does define him is internal. Ishmael observes, when Queequeg lies dying, that "as all else in him thinned, and his cheekbones grew sharper, his eyes, nevertheless, seemed growing fuller and fuller; they became of a strange softness of lustre; and mildly but deeply looked out at you there from his sickness, a wondrous testimony to that immortal health in him which could not die, or be weakened" (p. 365). This internal nobility which undercuts artificial and meaningless societal barriers is the bond between Queequeg and Ishmael. And it is this internal nobility, uncontaminated by "civilization", that Ishmael discovers in Queequeg, and through Queequeg, in himself. The love inspired by Queequeg triggers a release of emotional energy that not only deepens and broadens Ishmael's sensitivity and intellect, but also revitalizes his belief in the potential of universal democracy and brotherhood.

The Ishmael who first quit the "city of old Manhatto", with a "damp drizzly November in his soul", feeling himself "growing grim about the mouth", and "involuntarily pausing before coffin warehouses . . ." may be a proletarian, but he is not the same exultant Ishmael who chants a joyous hymn to the Great God Democratic and the nobility of his human creation:

Men may seem detestable as joint stock-companies and nations; . . . but man, in the ideal, is so noble and so sparkling, such a grand and glowing creature, that over any ignominious blemish in him all his fellows should run to throw their costliest robes. That immaculate manliness we feel within our selves, so far within us that it remains intact though all the outer character seem gone; bleeds with keenest anguish at the undraped spectacle of a valor-ruined man. . . . But this august dignity I treat of, is not the dignity of kings and robes, but that abounding dignity which has no robed investiture. Thou shalt see it shining in the arm that wields a pick or drives a spike; that democratic dignity which, on all hands, radiates without end from God; Himself! The great God absolute! The centre and circumference of all democracy! His omnipresence, our divine equality!

If, then, to meanest mariners, and renegades and castaways, I shall hereafter ascribe high qualities, though dark; weave round them tragic graces; if even the most mournful, perchance the most abased, among them all shall at times lift himself to the exalted mounts; if I shall touch that workman's arm with some ethereal light; if I shall spread a rainbow over his disastrous set of sun; then against all mortal critics bear me out in it, thou just Spirit of Equality, which has spread one royal mantle of humanity over all my kind! Bear me out in it, thou great democratic God! . . . Thou who, in all Thy mighty earthly marchings, ever cullest Thy selectest champions from the kingly commons; bear me out in it, O God! (p. 105)

Matthiessen remarks about this passage that "its crescendo completes his [Melville's] fusion of Christianity and democracy".[12] This may be, but it is certain that the passage marks Ishmael's fusion of the two. And in this fusion lies the difference between the Ishmael who sets out awhaling and the one who chants this ecstatic hymn. True, some critics feel that this change in tone is

[12]   Matthiessen, p. 445.

to be explained by Melville's own change of heart, his decision to write as far as possible what he was most moved to write. But this is no objection. As he moves through his relationship with Queequeg, and begins to feel the blossoming grandeur of the world rising within him, he becomes both more poetic and more profound. Perhaps this is merely to say that Melville found the objective-correlative for his own response to his reading in Ishmael's response to Queequeg.

But while Ishmael's relationship with Queequeg deepens both his understanding of and respect for the possibilities of democracy, it threatens also to strand him in a banal Transcendental optimism. The danger of an unbridled democratic idealism is that it tends to distend into infinite nothing. Ishmael himself asks, "How many, think ye, have ... fallen into Plato's honey-head, and sweetly perished there?" (p. 271). This danger is averted through Ishmael's contact with Ahab, for in Ahab the expanding radiance of Ishmael's love runs into the constricting blackness of Ahab's hate.

"Ahab", writes Alfred Kazin, "is a hero; we cannot insist enough on that. Melville believed in the heroic and he specifically wanted to cast his hero on American lines – someone noble by nature, not by birth, ... And because Ahab, as Melville intended him to, represents the aristocracy of intellect in our democracy, because he seeks to transcend the limitations that good conventional men like Starbuck, philistine materialists like Stubb, and unthinking fools like Flask want to impose on everybody else, Ahab speaks for the humanity that belongs to man's imaginative vision of himself".[13]

It may be that Ahab represents "the aristocracy of intellect", but he represents it as aristocracy run wild. Alienated from mankind, Ahab bends all his great intellectual powers first to obliterating the individuality of the members of the Pequod's crew. Then, in his dealings with Fedallah, he manifests the Faustian urge to impose his intellect on the entire universe. In the magnitude of his ambition, Ahab is indeed heroic. But whether he is a

[13]   Page x.

hero or not is another question: the same question raised by the defiant magnificence of Milton's rebellious Satan.

The finest description of Ahab as the modern embodiment of the classical tragic hero is Newton Arvin's:

Ahab is ... for his time and place, the noblest and most complete embodiment of the tragic hero. He is modern man, and particularly American man, in his role as 'free' and 'independent' Individual, as self-sustaining and self-assertive Ego, of forcible will and unbending purpose all compact, inflexible, unpitying, and fell, but enlarged by both his vices and his strength to dimensions of legendary grandeur. About Ahab's moral largeness there can be no uncertainty; the cleansing effect of *Moby-Dick* depends vitally upon that. He is described as not only 'grand' but even 'godlike,' and godlike – in a sense that is at once Greek and Yankee, at once classical and contemporary – everyone feels him to be. He has such Arete, says Melville in effect, as a grim and shaggy old whalehunter from Nantucket can have, and that is much; his very appearance suggests a demigod. ... He calls himself 'proud as a Greek God,' and indeed his pride is noble enough to endure the comparison. In its highest expression it is the heroic self-trust and self-regard of the modern Western man asserted in the teeth of all that would overbear and diminish him, whether natural or beyond nature.[14]

This view of Ahab as tragic hero makes sense when *Moby-Dick* is discussed in terms of Greek or Shakespearean tragedy. And that the influence of both, especially Shakespeare, is there cannot be denied; no doubt, part of Melville's genius is his ability to adapt to his needs the most widely varied materials. But the work as a whole is much more meaningful when it is viewed as an epic. Arvin himself writes that "if one must look for analogies that will do a little to express the effect *Moby-Dick* has on us in form ... it is not to tragedy that one should turn but to heroic poetry, to the epic. ... The kind of life Melville was raising to the fictive level in this book ... was a life in some of its aspects reminiscent of that led by the Achaean peoples in the days of the folk-wanderings or by the Germanic peoples in the days of theirs. ... It genuinely helps to define the formal quality of *Moby-Dick* if one says that what he feels in its spacious narrative movement

[14] *Melville* (New York, 1957), p. 176.

is not unlike what he feels in the narrative movement of the *Iliad*, [and] of the *Odyssey* . . .".[15]

And Richard Chase calls *Moby-Dick* an "epic romance". "But", he says, "although superficially resembling the *Odyssey*, *Moby-Dick* lacks, among other things, the rich observation of *ethos*, of ways of life, real and fabulous, which we find in Homer's poem. The *Odyssey* is extremely sophisticated about manners and morals and is actually more novelistic than *Moby-Dick*".[16]

Chase has an insight here, but does not follow it up. He is right when he says that the resemblance between *Moby-Dick* and the *Odyssey* is superficial. And yet, if this is so, how explain the fact that no serious reader or critic of the book has failed to notice the epic qualities? The answer, I think, is that *Moby-Dick* is an epic, but an epic in the Biblical tradition rather than in the Homeric and Classical. This is suggested by Nathalia Wright in her book, *Melville's Use of the Bible*, and is certainly indicated both by Melville's language and by the fact that the main characters, Ishmael and Ahab, have Biblical names. But though the fact seems obvious, no one has explored it fully.

And yet, once we recognize it, so much is explained. What I have in mind here, let me emphasize, is not merely the matter of characters, names and plots, but the Biblical spirit that informs the entire book. This spirit of the Biblical epic style as opposed to the Classical, is brilliantly analyzed in the first chapter of Erich Auerbach's *Mimesis*. He concludes, there, that the Homeric style is characterized by "fully externalized description, uniform illumination, uninterrupted connection, free expression, all events in the foreground, displaying unmistakable meanings, few elements of historical development and of psychological perspective . . .", while the Biblical, on the other hand, contains "certain parts brought into high relief, others left obscure, abruptness, suggestive influence of the unexpressed, 'background' quality, multiplicity of meanings and the need for interpretation, universal-historical claims, development of the concept of the historically

---

[15]   *The American Novel and Its Tradition*, pp. 156-57.
[16]   Page 101.

becoming, and preoccupation with the problematic".[17] The apt-
ness with which the latter qualities describe *Moby-Dick* is striking;
investigating them might well be the subject of a separate book.
Let it suffice here to draw some brief parallels. The universal-
historical claims of *Moby-Dick* are beautifully established in the
opening and closing sentences of the book: "Call me Ishmael",
with its quality of timelessness, and "Now small fowls flew
screaming over the yet yawning gulf; a sullen white surf beat
against its steep sides; then all collapsed, and the great shroud of
the sea rolled on as it rolled five thousand years ago". The profu-
sion of critical books and exegetic articles, most of them containing some truth, certainly demonstrates the need for interpretation. Finally, Ishmael's inability to encompass the characters or
himself testifies both to the multiplicity of meaning and "unexpressed 'background' quality" which pervades the book, and its
preoccupation with the "problematic". Both these characteristics
are demonstrated in the following passage:

> Here, then, was this grey-headed, ungodly old man, chasing with
> curses a Job's whale round the world, at the head of a crew, too,
> chiefly made up of mongrel renegades, and castaways, and cannibals
> – morally enfeebled also, by the incompetence of mere unaided virtue
> or rightmindedness in Starbuck, the invulnerable jollity of indifference
> and recklessness in Stubb, and the pervading mediocrity in Flask.
> Such a crew, so officered, seemed specially picked and packed by some
> infernal fatality to help him to his monomaniac revenge. How it was
> that they so aboundingly responded to the old man's ire – by what
> evil magic their souls were possessed, that at times, his hate seemed
> almost theirs; the White Whale as much their insufferable foe as his;
> how all this came to be – what the White Whale was to them, or how
> to their unconscious understandings, also, in some dim, unsuspected
> way, he might have seemed the gliding great demon of the seas of
> life, – all this to explain, would be to dive deeper than Ishmael can
> go. (p. 156)

The moment we begin to view *Moby-Dick* in perspective of
Biblical style, Ahab's heroic and tragic stature begins to diminish.
It becomes apparent, for example, that it is not Ahab's death that

17 (New York, 1957), p. 19.

makes the tragedy, but the wanton destruction of the entire crew. And let there be no mistake, it is for the crew we feel more than for Ahab. Had only the latter been ground in the maws of his own obsession, then there were no tragedy, or if there were, then the whale's destroying the Pequod and all aboard, becomes one of the most purposeless scenes in literature. It is the crew that we feel always surging up from below, always suppressed, yet all-important. We feel their presence in the same way that we feel the presence of the Children of Israel pressing against the authority of Moses and God. We need not know when each member of the crew scratches his back, for we feel the full portentousness of their human existence in Starbuck, Stubb, Flask, Queequeg, Tashtego, Daggoo, the Carpenter, the Blacksmith, Pip: we feel it in the dialogue that takes place at "Midnight in the Forecastle"; we feel it when Starbuck, helplessly watching Moby Dick's menacing onslaught on the Pequod, utters one of the most pathetic lines in the book: "Is this the end of all my bursting prayers? all my life-long fidelities? Oh, Ahab, Ahab, lo, thy work". And finally we feel it most magnificently in Ishmael himself, Ishmael the orphan, but not the alienated man; Ishmael who says, "I, Ishmael, was one of that crew; my shouts had gone up with the rest; my oath had been welded with theirs" (p. 149).

This total immersion explains, too, the disappearance of Ishmael that is so puzzling. He disappears because in his character of Everyman he has melted into the crew. This submergence of self is underlined by his description of the way in which he is saved from destruction: "Three of the oarsmen – were flung out [of Ahab's boat]; but so fell, that, in an instant two of them clutched the gunwhale again, and rising to its level on a combing wave, hurled themselves bodily inboard again; the third man helplessly dropping astern, but still afloat and swimming" (p. 429). The third man, of course, is Ishmael, and the fact that he was not able to return to the boat saves him. His silent third person reference to himself as the third man seems to indicate a complete suppression of ego. But at the same time that Ishmael's ego has been completely suppressed, Ahab is still raging "Towards thee I roll, thou all-destroying but unconquering whale; to the last I grapple with thee; from hell's heart I stab at thee; for hate's sake I spit my last breath at thee" (p. 431).

Ahab, then, is always there, always declaiming with the grandeur and unrestrained bombast of a Shakespearean hero, always maintaining his pose as a "Greek God". But the vision that comprehends him is Hebraic rather than Hellenic. Auerbach asserts that

we become conscious of the fact that in the Homeric poems life is enacted only among the ruling class – others appear only in the role of servants to that class. The ruling class is still so strongly patriarchial, and still itself so involved in the daily activities of domestic life, that one is sometimes likely to forget their rank. But they are unmistakably a sort of feudal aristocracy, whose men divide their lives between war, hunting, marketplace councils, and feasting, while the women supervise the maids in the house. As a social picture, this world is completely stable; wars take place only between different groups of the ruling class; nothing ever pushes up from below. In the early stories of the Old Testament the patriarchal condition is dominant too, but since the people involved are individual nomadic or half-nomadic tribal leaders, the social picture gives a much less stable impression; class distinctions are not felt. As soon as the people completely emerges – that is, after the exodus from Egypt – its activity is always discernible, it is often in ferment, it frequently intervenes in events not only as a whole but also in separate groups and through the medium of separate individuals who come forward; the origins of prophecy seem to lie in the irrepressible politico-religious spontaneity of the people. We receive the impression that the movements emerging from the depths of the people of Israel-Judah must have been of a wholly different nature from those even of the later ancient democracies – of a different nature and far more elemental.[18]

What we sense in *Moby-Dick* is the social condition that Auerbach describes as inhering in the Old Testament. We are conscious of Ahab's kingliness and of his alienation. We are conscious of his indomitable romantic will. But we are also conscious of his relation to and interaction with the crew, which cannot be regarded as simply a chorus. Agamemnon must satisfy the gods by sacrificing Iphigenia, and he must mollify obdurate princes, but never does he have to pay any attention to the people, the chorus which deplores the act. Ahab, on the other hand, is involved in

[18]   Page 18.

a constant struggle with his crew, as well as with the whale. He must raise the men to fever pitch, he must offer them a gold doubloon as a bonus, he must maintain the pretence of a conventional whaling voyage, and he must alternately cajole and bully them. To keep them from erupting, he must exert his fantastic will to the utmost. And in their weakness in letting themselves be bullied and bribed and mesmerized we feel the sweep of tragedy which extends infinitely beyond Ahab himself. We feel the tragedy of free men who have accepted authority too indiscriminately, who have subordinated their individuality to the will of one man, and who have therefore surrendered their manhood. When Samuel prays to the Lord, telling him that the people of Israel have asked him to appoint a king, God answers, "They have not rejected thee, but they have rejected me . . ." (I Samuel, 8:7).

Similarly, to follow Ahab, the men of the Pequod have ceased to follow "The Great God absolute! The centre and circumference of all democracy!" And when Ahab tells the "half mutinous" (p. 385) crew, "All your oaths to hunt the White Whale are as binding as mine; and heart, soul, and body, lungs and life, old Ahab is bound" (p. 385), they are just finding out what Samuel had told the Israelites: "This will be the manner of the king that shall reign over you: He will take your sons, and appoint them for himself, for his chariots, and to be his horsemen; and some shall run before his chariots. . . . And he will set them to ear his ground, and to reap his harvest, and to make his instruments of war, and instruments of his chariots. . . . And he will take your fields, and your vineyards and olive yards, . . . And he will take your menservants and your maidservants, and your goodliest young men, and your asses, and put them to his work. . . . And ye shall be his servants. And ye shall cry out in that day because of your king which ye shall have chosen you: and the Lord will not hear you in that day" (I Samuel 9:11-18). And so Starbuck cries out in vain. Once he has submitted his soul to another man's will, to a king, as it were, there is no one to hear his bursting prayers or reward his life-long fidelities.

Hearing from Peleg that "Ahab of old . . . was a crowned

king!" Ishmael can only observe that he was "a very vile one" (p. 80). But Ishmael finds all kings vile, for a king, by his very nature, stands between man and his God, or perhaps, in the romantic's view, between man and his own ego.

Hugh Henry Brackenridge, it will be recalled, had trouble in reconciling his democratic equalitarian beliefs with the mimetic devices he had inherited from his classical background. He could not portray the common man without treating him rather lightly and comically. In the Bible, however, Melville rediscovers the vision and style that enable him to write about the lower classes seriously.

Matthiessen observes that "without deliberately intending it, but by virtue of his intense concern with the precariously maintained values of democratic Christianity, which he saw everywhere being threatened or broken down, Melville created in Ahab's tragedy a fearful symbol of the self-enclosed individualism that, carried to its furthest extreme, brings disaster both upon itself and upon the group of which it is part" (p. 459).

I would agree with Matthiessen that Ahab's tragedy is the result of an unbridled individualism which leads him to conceive himself as "lord and dictator". But the disaster which befalls the crew is not, I think, a mere byproduct of Ahab's tragedy, it is an integral part of the tragic tone of the book. If Ahab's destruction results from his uncurbed individualism, then the destruction of the crew members results from their permitting him to ride roughshod over them.

Not only Ahab, however, was created out of Melville's concern for "the precariously maintained values of democratic Christianity", but Ishmael as well. For if Ahab represents the negative view, the destructive individualist and alienated intellectual aristocrat, Ishmael represents the liberal democratic intellectual who is not alienated from mankind, and who remains, in spite of his liberalism, capable of both deep love and deep thought.

We have seen Ishmael's capacity to love in his relationship with Queequeg. I would like, now, to turn to Ishmael as thinker. I must state at once that I do not pretend to encompass all of Ishmael's philosophizing. Since, as Kazin points out, his is "the single mind from whose endlessly turning spool of thought the whole story is unwound", to try to embrace his thought on all subjects would require a close textual analysis of almost the entire book. Hence, I must say with Ishmael himself, "I promise nothing complete; because any human being supposed to be complete, must for that very reason infallibly be faulty" (p. 117).

Instead, I would like to focus on an important undercurrent of thought which has not been widely noticed. This is Ishmael's intellectual response to another danger which menaces "the values of democratic Christianity": a shallow, mechanistic liberalism threatening to degenerate into a completely selfish materialism.

Ishmael's criticism of Transcendentalism and of the "young Platonists" who lose their identity in the mist of a vague idealism is rather appealing to the twentieth-century reader,[19] and has consequently received a great deal of attention. But if Ishmael cannot accept the extreme idealist who does not ground his thought in concrete facts, neither can he accept the shallow empiricist who posits a mechanistic universe in which all knowledge is obtained through the senses, and in which democracy is merely a civil order. What Ishmael wants to do is to deepen and broaden eighteenth-century liberalism. He does not want to conceive of man as merely a political or economic phenomenon but he wants to retain the ideals of Natural Rights and political freedom for the individual. In order to effect this, Ishmael returns to the chief source of both American liberalism and conservatism, John Locke, questioning his philosophy at two points: political theory and epistemology.

What Ishmael questions, primarily, in Locke's political theory is his glorification of property. *"Political Power"*, Locke had written in his *Second Treatise of Government*, "I take to be *a Right* of making Laws with Penalties of Death, and consequently all less penalties, for the Regulating and Preserving of Property, and of employing the force of the Community, in the Execution of such Laws . . .".[20] For Ishmael, who, despite his rejection of

---

[19] See Chap. XXXV, "The Mast-Head".
[20] John Locke, *Two Treatises on Government*, ed. Peter Laslett (Cambridge, 1960), Bk. II, Chap. 1, Par. 3 (p. 286).

extreme idealism, clings to an idealistic concept of democracy, a government that wields this kind of political power for such purposes becomes merely a device for perpetuating injustice. This, Ishmael makes quite clear in the chapter called "Fast-Fish and Loose-Fish", a chapter interesting not only for its slaughter of the Anglo-Saxon sacred cows of law and property, but also for its insight into the workings of Ishmael's mind.

Ishmael starts, as he often does, with a seemingly simple fact, the classification of wounded or hunted whales as property. What constitutes possession of a whale, he claims, is defined by two brief, but nonetheless comprehensive laws:

I.   A Fast-Fish belongs to the party fast to it.
II.   A Loose-Fish is fair game for anybody who can soonest catch it.
      (p. 308)

Having praised the clarity and succinctness of this code, Ishmael promptly proceeds to undermine it by introducing, in a tone of good-humored banter, some doubts as to its ultimate effectiveness. "But what plays the mischief with this masterly code", he slyly adds, "is the admirable brevity of it, which necessitates a vast volume of commentaries to expound it". It is ever thus with Ishmael's mind. What starts out self-evident soon becomes hopelessly ambiguous. But, always mindful of the reader, Ishmael goes on to "clarify" the code by citing some of the "commentaries".

First: What is a Fast-Fish? Alive or dead a fish is technically fast, when it is connected with an occupied ship or boat, by any medium at all controllable by the occupant or occupants, – a mast, an oar, a nine-inch cable, a telegraph wire, or a strand of cobweb, it is all the same. Likewise, a fish is technically fast when it bears a waif, or any other recognised symbol of possession; so long as the party waifing it plainly evince their ability at any time to take it alongside, as well as their intention so to do. (p. 308)

Ishmael's rambunctious good humor is engaging, and most of the ironies are almost too obvious to mention, but the questions they raise are not. For example, it is obvious that in common-sense terms, a strand of cobweb is not the same as a mast. In what way, then, are they the same? I would suggest that their sameness consists in the fact that the connection between possessor and possessed, metaphysically, if not legally, is always a tenuous one. There is the implication, also, that the concept of ownership of property is a human delusion. For how else is one to take the ludicrous suggestion that touching a whale with a strand of cobweb makes it the property of the person holding the other end of the strand. The tenuous nature of the relationship between mortal man and "his" property is further indicated by the fact that the possessor, in this "commentary", does not have to be able to control the fish to make it a Fast-Fish. All he must be able to do is to control the object which connects the fish to the ship or boat. Moreover, after all their involved explanation of the physical connection that must exist between owner and owned, the "commentators" then tell us that it is not necessary that there by any physical *connection* at all. Merely to say, "This is mine" coupled with the ability to make the saying good, is sufficient. Clearly, in all cases, the law recognizes that the right to own something depends on the power of the owner to keep it.

And this, indeed, is how the matter works out in practice. "These are scientific commentaries", says Ishmael, not without irony. "But the commentaries of the whalemen themselves sometimes consist in hard words and harder knocks – the Coke-upon-Littleton of the fist".

Ishmael now launches one of his seemingly irrelevant phallic jokes by describing "a curious case of whaletrover litigated in England". The defense lawyer compares the case to a recent one of adultery, in which a husband who abandoned his wife because "of the great stress of her plunging viciousness", tried to recover her, only to find that she had become the property of a "subsequent gentleman" who had "reharpooned her". The judge finds the parallel sufficiently convincing to grant the defense lawyer what he wants. The effect of the phallic joking is, as Robert Shulman points out, "to make the judge's decision immoral and corrupt in terms of the very standards of respectability which a Lord Ellenborough (the judge) piously upholds".[21]

[21] Page 181.

So though Ishmael seems to be digressing out of a sheer over-flow of high spirits, he is actually subverting the foundations of Anglo-Saxon law. He concludes his description of the case by saying, "These two laws touching Fast-Fish and Loose-Fish, I say, will on reflection, be found the fundamentals of all human jurisprudence; for notwithstanding its complicated tracery of sculpture, the Temple of the Law, like the Temple of the Philistines, has but two props to stand on".

Ishmael's association of the Temple of Law with the Temple of the Philistines is, no doubt, intended to be sacrilegious. At any rate, since Ishmael has begun his Samson's work, the temple of law is already a little shaky. But Ishmael, unlike the strong man, does not buckle the pillars with brute strength. Instead he ridicules them out of existence. For if we consider the two props of law in the light of the "commentaries", it becomes clear that the two props are in actuality one, and that the one is raw power. A Fast-Fish belongs to anyone who can keep it. But the same thing is also true of a Loose-Fish. That is, it also is the property of anyone who can hold onto it. Having thus reduced Anglo-American law to a vicious concentration of amoral power intended to preserve vested interests, Ishmael now proceeds to bring the entire temple down on the head of all the ruling Philistines:

Is it not a saying in every one's mouth, Possession is half of the law: that is, regardless of how the thing came into possession? But often possession is the whole of the law. What are the sinews and souls of Russian serfs and Republican slaves but Fast-Fish, whereof possession is the whole of the law? What to the rapacious landlord is the widow's last mite but a Fast-Fish? What is yonder undetected villain's marble mansion with a doorplate for a waif; what is that but a Fast-Fish? What is the ruinous discount which Mordecai, the broker, gets from poor Woebegone, the bankrupt, on a loan to keep Woebe-gone's family from starvation; what is that ruinous discount but a Fast-Fish? What is the Archbishop of Savesoul's income of £100,000 seized from the scant bread and cheese of hundreds of thousands of broken-backed laborers (all sure of heaven without any of Savesoul's help) what is that globular 100,000 but a Fast-Fish? What are the Duke of Dunder's hereditary towns and hamlets but Fast-Fish? What to that redoubted harpooneer, John Bull, is poor Ireland, but a Fast-Fish? What to that apostolic lancer, Brother Jonathan, is Texas but a Fast-

Fish? And concerning all these, is not Possession the whole of the law?

But if the doctrine of Fast-Fish be pretty generally applicable, the kindred doctrine of Loose-Fish is still more widely so. That is internationally and universally applicable.

What was America in 1492 but a Loose-Fish, in which Columbus struck the Spanish standard by way of waifing it for his royal master and mistress? What was Poland to the Czar? What Greece to the Turk? What India to England? What at last will Mexico be to the United States? All Loose-Fish. (pp. 309-10)

At this point we might expect that Ishmael is through. But, no. Once in flight, he does not rest until he achieves orbit. Having reached the utmost limits of social criticism, he recklessly plunges beyond phenomena into the infinite:

What are the Rights of Man and the Liberties of the World but Loose-Fish? What all men's minds and opinions but Loose-Fish? What is the principle of religious belief in them but a Loose-Fish? What to the ostentatious smuggling verbalists are the thoughts of thinkers but Loose-Fish? What is the great globe itself but a Loose-Fish? And what are you, reader, but a Loose-Fish and a Fast-Fish, too? (p. 310)

Ishmael's mind functions like a nuclear chain reaction. One explosion leads to a bigger explosion *ad infinitum.* Starting with the banal question of how to determine whom a captured whale belongs to, he expands into the larger question of property rights in general. This raises the question of property rights and political freedom, and as though this in itself were not perplexing enough, he cannot rest until he has set the question of political freedom in the larger perspective of the metaphysical problem of freedom of the human will. He cannot stop the flow of his symphonic prose until he has entangled the reader's soul in his verbal net, secured it, and made it a Fast-Fish, too.

Locke wrote that "The great and *chief end* . . . of Men's uniting into Commonwealths, and putting themselves under Government, *is the Preservation of their Property*".[22] That Ishmael could never have accepted such doctrine is patent. The bond that Ishmael recognizes between men is not preservation of property, but their common humanity and interdependence, the responsibility of

[22] *Second Treatise*, II: 9, 124 (pp. 368-69).

every man for his brother. Hence, at one point, Queequeg is on a dead whale's back, cutting in, while Ishmael is connected to him by a "monkey rope" which is supposed to keep Queequeg above water. If Queequeg should sink, then Ishmael is honor-bound to sink with him. As Ishmael sees it, "So then, an elongated Siamese ligature united us. Queequeg was my own inseparable twin brother; nor could I in any way get rid of the dangerous liabilities which the hempen bond entailed" (p. 253). It is this unbounded democracy of human brotherhood and love that Ishmael strives toward, not merely a democracy of the right to own property.

Much as he hates the property-worship in Locke's political theory, however, Ishmael detests the sterility he finds implicit in Locke's epistemology even more. This should not come as a sur-prise, since Melville himself could scarcely abide the light. What he was attracted to in both Shakespeare and Hawthorne was their ability to utter dark truths. Ishmael, too, loves blackness. He runs from both the pyrotechnic radiance of Emerson's idealism and the bright sunshine of Locke's empiricism. "When on one side", he remarks, "you hoist in Locke's head, you go over that way; but now, on the other side, hoist in Kant's and you come back again; but in very poor plight. Thus, some minds forever keep trimming boat. Oh, ye foolish! Throw all these thunderheads overboard, and then you will float light and right" (p. 259).

But Ishmael, in spite of his splendid advice, was himself un-able to throw either of the thunder-heads overboard. In him are joined the two currents of the American consciousness – the rational liberalism of the enlightenment so nobly embodied in Jefferson and Franklin, and the irrational foreboding darkness of Puritanism observable in the Mathers and Edwardses. Thus he is forever trimming boat between a Calvinist point of view which is essentially ontological, metaphysical and mysterious and the em-piricist point of view which is essentially epistemological, expe-riential and lucid. Living in a society in which the world-view of the enlightenment had triumphed, Ishmael is indeed part of that world to the extent that he accepts enlightenment egalitarian principles and denies the validity of established class structure

and hereditary privilege. But, accepting these enlightenment principles, Ishmael is unable to reject the residue of portentous irra-
tionality inherent in his Biblical heritage. And it is this inability,
no doubt, that explains the Biblical rather than classical orientation of *Moby-Dick*, and which also explains Melville's dissatisfaction with both Emersonian idealism and Lockean empiricism.
Nathalia Wright asserts that

> ... in his belief in the existence of this world beyond the world of
> sense Melville has often been called Platonic. Like the Platonists, he
> did believe truth resided in the unseen world of ideas and conceptions
> rather than in the world of material manifestations. But in his essen-
> tially romantic conception of this invisible sphere he was closer to the
> Hebrews than to the Greeks. Order, rhetoric, and logic did not re-
> present the primal truth to him as did elemental and undisciplined
> energy.
> For the Greeks there was clarity not only in this world but also in
> the world of gods and ghosts. The gods had a fixed abode, disem-
> bodied spirits followed a well-marked course, and converse with both
> was held natural and reasonable. In all their mythology there is no
> touch of fearful novelty. But to the Hebrews this world was vague
> .... And because it was vague it could be very dreadful to them.
> Whereas the Greeks could watch supernatural beings move among
> them, influencing their affairs, to the Hebrews such interference was
> utterly mysterious. It was a blow out of the dark, sudden and unex-
> plained.[23]

Ishmael's sense of the world, like Melville's, is closer to that
of the Hebrews than to that of the Greeks. Order, rhetoric, and
logic do not represent primal truth to him, as he makes clear
time and again in his humorously "learned" expository comments
on whaling lore. An example of Ishmael's logic: after citing the
evidence for classifying whales as mammals, he concludes, "Be it
known that, waiving all argument, I take the good old fashioned
ground that the whale is a fish, and call upon holy Jonah to back
me" (p. 118). Of his lack of system, he boasts, "Finally: it was
stated at the outset, that this system would not be here, and at
once, perfected. You cannot but plainly see that I have kept my
word" (p. 125). When he sets out, in "The Affidavit", to establish the "verity" of his narrative, he confesses, "I care not to

---

[23] *Melville's Use of the Bible* (Durham, 1949), p. 184.

perform this part of my task methodically" (p. 168). Before he describes "The Honor and Glory of Whaling", he avers that "there are some enterprises in which a careful disorderliness is the true method" (p. 283).

Moreover, the world for Ishmael remains dreadful and mysterious, dark and unexplained. Yet, he does not live in Biblical times. He lives, rather, in a world which has felt the impact of Locke's thought, as well as that of Kant's and Emerson's, and he himself is a part of that world, a world highly amenable to daylight. The enlightenment universe is an orderly one which reveals itself to our senses. In it we can be certain that we know what we know. Man can approach the objects of experience with confidence, and what he cannot experience he need not worry about. But it is precisely this view of the universe that Ishmael cannot wholly accept. He sees in the world around him an element that is not orderly. The universe is surrounded, as a matter of fact, with the irrational and unknowable. And it is the dimension of the unknowable that he tries to graft onto Locke's experiential world. In order to do this he must first break through the wall of Locke's sensational epistemology. And this is what he accomplishes in his attempts to describe whales in general and Moby Dick in particular.

The trouble with whales, the reader soon discovers, is that though they are objects of experience, and consequently a proper subject for scientific inquiry and classification, they are not knowable in their entirety. Discussing pictures of whales, Ishmael reveals that he has never found one that is perfectly accurate. Consequently, he avers "Any way you may look at it, you must needs conclude that the great Leviathan is that one creature in the world which must remain unpainted to the last. True, one portrait may hit the mark nearer than another, but none can hit it with any very considerable degree of exactness. So there is no earthly way of finding out precisely what the whale looks like" (p. 215).

And yet, while the whale in its wholeness is unfathomable, one portrait, as Ishmael says, "may hit the mark nearer than another". Ironically, however, it is not those who have had the most experience with whales who paint them best. Ishmael claims that "with not one-tenth of England's experience in the fishery, and not one thousandth part of that of the Americans, . . . [French painters] have nevertheless furnished both nations with the only finished sketches at all capable of conveying the real spirit of the whale hunt. For the most part, the English and American whale draughtsmen seem entirely content with presenting the mechanical outline of things, such as the vacant profile of the whale . . ." (p. 217). The implication is that the empirical method does not necessarily lead to a knowledge of truth. The empirical mind, which is a sort of file catalogue of sense perceptions can reproduce only surfaces, and the spirit of a "thing" ("the-thing-in-itself") is not to be found in its surface. Knowledge of truth, then, seems to require a leap beyond experience.

This becomes more and more evident as Ishmael continues to pile up information about the whale, for no matter how much information he gathers, he still despairs of encompassing leviathan. Worse still, as the factual evidence accumulates, the whale becomes more mysterious rather than more familiar. Describing the whale's head, Ishmael becomes concerned with the "problem" of how one can tell where it ends, since there is no neck to separate head and trunk. Speaking of the skin of the whale, he raises the problem of whether the skin is a thin outer coating or the full coat of blubber. Ishmael's perception of the problematic nature of even the seemingly simplest portions of the whale's anatomy could be documented almost endlessly. Let two more crucial examples suffice: the whale's fountain and Moby Dick's whiteness.

Ishmael begins the chapter on "The Fountain", as is his wont, by converting an apparently simple phenomenon into a mystery and a metaphysical problem: "That for six thousand years – and no one knows how many millions of ages before – the great whales should have been spouting all over the sea, and sprinkling and mistifying the gardens of the deep, . . . and yet, that down to this blessed minute . . ., it should still remain a problem, whether these spoutings are, after all, really water, or nothing but vapor – this is surely a noteworthy thing" (pp. 288-89).

Ishmael then launches a lengthy discussion on human and cetological respiration, and the relationship between the latter and the whale's breathing and its spout. From it all, he finally concludes, "But why pester one with all this reasoning on the subject? Speak out! You have seen him spout; then declare what the spout is; can you not tell water from air? My dear sir, in this world it is not so easy to settle these plain things. I have ever found your plain things the knottiest of all. And as for this whale spout, you might almost stand in it, and yet be undecided as to what it is precisely" (p. 291). So after all his involved and painstaking reasoning, he decides that reason, in this case, cannot decide anything. Nor does experience fare any better. For it is possible to experience the spout directly, to stand right in the middle of it, and still not know what it is. He concludes, finally, "The wisest thing the investigator can do then, it seems to me, is to let this deadly spout alone".

There is, then, no way of knowing the whale. If each of his parts is impossible to describe clearly, and if the whale himself is more than the sum of his parts, then how unfathomable must he be in his entirety? And yet, as mysterious as is the ordinary whale, Moby Dick is infinitely more inscrutable and terrifying, and this largely because of his whiteness.

"It was the whiteness of the whale", says Ishmael, "that appalled me". He has no hope of explaining himself, but he will try. As is his custom, he starts rather calmly by enumerating, in a long, periodic sentence, the ways in which "whiteness refiningly enhances beauty", resolving the sentence in a paradox: "yet for all these accumulated associations, with whatever is sweet, and honorable, and sublime, there yet lurks an elusive something in the innermost idea of this hue, which strikes more of panic to the soul than that redness which affrights in blood" (p. 158).

Whiteness, a simple conceit: and yet, by the time Ishmael has finished piling up what seems to be almost an infinitude of concessive clauses, the reader begins to feel the terror that Ishmael finds in it. But whiteness, and color in general, it should be added, gave Locke trouble, too. He could not quite convince himself of its objective existence, and therefore categorized it as a secondary quality, as opposed to such primary qualities as "extension, figure, number, and motion of bodies".[24] These secondary qualities "are in truth nothing in the objects themselves but powers to produce various sensations in us . . .".[25] Moreover, the "ideas produced in us by these secondary qualities have no resemblance of them at all. There is nothing like our ideas existing in the bodies themselves. They are, in the bodies we denominate from them, only a power to produce those sensations in us; and what is sweet, blue, or warm in idea, is but the certain bulk, figure, and motion of the insensible parts in the bodies themselves, which we call so".[26]

For Locke, then, it is impossible to conceive of color without first conceiving of a substance in which it inheres. In itself it has no reality, no existence. But the very thing that so terrifies Ishmael is that he *can* conceive of the existence of color, specifically of whiteness, without substance. And this is precisely what he does. It becomes the whiteness that invests substance with reality rather than the other way round, as Locke would have it. The "elusive something" that terrifies is in the whiteness itself. And "this elusive quality it is, which causes the thought of whiteness, when divorced from more kindly associations, and coupled with any object terrible in itself, to heighten that terror to the furthest bounds. Witness the white bear of the poles, and the white shark of the tropics; what but their smooth, flaky whiteness makes them the transcendent horrors they are?" (p. 158). What, indeed? And again, Ishmael proceeds to pile up instance after instance, this time heaping horror on horror: the "albatross", "the White Steed of the Prairies", the "Albino", the "White Squall", and so on. He climaxes this series with a terrifying reference to what seems to be Jung's racial unconscious: "Nor, in some things, does the common hereditary experience of all mankind fail to bear witness to the supernaturalism of this hue. It cannot well be doubted, that the one visible quality in the aspect of the dead which most appals the gazer, is the marble pallor lingering there;

---

[24] John Locke, *An Essay Concerning Human Understanding*, ed. A. S. Pringle-Pattison (Oxford, 1950), Bk. II, Chap. 8, Par. 12.
[25] II: 8, 14.
[26] II: 8, 14.

as if indeed that pallor were as much like the badge of consterna-
tion in the other world, as of mortal trepidation here". And he
concludes this section by affirming, "Therefore, in his other
moods, symbolize whatever grand or gracious thing he will by
whiteness, no man can deny that in its profoundest idealized
significance it calls up a peculiar apparition to the soul" (p. 160).

In the next section, Ishmael takes another approach. He tries
to account for the terrifying quality of whiteness by considering
instances in which whiteness, though divorced from any directly
terrifying associations, is terrifying still, adding that "without
imagination no man can follow another into these halls". Again
the evidence is poured on: "Whitsuntide", "a White Friar or a
White Nun", "the White Tower of London", "the White Moun-
tains of New Hampshire", "the White Sea", "the tall, pale man of
Hartz forests" – all these, according to Ishmael, terrify by their
very whiteness rather than by any "primary quality". But at this
point he is drawn up short by a question. Is he merely suffering
from an unfounded hypochondria? He answers with another
question. What terrifies a young colt in Vermont when he hears
the rustle of a buffalo robe behind him? It is not, says Ishmael,
"anything associated with the experience of former perils". It is
something more basic still, "the instinct of the knowledge of the
demonism in the world". And the same instinct is what inspires
Ishmael's terror, but in Ishmael's case, the instinct is awakened
not by the shaking of a buffalo robe, but by whiteness. And yet,
after all the "evidence" he has given of the terror inherent in
whiteness, he is willing to concede that the terror may exist not
externally, but only in Ishmael himself. "Though neither knows
where lie the nameless things of which the mystic sign gives forth
such hints; yet with me, as with the colt; somewhere those things
must exist".

Still, Ishmael finds, the spell of whiteness with its "appeal to
the soul" and its ability to symbolize both what is spiritual and
what is appalling, is unsolved. Perhaps this stems from its "in-
definiteness", which "shadows forth the heartless voids and im-
mensities of the universe". Or perhaps it is the sheer ambiguity,
since white is both the absence of color and the "concrete of all

colors". Or perhaps, Ishmael concludes, its power stems from the very theory of the "natural philosophers" themselves.

> When we consider that . . . all other earthly hues . . . are but subtile deceits, not actually inherent in substances, but only laid on from without; so that all deified Nature absolutely paints like the harlot, whose allurements cover nothing but the charnel house within; and when we proceed further, and consider that the mystical cosmetic which produces every one of her hues, the great principle of light, for ever remains white or colorless in itself, and if operating without medium upon matter, would touch all objects, even tulips and roses, with its own blank tinge – pondering all this, the palsied universe lies before us a leper. . . (p. 163)

Ishmael takes the definition of secondary qualities, which Locke had intended to be perfectly lucid, and in his usual fashion converts it into a source of inscrutable mystery. But he does not criticize Locke as Berkeley and Hume did, by questioning his logic in some instances, and pushing it to extremes in others. What he does, instead, is to accept Locke's fully accessible universe as given, and invest it with a horror and mystery that is implicit in it, and yet that it would have appalled Locke to imagine. For Locke, the category of secondary qualities was a source of clarification. It distinguished tangible substance from its intangible concomitants, such as odor, taste, color, sound. But what impresses Ishmael in contemplating this category is that it posits the paradox of non-existent existence, that which both exists and does not. But in this inscrutable universe, the greatest of mysteries remains the White Whale. Ishmael is most appalled by his whiteness. But there are those who dread more than any other quality his seeming ubiquity, and still others who suspect and fear his immortality.

2.

What I should like to do at this juncture is to dwell somewhat on this immortality, to call attention to the way in which Melville uses word play and his own unsystematically acquired learning to create this inscrutable and immortal "symbolic" side of the White

Whale. For if Ishmael is the dramatized presentation of the democrat as Man Thinking, Melville himself is the most brilliant American manifestation of the writer-democrat as Man Naming and Man Creating.[27]

In *The Philosophy of Literary Form*, Kenneth Burke discusses the use of the literary pun as a means of perpetrating a "concealed offence". With characteristic insight, he describes the use of *ablaut* as a way of articulating "unutterable words". Burke gives as illustrative material a passage from Coleridge's *Table Talk*, where Coleridge "... says that the consonants are 'the framework of the word,' and cites an example of a simple shorthand, understandable without vowels: 'Gd crtd th hvn nd th rth'".[28]

Continuing his discussion, Burke asserts that the concealed offense may mask "... two kinds of 'unutterable,' the unutterably good as well as the unutterably bad. ... The name of Jehovah was 'unspeakable,' for it represented the Almighty Power. In Greek it was called the 'Tetragrammaton,' which by a cunning, punning accident means 'four-letter word'".[29] And finally, Burke puts the intriguing and inevitable question: "As there are cases where we, in roundabout ways, pronounce the unutterable 'four-letter words,' might there not be corresponding cases where we, in roundabout ways, pronounce the unutterable 'Tetragrammaton'?"[30]

---

[27] Leo Spitzer writes that "... Spain ... gave us a narrative which is a monument to the narrator qua narrator, qua artist. For let us not be mistaken: the real protagonist of this novel is not Quijote, with his continual misrepresentation of reality, or Sancho with his skeptical half-endorsement of quixotism – and surely not any of the central figures of the illusionistic by-stories: the hero is Cervantes, the artist himself, who combines a critical and illusionistic art according to his free will. From the moment we open the book to the moment we put it down, we are given to understand that an almighty overlord is directing us, who leads us where he pleases". And in an elucidating footnote, Spitzer describes Cervantes as the founder of "that genre of 'subjective story-telling' which, before him, is found at its incipient stage with Boccaccio and which, later, was to inspire Goethe, ... Laurence Sterne, Fielding, Melville ('Call me Ishmael')". "Perspectivism in 'Don Quijote'", pp. 69, 83.

[28] New York, 1957, pp. 44-51.

[29] Pages 46, 47.

[30] Page 48.

What I would like to suggest here is that Yojo, the name of Queequeg's little idol-god in *Moby-Dick*, is exactly this kind of "good" pun on the Hebrew יהוה (YHWH) – a name so powerful that the third Commandment expressly forbids pronouncing it in vain, and which ultimately was transliterated into the English Jehovah, which is generally taken as the personal name of the God of Israel. By a kind of inversion of Coleridge's procedure, Melville substitutes for the consonant H the vowel O.[31]

Luther Mansfield and Howard P. Vincent, in their indispensable notes to the Hendricks House edition of *Moby-Dick*, assert – undoubtedly quite correctly – that Melville "was no Hebrew scholar",[32] but this constitutes no objection, for the sources from which Melville might have learned about both the Hebrew Tetragrammaton itself and its significance are numerous. For example, the 1848 edition of Noah Webster's *An American Dictionary* defined Jehovah as "The Scripture name of the Supreme Being, Heb. יהוה ". Perhaps a likelier source was John Kitto's *Cyclopedia of Biblical Literature*, which gives for Jehovah: " יְהֹוָה , or rather perhaps Jahveh יַהְוֶה , ... the name by which God was pleased to make himself known, under

---

[31] This kind of pun was not a new departure for Melville. Dorothee Metlitsky Finkelstein, *Melville's Orienda* (New Haven and London, 1961), while discussing Melville's use of Islamic names for purposes of creating characters and symbols, states that "Melville's interest in the meaning of words also shows itself in his coinages from the Hebrew .... The name of the 'sacred lake' Yammo in *Mardi* is clearly a derivation from the Hebrew word for 'sea' or 'lake', i.e. 'yam'". Page 222. Cf. Lawrance Thompson, *Melville's Quarrel with God* (Princeton, New Jersey, 1952), p. 187: "The 'Etymology' of the word 'Whale' which Melville presents on a preliminary page becomes much more entertaining when the whale-God interchange is carried over. Some Biblical commentaries, even some Bibles, carry a similar page which summarizes the etymology of the word 'God', and gives the form as it occurs in different languages, starting always with the Hebrew Tetragrammaton JHVH. Melville's play-on-words Tetragrammaton, in his etymology, is HVAL, and the initial passage which provides a brief commentary from Hakluyt would more pertinently apply to JHVH: 'While you take in hand to school others, and to teach them by what name a whale-fish is to be called in our tongue, leaving out, through ignorance, the letter H, which almost alone maketh up the significance of the word, you deliver that which is not true".
[32] New York, 1952, p. 579.

the covenant to the ancient Hebrews . . .". Moreover, in his article on "God", Kitto is careful to emphasize the distinction between the two most common names of God, *Jehovah* and *Elohim*, calling the latter "the abstract expression for absolute Deity", while citing, in reference to the former the theory of "Dr. Havernick, [who] . . . proposes the reading יַהְוֶה *Jahveh* instead of Jehovah, meaning 'the Existing One . . .'".[33]

One of the most impressive discussions of the Tetragrammaton that Melville might have known, however, occurs in John Gill's *Exposition of the Old Testament*. In his commentary on Genesis 2:4, Gill writes of the first appearance of the Tetragrammaton:

Here another name is added to God, his name *Jehovah*, expressive of his being and perfections, particularly his eternity and immutability, being the everlasting and unchangeable *I am*, which is, and was and is to come: this name, according to the Jews, is not to be pronounced, and therefore they put the points of *Adonai*, directing it so to be read; and these two names *Jehovah Elohim* or *Adonai* and *Elohim*, with them make the full and perfect name of God, and which they observe is here very pertinently given him, upon the perfection and completion of his works.[34]

Given both the information readily available to Melville and his interest in theological and Biblical matters, it does not seem implausible that he would conceive the name Yojo as a pun on *YHWH*. And the pun goes beyond the sacred letters themselves, involving not only the *word* that indicates God's identity but also the identity itself as it is revealed in the Divine Name. That identity insofar as the Divine Name reflects it, is, as Melville could have discovered in Gill's commentaries, pure Being. In explicating the "I am that I am" of Exodus 3:14, Gill expounds the full significance of the unutterable name:

And God said unto Moses, I am that I am, &c./ This signifies the real being of God, his self-existence, and that he is the being of

33 New York, 1846.
34 Although Gill seems to offer the most stimulating line of investigation, there were other similar commentaries accessible to Melville, such as Patrick, Lowth, Arnald, Whitby, and Lowman, *A Critical Commentary and Paraphrase on the Old and New Testament and the Apocrypha*, 4 Vols. (Philadelphia and New York, 1846).

beings; as also it denotes his eternity and immutability, and his constancy and faithfulness in fulfilling his promises, for it includes all time, past, present and to come; and the sense is, not only I am what I am at present, but I am what I have been, and I am what I shall be, and shall be what I am .... The words may be rendered, *I shall be what I shall be*, the incarnate God, God manifest in the flesh; *thus shalt thou say unto the children of Israel, I am hath sent me unto you*; or as the *Targum* of Jonathan has it, "I am he that is, and that shall 'be'": This is the name of *Ehjeh*, or *Jehovah, Moses* is empowered to make use of, and declare, as the name of the Great God by whom he was sent. . .

The *Ehje*, or *I am*, too, may account for the medial "j" in Yojo.

Yojo, however, is bodied forth as the exact opposite of *YHWH*. He is, like *YHWH*, a personal god, but so personal that his stature is diminished to the point of absurdity. This is immediately obvious in Ishmael's initial representation of Yojo. As Ishmael secretly watches from under the counterpane, Queequeg produces from the pocket of his "heavy grego, or wrapall, or dreadnaught, which he had previously hung on a chair, . . . a curious little deformed image with a hunch on its back, and exactly the color of a three day's old Congo baby". Yojo's absurdity seems to be further underlined by the "pagan" [35] ceremonies which ensue. Queequeg "sets up the little hunchbacked image, like a tenpin, between the andirons", in the empty but sooty fireplace, which in Ishmael's view, makes "a very appropriate little shrine or Chapel . . ." (p. 38).

Here we have a reversal of the process undergone by the whale. Whereas the whale eventually assumes majestic and even divine proportions, the awesome four-letter name is mock-heroically attached to a comic idol. It is only by examining this counter-process of the elevation of the whale as it resonates against the comic diminution of the Tetragrammaton that the full richness of Melville's word-play can be discovered. Although the Biblical and mythological sources have been studied meticulously and are now taken as a matter of course, there remains as yet no full scale

---

[35] For an analysis of the incongruities in Queequeg's observance – i.e., the mixture of Christian, Moslem, Pagan rites – see James Baird, *Ishmael: A Study of the Symbolic Mode in Primitivism* (New York, 1960), pp. 236-38.

attempt to isolate and analyze Melville's exploitation of the verbal intricacies of the Biblical Leviathan imagery.

This Leviathan imagery is first introduced in the "Etymology" and "Extracts" which precede the beginning of the narrative proper. In the "Etymology", the Hebrew word that Ishmael gives for whale is תָן (*tan*). Mansfield-Vincent annotates this etymological entry as follows:

The most accurate Hebrew word for whale was used in Genesis i, 21 and Job vii, 12, which is transcribed in the Roman alphabet as *tannin*. What Melville apparently wrote was תָן (*tan*), the hypothetical singular, which did not occur in the Old Testament, of the plural noun תַנִּים (*tannim*), used in Ezekiel xxix, 3 and xxxii, 2 – the latter verse quoted by Melville [in the chapter, 'The Honor and Glory of Whaling'].... The best scholarship of Melville's day, however, translated this hypothetical singular as 'jackal.' But the King James version rendered both plurals in Ezekiel as 'whale' .... Melville was no Hebrew scholar, but the nature of this error ... suggests that with the aid perhaps of some scholarly friend he was diligently attempting to get the most inclusive Hebrew term, one that would evoke for him *all* of the significant Biblical allusions to the whale.[36]

The Mansfield-Vincent note is illuminating, but there seems to be no need to invoke a "scholarly friend". A more tangible source for the *tan* is Kitto, who writes, in his "Whale" article: "(תָן *than*, and תַנִּין *thannin*; Sept. and Matt. xii. 40 Κητος), occurs in several places of the Old Testament, and once in the New Testament." The words *tannin, tanninim,* and *tannim* were in Melville's day, and remain to the present, problematic, being rendered variously as "dragon", "dragons", "whale", "whales", "croco-

---

[36] Page 579. H. Bruce Franklin, *The Wake of the Gods: Melville's Mythology* (Stanford, Cal., 1963), argues strenuously, and somewhat ingeniously, it seems to me, that Melville thought of the Leviathan myth as exclusively "an Egyptian, not a Hebrew, conception", even though he must grant that Melville found the Leviathan first in the Biblical texts (pp. 70, 71 ff.). Franklin's attempt to restrict Melville to one myth violates Melville's own method of mythmaking, which was syncretic rather than exclusivist. The method Franklin pursues ends only in limiting the profundity and universality of Melville's imaginative reconstructions of primordial archetypes. The materials I am about to deal with, the *tan-lvytn-Rahab-tehom* (watery chaos of Genesis 1:2) imagery of the Old Testament, are lucidly discussed in relation to Babylonian mythology by Alexander Heidl, *The Babylonian Genesis* (Chicago, 1963), pp. 98-116.

dile". Recent translations generally prefer vaguer terms, such as "sea monsters", "huge sea creatures", "sea animals", a tendency already afoot in early nineteenth-century Biblical scholarship, as Melville could easily have learned from Kitto's "Whale" article:

In the passages where scales and feet are mentioned as belonging to *than*, commentators have shown that the crocodile is intended, which then is synonymous with leviathan; and they have endeavoured also to demonstrate, where *thannin* draw the dugs to suckle their young, that seals are meant, although cetacea nourish theirs in a similar manner. It may be doubted whether, in most of the cases, the poetical diction points absolutely to any specific animal, particularly as there is more force and grandeur in a generalized and collective image of the huge monsters of the deep, not inappropriately so called, than in the restriction to any one species, since all are in Gen. i, 26 made collectively subservient to the supremacy of man.

The key to Melville's method of using Leviathan imagery to invest Moby Dick with "symbolic significance" lies in the first five "Extracts", where Melville develops the etymological and philological problems raised by the Biblical word clusters growing out of what he apparently conceived to be the root *tan*. In the first "Extract" (Gen. 1:21), "And God created great whales", the Authorized Version translates the Hebrew phrase *h'tanninim h'gdolim* as "great whales". In the second "Extract" (Job 41:31), "Leviathan maketh a path to shine after him; One would think the deep to be hoary", the terminology shifts from the whales (*tanninim*) of Genesis to Leviathan (a transliteration of the Hebrew *lvytan*). But though whale and leviathan had been linked to each other, they were not, in lexicographical practice, considered synonymous.

A clear link, however, is to be found in Gill's *Exposition*. He comments on Genesis 1:21 "*And God created great whales, &c.*] Which the Targum of Jonathan and Jarchi [sic] interpret of the Leviathan and its mate, concerning which the Jews have many fabulous things; Large fishes are undoubtedly meant, and the whale being of the largest sort, the word is so rendered".[37] Gill

---

[37] Gill gives as one of the sources of his commentary the Talmudic text, T. Bab Bava Bathra, fol. 74:2. This text contains the "fabulous things" about leviathan that Gill mentions. Most striking is the similarity between Gill's

makes this connection between *tannim* ("whales" in A.V.) and *lvytan* (Leviathan) even firmer in the commentaries he offers in explication of the first verse of the forty-first chapter of Job:

Canst thou draw out leviathan with an hook? &c.] That is, draw it out of the sea or river as anglers draw out smaller fishes with a line or hook? The question suggests it cannot be done; whether by the

---

commentary on this verse (Genesis 1:21) and that of the great rabbinical commentator, Rashi, who defines *h'tanninim h'gdolim* as follows: " – the large fishes that are in the sea; and according to the statement of the Agada (B. Bath 74b) it means here the Leviathan and its consort which He created male and female. He, however, killed the female and preserved it in salt for the benefit of the righteous in the time to come, for had they been permitted to be fruitful and to multiply the world could not have endured because of them". (*Pentateuch with Targum Onkelos, Haphtaroth, and Rashi's Commentary*, trans. M. Rosenbaum and A. M. Silbermann [New York], I, 5-6.) One is tempted, at this point, to speculate on the possibility of Melville's having known directly either Rashi's commentary or the Talmudic tale itself. Stubb's midnight whale-steak banquet, for example, eaten in the company of "thousands on thousands of sharks, swarming round the dead leviathan [not whale], [who] feasted on its fatness", seems to be a diabolic reversal of the banquet of the righteous referred to in Rashi (and Gill). Also, the "salting away" of lvytan is recalled when the cannibalistic Stubb tells the black cook to "be sure you stand by to get the tips of his fins; have them put in pickle" (p. 238).

Conceivably, Melville could have gotten at the Talmudic tale through John Dove's *The Importance of Rabbinical Learning* (London, 1746). Attacking Gill for his acceptance of rabbinical sources, Dove attempts to discredit these sources by giving in translation the "fabulous things about Leviathan and its mate" that Gill found in Bava Bathra 74:2: "A great Feast is to be made *here*; and not in Heaven ... The Provisions at this Feast are to be the greatest Beasts, Birds, and Fishes God ever made; their Wine only what grew in Paradise; which has been, and will be kept in Adam's Cellar till the Feast begins; then the great stalled Ox, Behemoth, Job xl:10. Ps. v. 10. will be brought forth. This is he that feedeth on a thousand Hills, and to prevent his want of Food, what he eats in the Day, grows in the Night. The huge Leviathan is also to be part of the Repast; and least the World should be overrun with these Monsters, God has gelded the Male Leviathan, and killed the Female, and preserves her in Pickle, for the Entertainment of the righteous in the Days of Messiah, IS. xxvii ... Before the Feast begins, Behemoth and Leviathan shall play together, to divert the Assembly, Job xl. 15. Psalm. civ. 6, when they have wearied themselves, Messiah with his Sword shall kill them both: Now followeth the Feast, and then the Marriage of Messiah, Psal. xlv. 10". Lowth's commentary on Gen. 1:21 is also of interest. He writes, in part, "The Hebrew word tanim [sic], which we translate whales, comprehends several sorts of great fishes ...".

leviathan is meant the whale, which was the most generally received notion; or the crocodile as *Bochart*, who has been followed by many; or the *orca* a large fish of the whale kind with many teeth, as *Hassaeus*, it is not easy to say. *Leviathan* is a compound word of *than*, the first syllable of *thannin*, rendered either a whale, or a dragon, or a serpent and of *levi*, which signifies conjunction, from the close joining of its scales, v. 15, 16, 17. The patriarch *Levi* had his name from the same word; see Gen. xxix 34, and the name bids fairest for the crocodile, which is called *thannin*, Ezek. xxix, 3, 4, and xxxii. 2. Could the crocodile be established as the leviathan, and the behemoth as the riverhorse, the transition from the one to the other would appear very easy.

Whatever the validity of Gill's exegesis in the light of modern philological and Biblical scholarship, what is important here is that his commentary could have served as a stimulus to Melville's receptive imagination. Certainly, the commentary cited could have provided Melville, if not with the idea itself, at least with powerful scholarly and theological support for the fusion that he was ultimately to make between the natural historical whale and the mythological-historical Leviathan. The fusion is already several ways implicit in the very word as Gill reconstructs it. First, there is the suggestion that Leviathan, as a compound of *levi* plus *than*, contains within itself the root of *h'tanninim h'gdolim*, the "great whales" of Gen. 1:21. In addition, Gill's commentaries on Genesis 1 and Job 41 not only link those chapters, they also establish a connection between these chapters and the next three Biblical quotations that appear in Melville's "Extracts".

In the third "Extract" (Jonah 1:17) "Now the Lord had prepared a great fish to swallow up Jonah", the terminology shifts again, this time from the *lvytan* of Job to the דג גדול *dag gadol* of Jonah, suggesting a connection that is, at once, more intangible and more problematic than the connection between *tanninim* and *lvytan*.

The precise identity of the "great fish" had already inspired a great deal of learned comment by the time Melville wrote *Moby-Dick*, much of it being discussed by Kitto in his article on "Jonah". He concludes, there, that ". . . the species of marine animal is not defined, and the Greek is often used to specify, not the genus whale, but any large fish or sea-monster". In denying the necessity for taking the *dag gadol* "great fish" as a whale, Kitto nonetheless implies a connection between the *dag* and the *"tan"*, refering to the former as a "sea-Monster", and to the latter as "huge monsters of the deep". Again, however, it is Gill who sets the relationship explicitly when he says that *h'tanninim h'gdolim* of Genesis 1:21 are "Large fishes".[38]

Melville's fourth "Extract" (Psalms 104:26), "There go the ships; there is that Leviathan whom thou hast made to play therein", shifts the terminology back to *lvytan*. Gill comments on this verse, "The *Targum* adds, 'for the righteous at the feast of the house of his habitation.'" Nor is this all, for Gill adds a cross reference to Job 41, the same chapter that Melville had drawn on for his second "Extract":

of this creature there is an account in Job xli. Some take it to be the crocodile, which is both a sea and river-fish; the *Septuagint, Vulgate Latin, Ethiopic*, and *Arabic* versions, and so Apollinarius, call it, the dragon; it is more generally thought to be the whale; *Aben Ezra* says it is the name of every great fish; it is a sportive creature, tumbles about in the great sea, and plays with the waters of it, which it tosses up in great quantities; and with the fishes of the sea, which it devours at pleasure; and laughs at the shaking of the spear; and which mariners throw out their empty casks to play with, when near them, and they in danger by it; see *Job* xli 5, 29.

Gill's cross reference, then, not only connects the *lvytan* of Psalms with the *lvytan* of Job, but also connects both of them to the crocodile, the whale, and the dragon, all part of the *"tan"* complex, and, finally, all of these to the "great fish", the *dag gadol* of Jonah.

But there remains still one more crucial Biblical verse in which *"tan"* and *"lvytan"* mingle directly, and that is Isaiah 27:1, which

---

[38]   The connection is even more striking in Rashi, for he identifies *h'tanninim h'gdolim* as *daggim gdolim*, the plural form of the phrase that appears in Jonah. Melville himself seems to echo Rashi jokingly by reversing the philological problem in Jonah: he has Ishmael say, in the "Cetology" chapter, "Be it known that, waiving all argument, I take the good old fashioned ground that the whale is a fish, and call upon holy Jonah to back me" (p. 118).

turns up, not unexpectedly, as Melville's fifth "Extract", "In that day, the Lord with his sore, and great, and strong sword, shall punish Leviathan the piercing serpent, even Leviathan that crooked serpent; and he shall slay the dragon that is in the sea". Within the context of Biblical commentary the verse is a most fitting coda to the first four "Extracts", drawing together not only the already problematic *tannin* and *lvytan*, but also two other Hebrew words: *nachash*, the serpent who first appears in the third chapter of Genesis, and who tempts man to sin; and, as William G. Braude has pointed out, *pequod*, the Hebrew word for punish.[39] Substituting the key Hebrew words, the verse then reads, "In that day *YHWH* with his sore, and great, and strong sword shall *pequod lvytan* the piercing *nachash*, even *lvytan* the crooked *nachash*; and he shall slay *h'tannin asher b'yam*". In both instances in which it is named in this verse, serpent stands as an appositive used to elaborate the nature of Leviathan, while the last clause seems to imply that the *tannin* dragon-whale in the sea is *lvytan-nachash* Leviathan-serpent, thus setting up all four as representative of evil which will eventually be punished (*pequod*) by Yahweh.

Although the verse itself is not entirely clear, it seems likely that Melville would have preferred a reading that took the two Leviathans and the dragon as a single being. Support for such a reading could have been found in Gill's commentary on Psalms 104:26 ("Extract" four), where he writes that Leviathan ". . . is generally reckoned by the ancients a figure of Satan, it being king over all the children of pride, *Job* xli. 34, as he is the prince of the power of the air, and god of this world; who has been playing

---

[39] *Explicator*, XXI (November, 1962): "The root of the word for 'punish' " writes Rabbi Braude, "is represented in the Hebrew by *Pequod* – so voweled . . . . But why does not Melville say plainly that Pequod has an underlying Hebrew meaning? The answer may lie in the structure of the novel. Even as Ahab conceals from the owners the presence of Fedallah and his companions, and as he conceals from the crew the main purpose of the trip, so also Melville conceals from his readers the secret and blasphemous meaning of the Pequod [and of Yojo?] that they may not be shocked by the wickedness of the venture". I would like to express my thanks here to Rabbi Braude for generously permitting me to see a longer manuscript on *Moby-Dick*.

his tricks in it from the beginning of it, not only deceiving our first parents, but all the nations of the world . . .". Having linked leviathan-Satan-serpent, Gill then gives a cross reference to Revelation 13:1, 4, the latter reading: "And they worshipped the dragon which gave power unto the beast: and they worshipped the beast, saying who is like unto the beast? Who is able to make war with him?"

An instance of the way in which Melville pounces on the mysterious Biblical image cluster and makes it function in his own art occurs in the chapter which establishes "The Honor and Glory of Whaling". Ishmael begins the chapter in typically playful fashion by associating the story of Perseus and Andromeda with the story of Jonah, linking both events, somewhat spuriously, if not unjustifiably, with the whale. He claims that ". . . as Leviathan was in the very act of carrying [Andromeda] off, Perseus, the prince of whale men, intrepidly advancing, harpooned the monster, and delivered and married the maid". He then goes on to give the reader the additional information that ". . . in the ancient Joppa, now Jaffa, on the Syrian coast, in one of the Pagan temples, there stood for many ages the vast skeleton of a whale, which the city's legends and all the inhabitants asserted to be the identical bones of the monster Perseus slew. . . . What seems most singular and suggestively important in this story, is that: it was from Joppa that Jonah set sail" (p. 283).[40]

_____

[40] Mansfield-Vincent note that the connection between Peresus and Jonah is made in three of the established Melville sources: "Sir Thomas Browne . . . noted in 'Extracts from Common Place Books' in the edition of Simon Wilkin (1836), Vol. 3, p. 362: "The story of Jonah might afford the hint unto that of Andromeda, and the sea monster that should have devoured her; The scene being laid at Joppa by the fabulists . . .' [Pierre] Bayle cited authorities who believed 'that Jonah's adventure laid a foundation for the poetical accounts concerning Andromeda's being exposed to the fury of a sea monster, which happened at Joppa' ". But the editors conclude that "Melville was closer to Kitto's 'Whale' article: 'Joppa: now Jaffa, the very place whence Jonah set sail, displayed for ages in one of its pagan temples huge bones of a species of whale, which the legends of the place pretended were those of the dragon monster slain by Perseus, as represented in the Arkite mythus of that hero and Andromeda: And which remained in that spot till the conquering Romans carried them in triumph to the great city' " (pp. 778-779). Melville's having found these connections elsewhere, how-

Having made these tenuous connections, Ishmael goes on to make one that is even more unlikely from a strictly empirical point of view:

Akin to the adventure of Perseus and Andromeda – indeed, by some supposed to be indirectly derived from it – is that famous story of St. George and the Dragon; which dragon I maintain to have been a whale; for in many old chronicles whales and dragons are strangely jumbled together, and often stand for each other. 'Thou art as a lion of the waters, and as a dragon of the sea,' said Ezekiel; hereby, plainly meaning a whale; in truth, some versions of the Bible use that word itself. Besides it would much abstract from the glory of the exploit had St. George but encountered a crawling reptile of the land, instead of doing battle with the great monster of the deep. Any man can kill a snake, but only a Perseus, a St. George, a Coffin, have the heart in them to march boldly up to a whale. (pp. 283-284)

"Melville", writes James Baird, "seems to have been only darkly aware of what he had touched in *Moby-Dick* when he spoke of 'whales and dragons strangely jumbled together.' At that moment when Melville sounds to the sea floor with Vishnu incarnate in *Moby-Dick*, he reaches the domain of the old sea-dragon: and there he feels the antiquity of his God".[41]

Without denying the basic validity of Baird's thesis, that is, that Melville "reaches the domain of the old sea-dragon and feels the antiquity of his God", one must, I think, differ with him on the extent to which Melville was aware of what he was doing. For though Melville's knowledge may be largely intuitive, he reaches the depths of intuition through his insights into the verbal structure of the traditional lore he inherited as a Christian. What Melville evidently has in mind, then, when he has Ishmael complain that "in many old chronicles whales and dragons are strangely jumbled together, and often stand for each other", is that the word translated as "dragon" in Isaiah 27:1 (*h'tannin*) is the singular of the word translated as "whales" in Genesis 1:21.

ever, does not invalidate the contention that in kneading these myths he was involved in a process of personal discovery. What is perhaps most noteworthy in Melville's manipulation of his particular sources here is the fact that all three accounts cited by Mansfield-Vincent speak of Andromeda as threatened by a "sea monster", whereas Melville converts the threatening creature into "Leviathan". This conversion can hardly be accidental.

41   Baird, p. 332.

Similarly, the word translated as "dragon" in Ezekiel 29:3 (*h'tannim*) is translated as "whale" in Ezekiel 32:2 (all references here to the King James Bible). Moreover, dragon-whale is also being commingled with Leviathan, for in the previous paragraph, Ishmael has asserted that ". . . as Leviathan was in the very act of carrying Andromeda off, Perseus, the prince of whale men, harpooned the monster". Finally, all of these crucial terms are stewed into a verbal chowder by the diction of the entire paragraph which, though relatively short, bristles with charged words. Dragon appears four times, whale four, snake once, monster-of-the-deep once, and reptile once. Considering superficial connections only, dragon is identified with whale on three occasions; dragon with reptile once; dragon with monster-of-the-deep once; dragon with snake once, and snake with whale once: all of these words but "snake" belong to the *tannin-lvytan* nexus of Biblical words, and "snake" is connected to the entire grouping by Isaiah 27:1.

But to give the screw one turn more, Ishmael adds some jumbling of his own. In the King James Bible, the portion of Ezekiel 32:2 that Ishmael ostensibly quotes in the paragraph reads, "Thou art like a young lion of the nations, and thou art as a *whale* in the seas". Ishmael's version reads, "Thou art as a lion of the *waters*, and as a *dragon* of the sea", which is actually closer to the translation in the Douay Bible: "Thou art like a young lion among the nations, and as a *dragon in* the sea". In having Ishmael say that Ezekiel "hereby plainly [means] a whale", and that "some versions of the Bible use that word itself", Melville shows his awareness of the linguistic problems he has conjured.

To recapitulate, the Leviathan imagery centers around three vaguely related Biblical word complexes which occur in five Biblical texts, among others,[42] that Melville uses in the "Extracts" preceding the whaling narrative. The *tan* complex indicates either natural or supernatural creatures ranging from whales to croco-

---

[42]   There are eleven other passages in which variants of *tannin* appear. In seven of these it is rendered as dragon or dragons, in one as whale (Job 7:12), and in the other three it is, interestingly enough, translated as serpent (Ex. 7:9, 10, 12).

diles to mythical monsters which prefigure Satan and the dragon. The *lvytan* complex also denotes either natural or mythical creatures, and in addition stands as an allegorical representation of Egypt and as possible symbolic foreshadowing or antetype of Satan or the dragon. Finally, the *dag gadol* is a large fish, perhaps natural, perhaps allegorical or mythical, which the Lord uses to bring man round to His own purposes. All three words denote things marine or amphibious, earthly or unearthly, historical or figural, and intertwine with each other in the dense fabric of talmudic literature and rabbinical commentaries.

What Melville's use of these materials suggests is that in writing *Moby-Dick* he did not naively create the symbolic Leviathan out of the naturalistic whale, but that he combined two levels of fiction – the quasi-biographical whaling voyage and the quasi-mythical Leviathan literature which was already traditionally problematic. That is, instead of starting with an "ordinary" whale and elevating it to the symbolic by means of poetic style, Melville started with both the palpable swimming whale and the *tan-lvytan* poetry-legend-allegory-myth, fusing the levels of "reality" in such a way as to re-activate and give renewed viability to the symbolic meanings inherent in the Biblical groupings.

The counterpoint to this fusion is the mock-heroic presentation of the four-letter god. Leviathan's divine antagonist, or, rather, conqueror, appears now, not as Ehjeh-Yahweh, the Creator, the great "I-Am" who brings order out of primeval chaos, but rather in the diminished form of Queequeg's little hunchbacked Congo idol. Set against the omnipresent Leviathan, the pint-sized YHWH may be seen as an attempt – perhaps not fully conscious – on Melville's part to cope with what is now recognized as one of the obsessions of nineteenth-century man, the "disappearance" of God.

For nineteenth- and twentieth-century man, writes J. Hillis Miller, "God has become a *deus absconditus*, hidden somewhere behind the silence of infinite spaces, and our literary symbols can make only the most distant allusions to him . . .".[43] Melville's pun

[43] "The Disappearance of God", *Victorian Studies*, VI (Summer, 1963), 209.

appears to be this kind of distant allusion. But the romantics, Miller continues, "still believe in God, and they find his absence intolerable. At all costs they must attempt to re-establish communication. Romanticism defines the artist as the creator or discoverer of new symbols, symbols which establish a new relation, across the gap between man and God".[44] Melville, seeking to bridge the gap between man and God, does not so much create new symbols as attempt to re-invest old ones with their original primitive potency. He tries to recover a sense both of the ancient power of the old gods and of the mystery of their names – the first in the terrifying omnipresence of Moby Dick as he emerges out of the dark consciousness of the remembering Ishmael, and the second in the pun on the name of the Living God.

In being conjoined with the foreboding, unencompassable, monstrous White Whale, the Leviathan imagery becomes the palpable center of the book, dominating both the action and the atmosphere of Ishmael's narrative. For all the legerdemain in Melville's fusion of whale-Leviathan-dragon-chaos-Satan-serpent, the fused terms are always tangibly present, making a direct impact on the reader. It is as though they are incessantly in the process of being compressed into the one overpowering and inevitable presence that dominates the book, Moby Dick himself.

The pun on YHWH, however, works more quietly. Yojo, like Ishmael and Queequeg, and like the disappearing God, all but vanishes from the narrative once the whaling voyage is underway. Bearing the awesome name, Yojo fails to inspire awe. Consequently, the Leviathan, quintessential embodiment of evil, is opposed only by Ahab, that "ungodly godlike man", a self-styled messiah who, bearing the name of a "wicked king", tries to do the real messiah's work of slaying the male Leviathan and presiding over the feast of the righteous.

In his study of the shifting of names in *Don Quixote*, Leo Spitzer writes that in Cervantes's great novel, "there can be no certainty about the 'unbroken' reality of the events; the only unquestionable truth on which the reader may depend is the will of the artist who chose to break up a multivalent reality into

44   *Ibid.*, p. 211.

different perspectives". "But God", Professor Spitzer continues, "cannot be attracted into the artist's linguistic perspectivism; rather is Cervantes's God placed above the perspectives of language".[45]

In *Moby-Dick*, however, God is not only attracted into the artist's "linguistic perspectivism", but becomes a focal point for it. First, Yahweh, the One God, is divided between the absurd idol who mockingly echoes his name, and the *tan-lvytan*-whale who reflects Yahweh's attributes of mystery, awe, and unlimited Being. Secondly, God is split into a number of subjective responses manifest in a wide range of characters. Finally, the gods themselves appear in the world of linguistic phenomena in almost endless variety. The sense of a fragmented godhead is intensified by the articulation (with varying degrees of seriousness) of the name of almost every god, demigod, demon, and prophet conceived by the religious imagination of man: Brahma, Allah, Jupiter, Prometheus, Typhon, Zoroaster, Moses, Dagon, Perseus, Mohammed, St. George, Ezekiel, among others.

One effect of this fragmentation is that Melville discovers the paradox faced by modern man as he attempts to confront God on a cosmic level, that is, to probe and control the secrets of creation itself: man who "on the one hand ... beholds God in every nook and corner of creation, in the flowering of the plant, in the rushing of the tide, and in the movement of his own muscle, as if God were at hand close to and beside man, engaging him in a friendly dialogue. And yet the very moment man turns his face to God, he finds Him remote, unapproachable, enveloped in transcendence and mystery".[46] On the one side, then, is Queequeg with his personal god, a reduced Tetragrammaton who is literally close at hand, engaging man in a dialogue that is not only friendly but intimate and playful. On the other side is Ahab, who turns his face to a cosmic god only to find him "remote,

---

[45] "Perspectivism in 'Don Quixote' ", pp. 57, 61.
[46] Joseph B. Soloveitchik, "The Lonely Man of Faith", *Tradition*, VII (Summer, 1965), 31. Rabbi Soloveitchik distinguishes between the two sides of man as the Adam of Genesis 1 and the Adam of Genesis 2. The first is characterized by a drive to master the outside world, and the second by the need for "redemption".

unapproachable, enveloped in transcendence and mystery". In between is Ishmael, trying to be reasonable and sane, vacillating between the two ends of the paradox, and above Ishmael is Melville who has broken even the reality of God into different perspectives.

Another effect of this "linguistic perspectivism" from which nothing is exempt is the projection of a "reality" that is constantly in the process of turning into something else. In *Don Quixote*, as Professor Spitzer demonstrates, names are in constant flux, and changes in name are usually accompanied by a change in a character's personality or in the function of an object.[47] In *Moby-Dick,* the names outwardly remain the same, but the substance or identity of the referents is constantly being augmented or diminished. For example: Yojo, as a four-letter god is inevitably in the shadow of Ahab's malignant god, and yet at the same time he also casts shadows back on both Ahab's devil-god and on the Judeo-Christian four-letter god; the physical whale is continually being elevated and transformed into the mythological Leviathan and other mythic monsters, but at the same time it is also being reduced to the featured fish in a fish story.

Moreover, it is this "linguistic perspectivism" in *Moby-Dick* that makes conventional standards of social realism inadequate in interpreting and evaluating Melville's achievement. Such standards assume that the novelist's language is a transparent medium that may sometimes be beautiful in itself, but that is used primarily for the purpose of rendering character or creating a milieu that is a copy of something in the world of Phenomena; consequently, "social" or "manners" critics tend to forget that language itself has a phenomenal reality and that the phenomenon of language is part of the reality of the novel too, and not merely a means for representing another kind of reality outside itself. In *Moby-Dick*, especially, language is too substantial and too resistant to serve only as an invisible device.

Melville's multivalent "reality", then, seems to grow out of a belief in the ultimate potency and generative capacity of language

[47]   Spitzer, pp. 43, 60 *et passim*.

itself. Another of the great commentators on Cervantes, Americo Castro writes that

the ultimate reality of *Don Quixote* cannot be understood if we keep it enclosed within the strict orbit of Western history . . . . To feel books as a living, animate, communicable and inciting reality is a human phenomenon belonging to Oriental tradition, and is related to the belief that the word is content and transmitter of a revelation. The idea of religion revealed through sacred books is Oriental, and not Occidental. From the conjunction of Hebrew concepts with neo-Platonic thought in Philo Judaeus sprang forth the belief in the logos-word as a divinely emanative and creative spirit: 'And the word [logos] was made flesh and dwelt among us.'[48]

The pervasiveness of the Biblical-Hebraic influence in *Moby-Dick* is beyond question. It should not be surprising, then, that in his attempt to re-discover the substance of the old gods in their historical names, Melville happened to find his way back to a "reality" essentially Hebraic and Oriental, a reality in which "words become flesh".

Henry A. Murray expresses his sense of the vitality of the literary allusions in *Moby-Dick* most eloquently in a passage which seems to echo what Professor Castro has said of the "reality" of *Don Quixote*:

To this Columbus of the mind, the great archetypal figures of myth, drama, and epic were not pieces of intellectual Dresden China, heir-looms of a classical education, ornamental bric-a-brac to be put here and there for the pleasure of genteel readers. Many of the more significant constellations were inwardly expressed by Melville, one after the other, as each was given vent to blossom and assert itself. Thus we are offered a spectacle of spiritual development through passionate identification.[49]

For Melville as for Cervantes, words, and especially names, are not ornamental, they are vital and "inciting", and one of the sources of the richness and complexity of Melville's book is a verbal structure in which "the word is content and transmitter of

[48] "Incarnation in 'Don Quixote' ", eds. Angel Flores and M. J. Bernadete, *Cervantes Across the Centuries* (New York, 1947), pp. 160-161.
[49] "In Nomine Diaboli", eds. Tyrus Hillway and Luther Mansfield, *Moby-Dick Centennial Essays* (Dallas, 1953), p. 8.

a revelation". Thus the investigation of words, through puns and etymological jokes, becomes a method of probing into the nature of different levels of reality.

Leviathan, for example, exists as a phenomenon in linguistic and literary history; so much is empirically ascertainable from evidence to be found in Biblical texts. Whether Leviathan existed, however, as a physical phenomenon or merely as a mythological or allegorical creation, or whether he existed as some combination of the three, this remains an unsolved problem, in the twentieth, as well as the nineteenth, century. Moreover, if Leviathan "existed" as a physical phenomenon, there arises the question, what was his shape and form? Here, the linguistic evidence leads in several directions; consequently, a clear picture is impossible. If Leviathan "existed" only as a myth or allegory, then how did the myth or allegory originate, and what does one or the other mean? If Leviathan "existed" as a combination of the three, then in what way are they related to each other? Melville's awareness of these problems seems amply demonstrated by his manipulation of *tan, tannin, tannim, lvytan*. And the consequence of Melville's manipulating is that "reality" becomes a historical, linguistic, literary, sociological, and metaphysical problem in *Moby-Dick*. But Melville's mind would not rest satisfied with only a problematic Leviathan. He had to add a problematic whale.

The whale, too, exists as a linguistic phenomenon. It also exists as a historical phenomenon. (Ishmael quotes Surgeon Beal, A.D. 1839, as saying: "Utter confusion exists among the historians of this animal" [p. 116]). But much more clearly than Leviathan, the biological whale exists as a possible subject of scientific investigation, as is indicated by the chapter on Cetology, where we learn that the whale in his physical being can be subjected to the most meticulous kind of classification, and also that all the classification adds nothing to our usable knowledge. For all its accessibility as an object of sensual perception, the living whale remains unquestionable tangible, but ultimately unknowable. From these two sets of reality problems, Leviathan and whale, Moby Dick takes on his own problematic identity, drawing reality as it were, into the magnetic field of the book from the outside world of historical, mythological, naturalistic, and linguistic phenomena with which his name is associated.

Yojo, on the other hand, must be taken as a nonce word which acquires "reality" cumulatively from its context. Set in a milieu of Biblical names (Ahab, Ishmael, Elijah, Bildad, Peleg), partially concealed Biblical terms (Leviathan, *Pequod*), Biblical quotations, and Biblical diction, "Yojo" gathers "substance" from its surroundings. Originally, the name refers to no "reality" outside of its own existence in the book, resembling, in that respect, the other pagan non-Biblical names, such as Queequeg, Tashtego, Daggoo. Until Melville utters the word it has no existence in either linguistics or literary history. Once uttered, however, and set in context, the name inevitably makes for itself a place both in human consciousness and in the world of linguistic phenomena and literary history – as Queequeg's Congo idol, but also as a "good" pun on the four-letter name of God, that is, as one more "roundabout way" of pronouncing, and thereby making "real", the unutterable Tetragrammaton.

INDEX

Auerbach, Erich, 40, 46, 181, 184

Bage, Robert, 79

Barzun, Jacques, 67-68

Beowulf, 115

Berkeley, George, 199

Bible, 40-43, 61, 116, 117, 118, 120, 181-219 passim

Boccaccio, 21

Brackenridge, Hugh Henry, 47, 50-74, 75, 76, 101, 186; *Modern Chivalry*, 51-74

Bradley, F. H., 33

Brown, Charles Brockden, 47, 75-100, 122, 123, 124; *Arthur Mervyn*, 100; *Carwin the Biloquist*, 100; Journal, 76-77; *Ormond*, 78, 80-82, 92-100; "The Rhapsodist", 75; *Skywalk*, 77-78, 79, 99; *Wieland*, 78, 79-80, 84-92, 94, 96, 99, 100

Browne, Thomas, 43

Buber, Martin, 147-48

Burke, Edmund, 111

Capellanus, Andreas, 128

Cervantes, Miguel de, 34-35, 42, 43, 44, 47n., 51, 52-54, 68, 69, 70, 72, 74, 108, 200n, 214-15, 216, 217

Chase, Richard, 36-39, 40, 44

Chaucer, Geoffrey, 71, 128-29

Cicero, 61

Coleridge, Samuel Taylor, 45-46, 200, 201

Cooper, James Fenimore, 47, 51, 101-122, 123; *The Deerslayer*, 103; *The Prairie*, 106-21; *The Spy*, 101

Defoe, Daniel, 20, 21-25, 26, 30

Dickens, Charles, 39

Dostoevsky, Fyodor, 42, 58-59, 64, 147

Edwards, Jonathan, 136-38, 140

Eliot, T. S., 104, 105, 118

Emerson, Ralph Waldo, 47, 105, 123, 154-55, 161, 170, 192, 193, 194

Fielding, Henry, 25, 27, 29, 30, 39, 50, 51, 54, 68, 69, 72, 83, 108, 129

Forster, E. M., 38

Gill, John, 202-3, 205-10

Godwin, William, 79, 83-84, 87, 90, 91, 94, 99

Hawthorne, Nathaniel, 35-36, 39, 43, 44-45, 46, 47, 77, 102, 122, 123-64, 165, 166, 167, 168, 169, 172, 176, 192; *The Blithedale Romance*, 157-63, 167, 172; "The Custom-House", 44-45; "Ethan Brand", 153; *Fanshawe*, 123; *The House of the Seven Gables*, 44, 151-57, 163, 165, 166, 167, 176; *The Marble Faun*, 163-164, 165, 167; "Rappaccini's Daughter", 153; *The Scarlet Letter*, 39, 124-51, 152, 153, 163, 164, 165

STUDIES IN AMERICAN LITERATURE

16. JOHN D. BRANTLEY: *The Fiction of John Dos Passos.* 1968. 136 pp.   ƒ 23.—

17. GEORGE BRANDON SAUL: *Quintet: Essays on Five American Women Poets.* 1967. 50 pp.   ƒ 11.—

18. CLIFFORD D. EDWARDS: *Conrad Richter's Ohio Trilogy Its Ideas, Themes, and Relationship to Literary Tradition.* 1970. 210 pp.   ƒ 32.—

19. PHYLLIS FRANKLIN: *Show Thyself a Man: A Comparison of Benjamin Franklin and Cotton Mather.* 1969. 93 pp.   ƒ 21.—

20. JOSEPH J. WALDMEIR: *American Novels of the Second World War.* 2nd Printing. 1971. 180 pp.   ƒ 21.—

21. L. HUGH MOORE, JR.: *Robert Penn Warren and History: 'The Big Myth We Live'.* 1970. 201 pp.   ƒ 35.—

22. JONAS SPATZ: *Hollywood in Fiction: Some versions of the American Myth.* 1969. 148 pp.   ƒ 28.—

23. STEPHEN A. BLACK: *James Thurber: His Masquerades: A Critical Study.* 1969. 128 pp.   ƒ 24.—

24. MARION K. RICHARDS: *Ellen Glasgow's Development as a Novelist.* 1971. 203 pp.   ƒ 32.—

26. G. A. M. JANSSENS: *The American Literary Review: A Critical History, 1920-1950.* 1968. 341 pp.   ƒ 38.—

27. JOSEPH GALLEGLY: *From Alamo Plaza to Jack Harris's Saloon: O. Henry and the Southwest He Knew.* 1970. 213 pp.   ƒ 25.—

MOUTON • PUBLISHERS • THE HAGUE